THE SLOW STAIN

LESSONS FROM THE PAST, WARNINGS FOR TODAY

CONNOR BOYACK

SOCIAL HARMONY

To Gordon B. Hinckley

For sounding the alarm.

Social Harmony
2183 W. Main #A102
Lehi, UT 84043

The Slow Stain: Lessons from the Past, Warnings for Today

ISBN-13 **979-8-88688-044-1** (paperback)

CONTENTS

Part Three: Modern Stains

Other religious titles by the author:

Christ versus Caesar: Two Masters, One Choice

*Latter-day Responsibility: Choosing Liberty
through Personal Accountability*

*Latter-day Liberty: A Gospel Approach
to Government and Politics*

INTRODUCTION

There's a tense scene in *The Matrix* where Morpheus has been captured by the Agents and is being forcibly drugged and interrogated. The year is close to 2197, and Agent Smith is hoping to procure the codes needed to invade Zion so the machines could crush humanity once and for all. As the drugs take their course, Smith explains that keeping the lab-grown humans comfortably plugged into the virtual reality required designing a system that reflected "the peak of your civilization."[1]

Thus, the machines chose the late 1990s—the era of AOL chat rooms and dial-up modems, pop bands like NSYNC and Britney Spears, and the Beanie Babies craze. Perhaps the last few decades of lived experience offer reasons to agree with Agent Smith and his artificially intelligent associates. Maybe it's nostalgia distorting things, but, in many respects, it does seem like the late 1990s was an idyllic time in contrast to the social degeneracy that has followed. Public optimism ran high, driven by economic growth and burgeoning tech ventures. Television provided communal water cooler moments, with shows like *Friends* and *Seinfeld* reflecting an upbeat cultural milieu. The grow-

---

1   Lilly and Lana Wachowski, dir. *The Matrix*, Warner Bros., 1999.

ing World Wide Web connected humanity like never before. Mental health was generally strong. In fact, Gallup's data bears out this theory. Since 1979, they've been polling multiple times a year to ask Americans if they are satisfied with the way things are going in their country. In the nearly half a century since, the highest score achieved, 71 percent, came in 1999.[2] (The scores in recent years have been in the low 20s.)

But not everything was sunshine and rainbows—certainly not from the perspective of President Gordon B. Hinckley. Barely two months after he became president of The Church of Jesus Christ of Latter-day Saints in early 1995, he spoke to a group of local leaders at a regional conference in Springville, Utah. Contrasting the nostalgic perception of positivity, Hinckley warned against the tendency God's followers had to take on the negative ways of the world. "We don't adopt them immediately," he said, "but we slowly take them on, unfortunately."[3]

Perhaps he was testing the reaction to this idea with a smaller audience before sharing it more widely, which he did later that same year in the October 1995 General Conference. Speaking to the women in the Relief Society session, Hinckley shared for the first time what most Mormons are now very familiar with—"The Family: A Proclamation to the

---

2   "Satisfaction With the United States," Gallup, accessed December 13, 2024, https://news.gallup.com/poll/1669/general-mood-country.aspx.

3   Quoted in Earl C. Tingey, "The Sabbath Day and Sunday Shopping," *Ensign*, May 1996, https://www.churchofjesuschrist.org/study/general-conference/1996/04/the-sabbath-day-and-sunday-shopping.

World." Far less known is what he said just prior to reciting this proclamation's text:

> With so much of sophistry that is passed off as truth, with so much of deception concerning standards and values, with so much of allurement and enticement to take on the slow stain of the world, we have felt to warn and forewarn.[4]

The decades since have borne out what was warned against: deceitful and fallacious arguments being proclaimed as true by academics, celebrities, politicians, and professional propagandists; the accelerated degradation of societal standards and values; and the seductive pull of peer pressure and social conformity enabling the "slow stain of the world" to persistently spread among Latter-day Saints.

The scriptures are filled with examples of God's people embracing—slowly, then suddenly—the idolatrous ideas and corrupt behaviors of those who lived near and among them. Things were so bad in Noah's day that "God looked upon the earth, and, behold, it was corrupt; for all flesh had corrupted his way upon the earth."[5] The rescued Israelites embraced Egyptian paganism to the point of creating and worshiping a golden calf.[6] After settling in Canaan, they "followed other gods, of the gods of the people that were round about them,

---

4   Gordon B. Hinckley, "Stand Strong against the Wiles of the World," *Ensign*, November 1995, https://www.churchofjesuschrist.org/study/general-conference/1995/10/stand-strong-against-the-wiles-of-the-world.
5   Genesis 6:12.
6   Exodus 32:1–6.

and bowed themselves unto them."[7] Rejecting the prophetic
judgment of Samuel, a later generation of Israelites demanded
a monarchy "to judge us like all the nations."[8] King Solomon,
influenced by his foreign wives, built high places for false
gods, gradually integrating their religious rites into Israel's
worship.[9] The northern kingdom of Israel incorporated idol
worship and pagan rituals introduced by neighboring peoples.[10] The people of Judah adopted foreign idols and forsook
their covenant. God had planted them "a noble vine, wholly
a right seed," yet by adopting the beliefs of surrounding pagan cultures, they had "turned into the degenerate plant of a
strange vine."[11] Jesus rebuked the Pharisees and scribes for
clinging to the traditions of men and rejecting the commandments of God.[12] Paul warned of those who had "changed the
glory of the uncorruptible God into an image made like to cor-
ruptible man."[13] The list goes on.

Of course, the slow spread of society's degenerate practices is not reserved for scripture stories of yesteryear; we,
too, can be, and are, guilty of the same. President Hinckley's
observation was not in the abstract. It's already happening,
and we were warned of that outcome in revealed scripture.
Nephi foresaw that in the latter days many would be paci-
fied into carnal security, their souls being led away "carefully

7   Judges 2:12.
8   1 Samuel 8:5.
9   1 Kings 11:1–10.
10   2 Kings 17:7–17.
11   Jeremiah 2:11–13, 20–23.
12   Mark 7:8–9.
13   Romans 1:23.

down to hell."[14] Others would fall to flattery, being deceived into ignoring the devil's influence in their own lives, "until he grasps them with his awful chains."[15] Secret combinations seduced the once-righteous Nephites "until they had come down to believe in their works and partake of their spoils, and to join with them in their secret murders and combinations."[16] We are directly commanded by the Lord to "repent of [our] sins, and suffer not that these murderous combinations shall get above [us]." Moroni's warning makes clear this outcome is not a matter of *if*, but "*when* ye shall see these things come among you."[17] And in a revelation given to Joseph Smith, God lamented the many covenant breakers who "seek not the Lord to establish his righteousness, but every man walketh in his own way, and after the image of his own god, whose image is in the likeness of the world, and whose substance is that of an idol..."[18]

The purpose of this book is to help you better understand historical examples of idolatry and spiritual decay as well as what these challenges look like in our day. Because the intent of education is to lead to improved action, the book's goal is to empower you to recognize, avoid, and even fight against the slow stain corrupting Christ's followers. A solution is not relevant until a problem is adequately understood. To immunize ourselves from the stain, we must be fully aware of what it is and how it spreads.

---

14 2 Nephi 28:21.
15 2 Nephi 28:22.
16 Helaman 6:38.
17 Ether 8:23–26.
18 D&C 1:15–16.

Before we begin, a word of caution: Hinckley's choice of words may be a bit deceptive. Yes, the stain begins to spread slowly—but like a snowball going down the hill, increasing in size and momentum, wickedness can compound over time. After the Proclamation was shared in that 1995 Relief Society meeting, it was met with what can best be described as a collective shrug. It was not a radical restatement of doctrine or a provocative declaration dividing society into opposing camps. Nearly nobody disputed that human beings were "male and female" and that "gender is an essential characteristic" of one's identity that is not fluid or simply "assigned" at birth. Sure, there were intellectual radicals pushing the envelope, such as feminist philosopher Judith Butler in her 1990 book *Gender Trouble: Feminism and the Subversion of Identity*. Butler's academic attack on traditional gender roles offers us this word salad:

> The univocity of sex, the internal coherence of gender, and the binary framework for both sex and gender are considered throughout as regulatory fictions that consolidate and naturalize the convergent power regimes of masculine and heterosexist oppression.[19]

But Butler and her peers were in the strong minority—a social anomaly compared to the masses who recognized binary gender (male and female) not as a "regulatory fiction" but as plain reality. Literature, social commentary, most of academia, and more from the 1990s simply assume this fact

---

19 Judith Butler, *Gender Trouble: Feminism and the Subversion of Identity* (New York: Routledge, 2006).

and discuss gender issues in the context of men and women. When researchers analyzed "gender role attitudes" from 1977 to 2008 for the *American Journal of Sociology*, using data from the General Social Survey, a nationally represented interview-based survey to monitor social changes in America, the authors discuss men's issues and women's issues, without nary a mention of anything else even being within the realm of sociological possibility.[20] Transgender activism would soon change that and spread throughout academia in subsequent years, but certainly, in 1995, Hinckley's views on gender were noncontroversial and widely shared.

The same goes for marriage, which the Proclamation states is only "between man and woman." In a world that has largely legally codified same-sex marriage, it may be difficult to remember the political landscape that preceded it. For example, the most ardent supporters of legalizing same-sex marriage have been Democrats, yet the most prominent Democrats in the 1990s all affirmed their support of marriage between a man and a woman. President Bill Clinton, for example, signed the Defense of Marriage Act in 1996, which defined marriage for federal purposes as the union of a man and a woman; he also ran ads on Christian radio stations promoting his signing of the bill.[21] While running for president in 2008, Barack

---

20 David Cotter, Joan Hermsen, and Reeve Vanneman, "The End of the Gender Revolution? Gender Role Attitudes from 1977 to 2008," *American Journal of Sociology* 117, no. 1 (2011): 259–289.

21 "Listen to Bill Clinton's 1996 radio ad touting his passage of DOMA," CNN, October 10, 2016, https://www.cnn.com/2016/10/10/politics/bill-clinton-1996-radio-ad/index.html.

Obama explicitly stated, "I believe marriage is between a man and a woman. I am not in favor of gay marriage."[22] Joe Biden, as senator, voted in favor of the bill that Clinton signed. While there was a growing movement to campaign for same-sex marriage in the 1990s, the idea was still outside the Overton Window[23] and thus not publicly shared by most Americans. Here, too, Hinckley and his apostolic associates were saying something reflective of what was at the time the status quo.

A final example may suffice—and this one differs from the rest. The Proclamation also states, "Children are entitled to birth within the bonds of matrimony." While widely accepted as an ideal, by the 1990s there had already been a surge in births to unwed couples and a corresponding rise in single mothers rearing children. In decades past, nonmarital births were pretty rare. In the 1960s, for example, 43 percent of unwed pregnancies resulted in a shotgun marriage, in contrast to only 9 percent today.[24] By 1980, some 18 percent of all women in the United States who gave birth were unmarried. By 1995, the number had already risen to 27 percent.[25] Here, the Proc-

---

22 "Evolve: Obama gay marriage quotes," Politico, May 9, 2012, https://www.politico.com/story/2012/05/evolve-obama-gay-marriage-quotes-076109.

23 The Overton Window is the range of ideas and policies that are considered acceptable and mainstream in public discourse at a given time.

24 "How We Ended Up With 40 Percent of Children Born Out of Wedlock," Institute for Family Studies, December 18, 2017, https://ifstudies.org/blog/how-we-ended-up-with-40-percent-of-children-born-out-of-wedlock.

25 "Percentage of births to unmarried women in the United States from 1980 to 2022," Statista, accessed December 14, 2024, https://www.statista.com/statistics/276025/us-percentage-of-births-to-unmarried-women/.

lamation was sounding an alarm for a trend already spreading throughout society. Today, roughly 40 percent of all children are born out of wedlock.[26] Obviously, this is not merely an American problem: across developed nations, the average rate of births occurring outside of marriage is 42 percent.[27] Some countries rank very high, such as Mexico (70 percent), Costa Rica (73 percent), and Chile (75 percent).[28] Those at the bottom of the list include Japan and Korea with only two to three percent of births outside of marriage,[29] though this statistic is influenced by the fact that people in these countries are having almost no children at all.

The collective shrug given in reaction to the Proclamation was no doubt because the spread was indeed slow. Many of the issues it warned against were still only supported by those at the margins of society. But the compounding effect is real: ten people converted to an idea can, in turn, each influence dozens more, each of whom then goes on to reach countless more, and so on. The spread accelerates, as it certainly has with the issues Hinckley warned against. Conservatives and others opposed to same-sex marriage warned that its legalization would be a veritable slippery slope toward society's embrace of other unorthodox behaviors. For example, the Family Research Council warned:

---

26 Ibid.
27 "SF2.4: Share of births outside of marriage," OECD Family Database, accessed December 14, 2024, https://www.oecd.org/content/dam/oecd/en/data/datasets/family-database/sf_2_4_share_births_outside_marriage.pdf.
28 Ibid.
29 Ibid.

Once marriage is no longer confined to a man and a woman, and the sole criterion becomes the presence of "love" and "mutual commitment," it is impossible to exclude virtually any "relationship" between two or more partners of either sex. To those who scoff at concerns that gay marriage could lead to the acceptance of other harmful and widely-rejected sexual behaviors, it should be pointed out that until very recent times the very suggestion that two women or two men could "marry" would have been greeted with scorn. The movement to redefine marriage has already found full expression in what is variously called "polyfidelity" or "polyamory," which seeks to replace traditional marriage with a bewildering array of sexual combinations among various groups of individuals.[30]

In response to these and related concerns, advocates ardently reassured everyone that the slippery slope was nothing more than a fallacy and that, on its face, the giving of legal marriage status to two men or two women would not have the broader implications opponents predicted. Except, time has borne out many of these concerns and shown how quickly the stain can spread. What began as a quest for same-sex marriage soon turned into: using the legal system to compel business owners to offer their services in support of gay marriage celebrations; elevating transgender issues as the next frontier of activism, shaming those who don't use one's preferred pronouns; allowing minors to dance in front of sexually oriented

---

30 "Ten Facts About Counterfeit Marriage," Family Research Council, accessed March 23, 2025, https://downloads.frc.org/EF/EF11B07.pdf

drag performers; puberty blockers and permanent steriliza-
tion of minors who think they were born the wrong gender;
pedophiles rebranding as "minor-attracted persons"; biological men competing against women in sports; and all kinds of
other social degeneracy. What was a "love is love—we just
want acceptance!" campaign quickly became a Trojan horse
for a radical redefinition of societal norms. The slow stain accelerated into a swift contamination, saturating classrooms,
media outlets, academic institutions, civic movements, social
circles, and beyond. And that stain can affect everything it
touches, including the Church—which, despite its long-held
strenuous objections to same-sex marriage, ended up affirma-
tively supporting a federal same-sex marriage law in 2022.[31]

Though we'll certainly discuss many relevant examples of
marriage, children, and gender, this book is not limited only
to these issues. The slow stain of the world encompasses far
more than social threats to the family. We'll review, among
other things: secret combinations and the continuing war on
agency; government-run education and the dumbing down
of society; rising support for socialism and institutionalized
covetousness; feminism and the de-prioritization of motherhood; monetary debasement and the financial enslavement of
families; and government surveillance and the trading away of
liberty for "security" theater.

---

31 "Mormon church comes out in support of same-sex marriage
law," NBC News, November 15, 2022, https://www.nbcnews.
com/nbc-out/out-politics-and-policy/mormon-church-comes-
support-sex-marriage-law-rcna57393.

To understand these threats we face in the present, it would be instructive for us to gain insight by reflecting on the past. That is, after all, the whole point of scripture—and the reason God has given us additional insights to guide our actions today. We ought to liken the circumstances in these stories to our own lives and search for wisdom that can help us avoid the societal stains threatening to spread to our homes. What we'll find, and what any serious student of scripture already knows, is that a slow and subtle erosion of long-held values is first tolerated, then normalized, and eventually celebrated. What once was considered scandalous or morally unacceptable becomes fashionable. Once the foundation of shared virtues cracks, the entire structure of a community's moral order can collapse, often far more rapidly than one might expect.

In the pages that follow, we will examine ancient warnings and modern analogs. We will consider how various societies—Nephite, Israelite, early Christian, and others—gradually allowed contamination to creep into their midst. We will see how moral principles were quietly sidelined and ultimately replaced. This analysis will help us pinpoint where we stand in our own moment in history and, more importantly, what we can do to resist today's creeping cultural corruption. If we understand how the pattern unfolds, we will be better equipped to disrupt it.

PART ONE

HISTORICAL EXAMPLES

As a newly ordained Elder studying in the Missionary
Training Center in 2001, preparing to head to Honduras for
nearly two years, I quickly became aware of my scriptural
illiteracy. Despite years of seminary and regular church attendance, with irregular family and personal scripture study
along the way, I had work to do. There was a lot I didn't know.
Perhaps this situation is best demonstrated by the fact that, at
one point, I asked my teacher why the fifth chapter of Jacob
in the Book of Mormon had a lengthy story about gardening.
"I don't get it," I admitted. "Why all the fuss about fertilizing
and pruning in a book of scripture?"

Shake your head all you want. I was clearly scripturally
illiterate. Fortunately, that soon changed, but in that moment
the teacher kindly smiled and explained that the entire chapter is an allegory—a story with hidden meaning. As one schol-
ar wrote about Zenos's olive tree allegory, it is "at once simple
and complex, obscure and obvious."[1] Perhaps not obvious to
me but worth spending some time to understand.

Zenos uses olive trees as a metaphor for God's covenant
people, showing a careful and continual effort by the "master"
(representing the Lord) to nourish and preserve them over
long spans of history. Each step in planting, pruning, grafting,
and harvesting parallels God's active guidance of Israel and
other nations—teaching truth, calling prophets, and warning
against idolatry. When the chosen branches begin to decay,

---

1   Paul Y. Hoskisson, "The Allegory of the Olive Tree in Jacob,"
     Book of Mormon Central, accessed December 28, 2024,
     https://archive.bookofmormoncentral.org/sites/default/files/
     archive-files/pdf/hoskisson/2016-02-03/ch._5-the_allegory_
     of_the_olive_tree.pdf.

it signifies spiritual decline and an embrace of foreign philosophies or wicked traditions. As the master grafts in wild branches—other peoples—and carefully prunes away infected or lifeless parts, he is extending mercy, offering new covenants, and removing corrupt influences. This careful husbandry shows that God is willing to save and restore His people as long as they respond to His efforts, while also warning that neglect and the acceptance of cultural contamination can eventually lead to spiritual death if left unchecked.

Throughout the allegory, you can almost hear the anguish in the master's voice, asking his servant several times, "What could I have done more for my vineyard?"[2] His repeated attempts to save the varied trees and cultivate good fruit were frustrated by constant corruption among the vineyard, leading to "much fruit, and there is none of it which is good."[3] Indeed, the master observed "all kinds of bad fruit; and it profiteth me nothing notwithstanding all our labor; and now it grieveth me that I should lose this tree."[4] The master and his servant looked around the vineyard and "beheld that the fruit of the natural branches had become corrupt also; yea, the first and the second and also the last; and they had all become corrupt."[5] Things got so bad that the master threatened to burn it all to the ground: "all the trees of my vineyard are good for nothing save it be to be hewn down and cast into the fire."[6]

---

2   Jacob 5:41, 47, 49.
3   Jacob 5:32.
4   Ibid.
5   Jacob 5:39.
6   Jacob 5:42.

Why were these trees so prone to corruption? The allegory is mostly silent on this question, though it suggests that "the wild fruit... had overcome that part of the tree which brought forth good fruit,"[7] suggesting that the healthy parts of the tree were often overtaken by the invasive forces introduced into the vineyard. Let's infer a few things beyond what's in the text that might be relevant observations.

First, the trees can be viewed as inherently vulnerable because they are planted in a fallen world. Just as a pristine orchard can still be subject to pests, drought, or disease, so too can a covenant people remain susceptible to alluring philosophies, idolatrous rituals, and moral relativism prevalent in their environment. God does not seclude or segregate His children in greenhouse-like isolation. They are expected to grow amid adversity and opposition.

Second, the allegory illustrates that without constant nurturing and intentional effort, corruption flourishes. Even healthy branches need constant pruning, meaning that even strong believers require regular spiritual maintenance. Left untended, virtue and truth can grow stale, and worldly ideas can seem more appealing. The very absence of vigilance creates space for unrighteous influences to take root and spread, eventually deforming what was once solid and pure.

Third, the trees' proneness to corruption may reflect the gradual and subtle nature of spiritual decay. "Wild fruit" is not introduced as a bold, sudden intrusion easily recognizable to all. Instead, harmful influences blend quietly into the orchard,

---

7   Jacob 5:40.

grafted in and growing alongside the original stock. Over time, such influences gain ground because the difference between right and wrong, truth and error, can become blurred. As a result, sound doctrine and moral standards recede against a surging tide of shifting norms and comfortable compromises. In this sense, the allegory underscores that moral corruption rarely announces itself dramatically at the outset. Rather, it infiltrates gradually—spreading slowly at first.

Ultimately, the olive trees are prone to corruption because they exist in a dynamic environment of competing values, subject to the stewardship—or neglect—of the master's servants and the attentiveness—or apathy—of those tending their growth. Obviously, we humans have agency as well, unlike trees. Our own spiritual decay is not something that can be blamed on others. The lesson for us is that spiritual strength is not self-sustaining. It must be cultivated, protected, and periodically renewed to prevent the wild fruit of cultural contamination from overtaking the orchard. And the allegory packs a punch because it precisely describes what we see in scriptural history over and over again. Despite the best efforts of God and His prophets to call people to repentance and help them bear good fruit, they choose—typically as a result of the cultural contaminations to which they've been exposed—to abandon the gospel by trying to serve multiple masters at once. The scriptural narratives that follow provide case after case revealing how once-flourishing vineyards of believers succumbed, step by subtle step, to the pervasive influence of the world.

THE ISRAELITES

Long before the gardeners in Zenos's allegory were anxious over an orchard of corrupted trees, the Lord had chosen Israel as His 'peculiar treasure," establishing a covenant to make them "a kingdom of priests, and an holy nation."[1] Delivered from Egyptian bondage by miraculous power and bound to God by sacred commandment, these people were to remain distinct in belief, behavior, and worship—even when surrounded by hostile and idolatrous nations. The Lord urged them to "learn not the way of the heathen"[2] and commanded, "Thou shalt have no other gods before me."[3] He desired them to flourish like a well-tended vine,[4] devoted solely to Him and nourished by divine truth. In theory, Israel's covenant relationship should have yielded a people filled with spiritual vitality and true devotion, but, as we will see, this chosen nation repeatedly succumbed to the slow stain of foreign influences and fell far below the standard God had set.

---

1 Exodus 19:5–6.
2 Jeremiah 10:2.
3 Exodus 20:3.
4 Isaiah 5:1–4.

The Golden Calf at Sinai

Following their miraculous escape from Egyptian bondage and triumphant crossing of the Red Sea,[5] the Israelites stood poised to become a people wholly devoted to the Lord.[6] It was a defining moment—a fresh start after centuries under the shadow of a pagan empire that worshiped a vast pantheon of gods.[7] Yet only a short time later, while Moses communed with God on Mount Sinai,[8] the people reverted to what they knew from their former oppressors. Rather than patiently awaiting divine direction, they fashioned a golden calf reminiscent of the bull-gods worshiped in Egypt, bowing before it in revelry and sin.[9] This shameful scene was not merely a misstep—it was a sign that Egypt's religious traditions had left a deep imprint on their minds and hearts.

Though the Lord patiently gave them His law and prescribed strict worship practices,[10] this contamination from Egyptian culture resurfaced repeatedly. In the wilderness, many Israelites still clung to the idea that deities could be molded and manipulated to their liking,[11] rather than worshiping the one, invisible God who delivered them.[12] Their yearning for the food, comfort, and familiar religious customs of Egypt competed with the monotheism Moses tirelessly

5   Exodus 14:21–31.
6   Exodus 19:5–6.
7   Exodus 12:12.
8   Exodus 24:12–18.
9   Exodus 32:1–6.
10   Exodus 20; Leviticus 1–27.
11   Exodus 32:4.
12   Deuteronomy 4:15–19.

taught. The multitude "fell a lusting" and whined, saying, "Who shall give us flesh to eat? We remember the fish, which we did eat in Egypt freely; the cucumbers, and the melons, and the leeks, and the onions, and the garlick: But now our soul is dried away: there is nothing at all, beside this manna, before our eyes."[13] Even as God led them by a pillar of cloud and fire,[14] and fed them with manna,[15] lingering vestiges of Egyptian thought and idolatry undermined their faith and fidelity. The Lord said:

> In the day that I lifted up mine hand unto them, to bring them forth of the land of Egypt into a land that I had espied for them, flowing with milk and honey, which is the glory of all lands:

> Then said I unto them, Cast ye away every man the abominations of his eyes, and defile not yourselves with the idols of Egypt: I am the Lord your God.

> But they rebelled against me, and would not hearken unto me: they did not every man cast away the abominations of their eyes, neither did they forsake the idols of Egypt: then I said, I will pour out my fury upon them, to accomplish my anger against them in the midst of the land of Egypt.[16]

---

13 Numbers 11:4–6.
14 Exodus 13:21–22.
15 Exodus 16:4–5, 14–15.
16 Ezekiel 20:6–8.

This dual allegiance continued to surface throughout the lengthy sojourn in the desert.[17] By the time the Israelites finally stood ready to enter the Promised Land, the Lord had to repeatedly emphasize the importance of worshiping Him alone and shunning the idols of other nations.[18] Much of the purpose behind the Law of Moses was no doubt to isolate Israel from the influences of surrounding cultures—an isolation necessary because of how thoroughly Egyptian beliefs had penetrated the hearts of previous generations. Ceremonial purity, dietary restrictions, distinctive religious festivals, and centralizing worship at the Tabernacle (and later the Temple) all served to keep the people focused on their covenant with the one true God.[19] Without these preventative measures, the lingering memory of Egyptian idolatry would continue to corrode their spiritual integrity.[20]

Israel's experiences in Egypt left scars that would take generations to heal.[21] The golden calf episode was perhaps the most dramatic manifestation, but subtler forms of cultural contamination lingered long after.[22] By looking back to Israel's time under Egyptian rule, we see that even miraculous deliverance and divine instruction did not slow the spread of pagan ideas and influences resulting from their Egyptian exposure.

---

17 Numbers 14:2–4.
18 Deuteronomy 6:4–14; Joshua 24:14–23.
19 Leviticus 11–23; Exodus 25–27; Deuteronomy 12:1–14.
20 Psalm 106:19–21.
21 Ezekiel 23:3, 8.
22 Amos 5:25–27; Acts 7:39–43.

Moabite Idolatry at Baal–Peor

As the Israelites pressed closer to the Promised Land, word began to spread of their victories over formidable enemies—most notably Sihon, king of the Amorites,[23] and Og, king of Bashan.[24] These defeats rattled Moab and its king, Balak, who recognized that Israel's success was not due to sheer military prowess alone, but some sort of divine protection. So Balak sought a supernatural countermeasure to fight back and attempted to hire the soothsayer Balaam to curse Israel in order to make them vulnerable.[25]

The plan failed spectacularly. Instead of cursing God's people, Balaam was compelled by divine intervention to pronounce blessings upon Israel.[26] Balak's hopes were dashed, so he resorted to a more insidious strategy. There would be no open battle against Israel's armies, no bold challenge to their God. Instead, the Moabites would exploit Israel's vulnerabilities—its human desires and capacity for compromise.

> And Israel abode in Shittim, and the people began to commit whoredom with the daughters of Moab. And they called the people unto the sacrifices of their gods: and the people did eat, and bowed down to their gods.[27]

By inviting Israelite men to participate in ritual feasts to their god Baal-Peor and enticing them to indulge in immoral

---

23 Numbers 21:21–24.
24 Numbers 21:33–35.
25 Numbers 22:1–6.
26 Numbers 23–24.
27 Numbers 25:1–2.

acts tied to pagan worship, Moab aimed to accomplish what curses and swords could not. Having failed to defeat Israel in direct conflict or through spiritual cursing, they turned to seduction as their final, and tragically successful, weapon. The people who had only recently escaped Egypt's grip and witnessed God's mighty works now stumbled into idolatry and immorality, seduced by Moabite customs that were as enticing as they were destructive.

The Moabites did not need to directly challenge Israel's worship of the true God. They simply introduced a contrary model—one where divine favor could be obtained through celebratory feasting and immorality. Israel's participation in these rites implied that they viewed the Lord as just one more deity among an array of gods to be appeased rather than the only true God. This willingness to mingle their sacred identity with foreign religion exposed how susceptible the people were to cultural contamination. By partaking of the Moabites' sacrificial meals and bowing to their gods,[28] Israel proved that previous lessons and warnings had not fully taken root.

After Joshua's Death

Many years later, once settled and prospering under Joshua's leadership, Israel was entering the next phase of its history in a position of apparent strength and stability. The tribes were settling into their allotted territories, and some had already seen God's power demonstrated through resounding

---

28   Numbers 25:2.

military victories.[29] But after Joshua died, a new generation arose "which knew not the Lord, nor yet the works which he had done for Israel."[30] Without Joshua's leadership to guide them, and not having experienced God's deliverances themselves, the people became susceptible to the slow stain of surrounding cultures and their idolatrous influences.

All around Israel, the Canaanites had built altars and shrines to worship a wide range of fertility gods like Baal, Asherah, Astarte, Mot, and others. Their religious rites often involved immoral practices—ritual prostitution, child sacrifice, and superstitious customs to curry favor with these deities who, in their minds, controlled rainfall and agricultural success. Rather than firmly resisting these influences, Israel began to mingle more freely with Canaanite society, forging alliances and intermarriages that quickly diluted their distinct way of life.[31] Little by little, what had seemed foreign became familiar, and Israel's own worship practices were compromised. The stain spread.

> And the children of Israel did evil in the sight of the Lord, and served Baalim: And they forsook the Lord God of their fathers, which brought them out of the land of Egypt, and followed other gods, of the gods of the people that were round about them, and bowed themselves unto them, and provoked the Lord to anger. And they forsook the Lord, and served Baal and Ashtaroth.[32]

---

29 Joshua 24:31.
30 Judges 2:10.
31 Judges 1:27–36; 3:5–6.
32 Judges 2:11–13.

Israel was essentially saying that Yahweh was no longer the exclusive object of their devotion. As they adopted Canaanite customs, they brought pagan idols into their homes and communities, combining covenant worship with the agricultural gods and fertility rites that promised worldly prosperity. This syncretism—the blending of true worship with pagan elements—wasn't a dramatic overnight rebellion or sudden decision on their part. Instead, it spread gradually: the more Israel interacted with the Canaanites, the more they saw immediate benefits in fitting in, and the less they remembered the unique deliverances that had once made them a distinct nation. These choices paved the way for repeated cycles of apostasy, oppression, and eventual rescue by a judge whom the Lord raised up.[33] Each judge would restore monotheism momentarily, only for the people to slide back into the same pattern of cultural contamination once that strong leadership was gone.

Like All the Nations

Though judges arose periodically to rescue Israel from its idolatry and foreign oppression, the people's appetite for worldly acceptance persisted. Each time a deliverer restored the people to covenant faithfulness, complacency returned soon after. The closing chapters of the judges' era reveal a nation longing for more than just momentary stability—they wanted a permanent solution that matched the visible pomp and power of surrounding kingdoms. And they soon got it.

---

33 Judges 2:14–16.

Samuel was fulfilling his prophetic charge to warn Israel against the moral lapses that had repeatedly drawn them into bondage. "If ye do return unto the Lord with all your hearts," Samuel admonished them, "then put away the strange gods and Ashtaroth from among you, and prepare your hearts unto the Lord, and serve him only."[34] However, Samuel's leadership was not sufficient to quell the people's desire to embrace the ideas and practices of surrounding cultures. This became evident when Samuel, in his old age, had appointed his sons as judges in Israel, only for those sons to abuse their positions of authority for financial gain.[35] The elders in Israel approached the aged Samuel with a political solution similar to what everyone else was doing:

> Then all the elders of Israel gathered themselves together, and came to Samuel unto Ramah, And said unto him, Behold, thou art old, and thy sons walk not in thy ways: now make us a king to judge us like all the nations. But the thing displeased Samuel, when they said, Give us a king to judge us. And Samuel prayed unto the Lord. And the Lord said unto Samuel, Hearken unto the voice of the people in all that they say unto thee: for they have not rejected thee, but they have rejected me, that I should not reign over them.[36]

Instead of relying on God's direct guidance, Israel demanded the worldly structure they believed would ensure prestige, stability, and a reputation equal to neighboring pow-

---

34 1 Samuel 7:3.
35 1 Samuel 8:1–3.
36 1 Samuel 8:4–7.

ers. Samuel spelled out in stark detail the potential costs of such a path, warning of conscription into royal service, heavy taxation, and the loss of personal freedoms.[37] Even so, "the people refused to obey the voice of Samuel" and insisted, "We will have a king over us; That we also may be like all the nations; and that our king may judge us, and go out before us, and fight our battles."[38] In this statement, Israel disclosed its underlying motives—an ambition to conform to the prevailing norms of global power rather than maintain the unique covenantal bond that had distinguished them since the Exodus. Once again, the slow stain of worldly influence had tainted Israel. Their desire to replicate what they observed in surrounding cultures was clearly greater than their fidelity to the Lord and the warnings from His prophet. They were God's people in name, but in practice, they pursued and participated in the ways of the world.

Solomon's Foreign Wives

Israel's choice to enthrone a king led to a golden age under David and later Solomon—an age whose glory would soon be corroded by idolatrous entanglements. Solomon's reign began with the favor of God, marked by great wisdom and prosperity.[39] Yet the success of his kingdom soon clashed with the warnings the Lord had previously given about royal excess and foreign entanglements.[40] Over time, Solomon's

---

37　1 Samuel 8:10–18.
38　1 Samuel 8:19–20.
39　1 Kings 3:5–13.
40　Deuteronomy 17:14–17.

heart turned from the God of Israel to the deities venerated by the many nations surrounding him, such as Moab, Ammon, Edom, Sidon, and the Hittite kingdoms.

This slide into apostasy came because Solomon "loved many strange women"[41] and built high places and altars to accommodate their varied gods.[42] In direct defiance of the Lord's commandment that Israel should not intermarry with idol-worshipers,[43] these polygamous unions became a conduit for cultural contamination. Rather than maintaining the purity of Israel's worship, Solomon justified the integration of foreign deities—an outward display of his willingness to syncretize truth with pagan belief. By yielding to the political allure of diplomatic marriages—a practice embraced by many royal kingdoms throughout time—he introduced spiritual corruption into the highest level of Israel's governance. The outcome was catastrophic. Solomon's heart unsurprisingly became "turned away after other gods," and he "did evil in the sight of the Lord."[44] This behavior was especially egregious given that the Lord had twice appeared to Solomon to reaffirm His covenant and warn against apostasy.[45]

Solomon's personal choices reached far beyond his own household, infecting the very core of Israel's identity. By building shrines and worship sites for pagan gods, he effectively broadcasted that the throne sanctioned such practices. Once the king himself sanctioned idol worship, local leaders

---

41 1 Kings 11:1.
42 1 Kings 11:4–8.
43 Deuteronomy 7:3–4.
44 1 Kings 11:4–6.
45 1 Kings 11:9–10.

and commoners alike felt freer to participate. A monarchy previously united around the worship of Jehovah splintered into factions of competing religious loyalties. Royal officials, bureaucrats, and those seeking favor at court adapted to the shifting cultural climate, compromising the distinct covenant standards that had long defined Israel. Over time, the taboo of mingling pagan rites with the worship of the one true God dwindled. Foreign influences took root in places of high authority and bled down into everyday life. The influx of pagan shrines, alliances, and the open tolerance of polytheistic rituals contaminated Israel and undermined the purpose for which God had once set them apart. Stains spread slowly to start, but if they can contaminate people in positions of influence, their reach and impact accelerate significantly.

Apart from his pagan, polygamous relationships, Solomon is best known for overseeing the construction of Israel's first permanent temple in Jerusalem—a momentous feat that symbolized the nation's covenant bond with God.[46] Although David had long yearned to build such a house for the Lord, it was Solomon who brought the ambitious vision to fruition. Upon its completion, the temple became the focal point of Israel's faith. Its dedication was marked by solemn sacrifices and a visible demonstration of divine glory, with the cloud of the Lord's presence filling the sanctuary.[47] The people now had a centralized location for sacrifices and feasts—an unprecedented opportunity for them to unite in worship. But it wasn't the only game in town: Solomon's embrace of false gods ultimate-

---

46   1 Kings 5–9; 2 Chronicles 2–7.
47   1 Kings 8:10–11.

ly led to the construction of a competing cult temple only four miles away from the famed Temple of Solomon. Constructed in a similar fashion, this temple at Tel Moza—only recently discovered and still being excavated—includes an altar, an offering table, cult vessels and artifacts, and more.[48] The pagan worship at this nearby temple long succeeded Solomon's reign and became more pervasive as Israel divided into two kingdoms under Jeroboam and Rehoboam.

Jeroboam's Golden Calves

Following Solomon's death, the kingdom of Israel fractured into two realms: Judah in the south and the newly formed northern kingdom, ruled by Jeroboam. Once an official under Solomon, Jeroboam had fled to Egypt to escape the king's wrath.[49] While there, he encountered religious customs that would profoundly shape his leadership. Returning home to govern the north, he faced an immediate dilemma: how to ensure his subjects' loyalty when the temple—and thus the heart of Israel's worship—remained in Jerusalem. Fearing that ongoing pilgrimages to the southern kingdom would erode his influence, Jeroboam institutionalized idolatry instead:

> If this people go up to do sacrifice in the house of the Lord at Jerusalem, then shall the heart of this people turn again unto their lord, even unto Rehoboam king of Judah, and they shall kill me, and go again to Rehoboam king of Judah. Whereupon the king took

---

48 "Tel Moza Expedition Project," accessed December 22, 2024, https://www.telmoza.org/.

49 1 Kings 11:26–40.

counsel, and made two calves of gold, and said unto them, It is too much for you to go up to Jerusalem: behold thy gods, O Israel, which brought thee up out of the land of Egypt.[50]

By co-opting Egyptian iconography and reviving an idolatrous practice from Israel's distant past, Jeroboam ensured that religious devotion in the north pivoted away from the covenant-centered temple worship in Jerusalem. Priests were consecrated outside the Levitical order,[51] feasts were scheduled in competition with God's appointed times,[52] and the entire structure of Israel's relationship with Jehovah was corrupted at its core. What began as an attempt to secure national stability quickly became a slippery slope to deeper apostasy. Jeroboam's golden calves reintroduced idolatry on a grand scale: once the highest authority sanctioned it, the populace not only tolerated but also embraced foreign deities. Jeroboam had cemented his political power at the expense of his people's devotion to God. Once again, Israel's worship had become tainted.

Ahab and Jezebel

For generations after Jeroboam's reign, the northern kingdom lurched from one dynasty to another, each ruler seeming to outdo the last in rebellion against the Lord. Jeroboam's golden calves had sown the seeds of widespread idolatry, which soon choked out true devotion and entrenched for-

---

50 1 Kings 12:27–28.
51 1 Kings 12:31.
52 1 Kings 12:32–33.

eign practices among the people.[53] Baasha wrested the throne through conspiracy, yet repeated Jeroboam's errors,[54] and his successor Zimri ruled only a week before Omri emerged triumphant in a civil war.[55] Each regime further eroded what little remained of the nation's spiritual integrity, culminating in Omri's son, Ahab, who ascended to power at a time when the kingdom had already largely distanced itself from the worship of Jehovah.

It was into this moral quagmire that Ahab introduced his most ruinous decision: forging an alliance with the Phoenicians by marrying Jezebel, daughter of the king of Sidon.[56] Influenced by Sidonian customs, Ahab openly embraced the worship of Baal and built an altar in Samaria, effectively sanctioning idolatry as the state religion:

> And he reared up an altar for Baal in the house of Baal, which he had built in Samaria. And Ahab made a grove; and Ahab did more to provoke the Lord God of Israel to anger than all the kings of Israel that were before him.[57]

In clear contrast to the commandments, a once-chosen people now hoisted an emblem of foreign devotion in the seat of royal power. Under Ahab and Jezebel's guidance, Baal worship became the cultural norm: shrines proliferated, false prophets abounded, and those loyal to the Lord were per-

53   1 Kings 14:9–16.
54   1 Kings 15:27–34.
55   1 Kings 16:15–23.
56   1 Kings 16:31.
57   1 Kings 16:32–33.

secuted, fleeing to hide in a cave to escape.[58] By enthroning
Baal in the political and religious life of Israel, Ahab followed
in Solomon's footsteps by embracing idolatrous practices at
the highest levels and pushing it onto the people. With royal
sanction behind Baal worship, the northern kingdom swiftly
absorbed these corrupted practices—no public outcry, no
outpouring of protest. Time and again, Israel had shown that
the slow stain of foreign idolatry was no unwelcome invader.
They embraced it with open arms.

After the Assyrian Conquest

Eventually, Israel's persistent apostasy enabled the Assyrian conquest. By 722 BC, Samaria fell,[59] and the kingdom
of Israel was officially dismantled—a defeat they invited by
abandoning their only true protector. Following the fall of
Samaria, the Assyrians employed a strategy of deportation
and resettlement to maintain control over their new terri-
tory. They removed many Israelites from their homeland and
replaced them with people from other nations.[60] These new-
comers brought with them their own deities and customs,
further muddying whatever remained of Israel's religious
identity. These new residents adapted their rites to combine
with worship for the God of Israel.[61] The end result was a hy-
brid faith alien to the covenant that had once bound Israel to
the Lord. The Bible makes very clear where the fault lies:

---

58   1 Kings 18:4.
59   2 Kings 17:5–6.
60   2 Kings 17:24.
61   2 Kings 17:25–33.

For so it was, that the children of Israel had sinned against the Lord their God, which had brought them up out of the land of Egypt, from under the hand of Pharaoh king of Egypt, and had feared other gods, And walked in the statutes of the heathen, whom the Lord cast out from before the children of Israel, and of the kings of Israel, which they had made.

And the children of Israel did secretly those things that were not right against the Lord their God, and they built them high places in all their cities, from the tower of the watchmen to the fenced city. And they set them up images and groves in every high hill, and under every green tree:

And there they burnt incense in all the high places, as did the heathen whom the Lord carried away before them; and wrought wicked things to provoke the Lord to anger: For they served idols, whereof the Lord had said unto them, Ye shall not do this thing.

Yet the Lord testified against Israel, and against Judah, by all the prophets, and by all the seers, saying, Turn ye from your evil ways, and keep my commandments and my statutes, according to all the law which I commanded your fathers, and which I sent to you by my servants the prophets. Notwithstanding they would not hear, but hardened their necks, like to the neck of their fathers, that did not believe in the Lord their God.

And they rejected his statutes, and his covenant that he made with their fathers, and his testimonies which he testified against them; and they followed vanity, and became vain, and went after the heathen that were round about them, concerning whom the Lord had charged them, that they should not do like them.

And they left all the commandments of the Lord their God, and made them molten images, even two calves, and made a grove, and worshipped all the host of heaven, and served Baal. And they caused their sons and their daughters to pass through the fire, and used divination and enchantments, and sold themselves to do evil in the sight of the Lord, to provoke him to anger.[62]

In reality, the installation of new settlers with foreign deities only accelerated a process that was already far advanced. Now, the northern kingdom was hopelessly entangled in a patchwork of superstitions—some faintly reminiscent of the Mosaic law, many overtly pagan. This final phase of assimilation testified that Israel's flirtation with idolatry had come full circle: they had once yearned for security and prestige by copying other nations' ways, and now they became a vassal state drowning in a sea of false gods.

In this bleak aftermath, the scriptural record underscores the tragic irony: the people God once called "my people"[63] forfeited their identity by chasing after every imaginable deity. Their covenant inheritance, so precious and heavily guarded

---

62 2 Kings 17:7–17.
63 Hosea 1:9.

by prophets of old, was squandered in their pursuit of worldly allure. The Assyrian conquest exposed how deeply the slow stain of spiritual compromise had permeated the nation's heart. In a matter of generations, Israel had gone from being set apart to being hopelessly conformed.

Judah's Adoption of Surrounding Idols

While the northern kingdom collapsed beneath Assyrian power, Judah appeared, for a time, to stand on firmer ground— thanks in part to King Hezekiah's devotion to the Lord. Yet even Hezekiah's sweeping reforms,[64] which targeted pagan altars and images inherited from earlier apostasies, did not permanently shield Judah from the slow stain of surrounding cultures. In the decades following Assyria's conquest of Israel, Judah continued to face rampant spiritual threats, proving that no nation was immune to the corrosive lure of pagan practices. Enter Manasseh, who ascended to the throne at age twelve and promptly reversed the very reforms that had offered Judah a measure of holiness and divine protection:

> And he did that which was evil in the sight of the Lord, after the abominations of the heathen, whom the Lord cast out before the children of Israel.

> For he built up again the high places which Hezekiah his father had destroyed; and he reared up altars for Baal, and made a grove, as did Ahab king of Israel; and worshipped all the host of heaven, and served them.

---

64   2 Kings 18:1–6.

And he built altars in the house of the Lord, of which the Lord said, In Jerusalem will I put my name. And he built altars for all the host of heaven in the two courts of the house of the Lord.[65]

Like other apostates of his day, Manasseh embraced the excesses of these pagan rituals, which included child sacrifice, by killing his own son.[66] He desecrated the temple, installing the image of a pagan god[67]—symbolically signaling that foreign gods and worldly values were welcome at the heart of Judah's religious life. Manasseh's endorsement injected the practices of Canaanites, Assyrians, and other pagan nations deep into Judah's cultural bloodstream. People who had once flirted only occasionally with idol worship now found that compromise endorsed and prescribed by royal decree. What began as a smoldering temptation under lesser kings burst into a full blaze of syncretism, overshadowing the Mosaic Law and smothering any lingering reverence for the Lord's holiness.

Prior to the Babylonian Exile

Even after Manasseh's reign began to wane and subsequent kings tried—and often failed—to rein in idolatrous impulses, Judah's slide toward spiritual ruin continued. The prophet Jeremiah emerged during this turbulent period, crying repentance to a nation that had grown deaf to divine warnings. Despite sporadic efforts at reform, Judah's leaders persisted in

---

65   2 Kings 21:2–5.
66   2 Kings 21:6.
67   2 Kings 21:7.

turning to military alliances with Egypt, in adopting remnants of Canaanite fertility rites, in flirting with Assyrian astral worship, and in welcoming Babylonian deities into their religious pantheon. By the late seventh century BC, foreign infiltration had penetrated virtually every part of Judah's culture.

Echoing the allegorical reference from Zenos, Jeremiah shared the Lord's lament about the children of Israel pursuing worldly ways: "Yet I had planted thee a noble vine, wholly a right seed: how then art thou turned into the degenerate plant of a strange vine unto me?"[68] Their moral corruption was evident not only in pagan altars and public rituals but also in the daily sins of injustice, deceit, and oppression that arose when God's laws were cast aside. The prophet shared that Judah had "played the harlot with many lovers," referencing how they chased after deities from across the region, from Egyptian cults to Babylonian cosmic beliefs.[69] "My people," the Lord said, "have changed their glory for that which doth not profit."[70]

This wide-scale abandonment of God, as we've seen, did not happen overnight. As with earlier generations, it began with small compromises: treating foreign gods with a casual tolerance, allowing idols to remain in private homes, and accommodating alliances and marriages that bound Judah more deeply to pagan nations. Little by little, these influences chipped away at the identity Judah once held as a people uniquely set apart to serve Jehovah. The glitter of Egyptian

---

68 Jeremiah 2:21.
69 Jeremiah 2:20.
70 Jeremiah 2:11.

wealth, the awe of Assyrian power, and the rising star of Babylon all contributed to a culture that steadily forgot its true heritage.

By Jeremiah's day, the moral rot was nearly complete, setting the stage for the Babylonian exile that would soon follow—a tragic culmination of generations of escalating infidelity and a final consequence of Israel's refusal to forsake false gods. Long before the armies of Nebuchadnezzar razed Jerusalem and dismantled the Temple,[71] prophets had implored Judah to abandon its adulterous alliances with foreign deities and return to the God who had delivered them from Egypt. Their pleas went unheeded. Thus, when Babylon finally swept in to conquer the land, it was more than a political or military defeat—it represented divine judgment for a people who had consistently chosen idolatry over worship of the one true God.

Intermarriage and Cultural Contamination

After roughly seventy years of Babylonian captivity,[72] a humbled remnant of Israel returned to their homeland under the edict of King Cyrus.[73] Their exile had been a dramatic judgment upon centuries of escalating idolatry, forcibly ripping them from the temple and inheritance they had so often taken for granted. In many respects, the trauma of losing Jerusalem, combined with life in a pagan empire, served to chasten them. Now able to rebuild, Israel's overt idol worship

71   2 Kings 24–25.
72   Jeremiah 25:11–12; 29:10.
73   2 Chronicles 36:22–23.

had largely vanished. They meticulously reconstructed the Temple walls, reestablished its ordinances, and renewed their commitment to the Law of Moses, determined to break from the patterns of apostasy that led to their downfall.

Yet the pull of outside influences still persisted. Many Jews intermarried with Ashdodites, Ammonites, and Moabites. Their children "spake half in the speech of Ashdod, and could not speak in the Jews' language."[74] Nehemiah, a prominent Jewish leader, rebuked his peers over their idolatrous intermarrying:

> And I contended with them, and cursed them, and smote certain of them, and plucked off their hair, and made them swear by God, saying, Ye shall not give your daughters unto their sons, nor take their daughters unto your sons, or for yourselves.

> Did not Solomon king of Israel sin by these things? yet among many nations was there no king like him, who was beloved of his God, and God made him king over all Israel: nevertheless even him did outlandish women cause to sin. Shall we then hearken unto you to do all this great evil, to transgress against our God in marrying strange wives?[75]

Still, even Nehemiah's forceful protests could only do so much to contain the slow stain of surrounding cultures. His chastisement of the offenders and his impassioned plea highlighted a deeper reality: despite all that the Jews had suffered,

---

74 Nehemiah 13:24.
75 Nehemiah 13:25–26.

from Egypt all the way up to their Babylonian captivity, they persisted in repeating the practices they had been explicitly told to avoid. Israel had been chosen to be a "peculiar treasure" among the nations,[76] yet time and again the people drew near to customs that threatened their distinctiveness. Nehemiah is best known for helping Jerusalem rebuild its walls to repel physical assault, yet these obstructions were unable to keep out the spiritual threats that encircled Israel—especially since the people intentionally sought after and embraced them.

Marrying people from other faiths was not an isolated event. It represented a recurring pattern seen throughout Israel's history: each time the people began to prosper, external influences offered alluring alternatives to their full devotion. Whether in Solomon's grand palace, Jeroboam's northern kingdom, or Nehemiah's Jerusalem, the slow stain of worldly enticements continually undermined the Lord's call for unwavering fidelity. In Nehemiah's rebuke, we catch an echo of ancient warnings: no matter how many times God delivers His people, the risk remains that they will once again choose to absorb the beliefs and behaviors of those around them, jeopardizing the very inheritance that sets them apart. A stain you embrace will never be cleansed.

The Romans

Though the Jews had already weathered centuries of cultural contamination under successive empires, Rome's oc-

---

76 Exodus 19:5.

cupation introduced yet another slow erosion of their divine distinctiveness. By the time of Christ, Judea was firmly under Roman administration: taxes flowed to Caesar, Roman governors like Pontius Pilate wielded civil authority, and even the high priest was effectively installed or approved by political figures rather than by divine ordination. This hierarchical arrangement left the Jewish leadership caught between religious duties to God and pragmatic submission to Roman power. While devout Jews still clung to the rites and sacrifices of the Temple, many leaders learned to navigate Roman expectations and work within the system.

This wasn't mere politics. Coins stamped with the emperor's image circulated in Jewish markets, reminders of a foreign ruler revered by many as semi-divine. Meanwhile, factions like the Sadducees—who largely controlled the priesthood—embraced Hellenistic and Roman influences, prioritizing status, commerce, and power over doctrinal fidelity. Dynamics such as these intertwined Temple life with the apparatus of an empire that cared little for Israel's religious aspirations.

Over time, the weight of Roman taxes, the partial assimilation of Jewish elites, and the cultural infusion of Gentile customs conspired to wear down their spiritual identity and faithfulness to God. Although the Pharisees tried to maintain strict adherence to the Law of Moses, even they, in seeking to preserve certain traditions, became mired in a system that often placed legal technicalities and social standing above the true spirit of God's commandments. Thus, in the decades before Jerusalem's eventual destruction, the slow stain of Roman influence revealed itself in a people who, though outwardly devout, had largely accepted the daily symbols and demands of Caesar. Despite the Temple standing proudly on Mount Moriah, a powerful tension persisted between the official forms of worship and a practical submission to foreign rule—unsettling evidence that a once-theocratic nation had become ever more entangled in the empire's worldly sway.

The Israelites' story is one of compromise, idolatry, and assimilation of surrounding practices. They were chosen to stand apart as God's covenant people, yet time and again they invited outside influences into their belief system, displacing divine counsel with carnal desires. Rejecting God led to the outcomes His prophets warned of: foreign conquest, scattering, and prolonged chastening to prompt their repentance. It was not God's unwillingness to protect them—rather, the people themselves forfeited His favor by welcoming a slow infiltration of corrupt ideologies and immoral rites. Each wave of apostasy confirms that a heart divided between God and the world cannot retain heaven's blessings for long.

THE JAREDITES

In the olive tree allegory, Zenos shares that in order to preserve its natural branches, "the Lord of the vineyard went his way, and hid the natural branches of the tame olive tree in the nethermost parts of the vineyard."[1] He wanted to see good fruit produced but was grieved that he was losing the tree *and* its potential fruit.[2] The scattering of some branches into distant areas of the vineyard seemed to be an act borne out of desperation—pruning, digging, and nourishing the main tree had, despite his best efforts, resulted in corruption and evil fruit,[3] "good for nothing save it be to be hewn down and cast into the fire."[4]

The Jaredites were certainly one such branch that the Lord relocated elsewhere, to a promised land "which is choice above all the earth."[5] This new "nethermost part" of the Lord's vineyard—separated by vast waters and preserved for a righteous nation—was intended to be a haven where the "natural branches" could thrive, untainted by the idolatrous practices that had taken hold in the old world. By removing them from the immediate influence of Babylonian society, the Lord pro-

1   Jacob 5:13–14.
2   Ibid.
3   Jacob 5:39–40.
4   Jacob 5:42.
5   Ether 1:38.

vided an environment in which the Jaredites, like other hidden branches,[6] might take firm root and produce good fruit. Isolated on a fresh continent, they were free to build a society centered on their covenants with Christ. God's intent in isolating them was to spare them from the slow stain of worldly corruption that had spread so widely in their old homeland. That was the goal, anyway. Yet, as Ether's record reveals, even in this promised land, the seeds of apostasy could easily take hold.

Secret Combinations

The Jaredites' initial prosperity and fidelity to God soon succumbed to corruption within just a few generations. The tiny kingdom produced warring familial factions, with children, cousins, and siblings all warring one against another to wrest control of the fledgling monarchy. In one early example, Jared (named after the original Jared) dethroned his father, Omer, after winning over half of the people through flattery.[7] Omer was incarcerated for years, apparently allowed conjugal visits leading to the birth of many children who, years later, "were exceedingly angry because of the doings of Jared their brother, insomuch that they did raise an army and gave battle unto Jared."[8] These seditious siblings overpowered Jared's army and nearly killed Jared himself, who "pled with them that they would not slay him, and he would give up the

---

6   Jacob 5:13–14.
7   Ether 8:2–3.
8   Ether 8:4–5.

kingdom unto his father."[9] They agreed, Jared lost, and he was deeply upset about it "for he had set his heart upon the kingdom and upon the glory of the world."[10]

Observing her father's frustration, Jared's daughter contrived a cunning plan inspired by "the records which our fathers brought across the great deep"[11]—ancient documents describing secret oaths and conspiracies once used to gain power. She proposed that Jared promise her in marriage to a man named Akish, on the condition that Akish murder her grandfather, Omer, and secure the throne for her father, Jared.[12] Through this arrangement, Jared's daughter believed she could restore her father to power and position herself advantageously. Though the scheme initially succeeded in toppling Omer, it also revived the very corruption the early Jaredites had hoped to escape by leaving the Old World behind.

The slow stain of secret combinations—with their tools of deception, flattery, and legalized murder and plunder—intensified significantly as time went on. These conspirators bound themselves with unholy oaths to protect one another and their thirst for power, forging a hidden network of loyalty and fear that threatened anyone on the throne. Over generations, what might have been dismissed initially as just political maneuvering metastasized into the primary driver of societal decay. Moroni, in editorializing Ether's record, notes that they were the primary cause of the Jaredites' ultimate destruction.[13]

---

9   Ether 8:6.
10 Ether 8:7.
11 Ether 8:9.
12 Ether 8:10.
13 Ether 8:21.

A Com–plete Breakdown

Akish didn't stay in power forever. In what would eventually become a constant scene of blowback—with the faction out of power revolting against the faction in power, again and again—Omer's family regained control after a yearslong war between the two sides.[14] Omer's son Emer began to restore righteousness, which brought prosperity to the people. He even saw Christ himself.[15] Emer's son Coriantumr continued in his father's footsteps, doing "that which was good unto his people in all his days"[16]—as did his son Com. It was Com's son Heth who would give in to temptation and lust for power, breaking the fragile peace the people had been enjoying in recent decades. Com's throne became the object of his son's lust, leading Heth to "embrace the secret plans again of old, to destroy his father."[17] Heth wanted power, and Satan had a tried and true recipe to help him acquire it. Com soon thereafter died at the hands of his own son.[18]

Maybe there's something in a name, but the cycle repeated generations later with another Com (whose father was also named Coriantum). This Com grew up in a family who for generations had been living "in captivity," now under the authority of Amgid.[19] Finally, Com rose up against his oppressors and "drew away the half of the kingdom," ruling over this

---

14   Ether 9:12–13.
15   Ether 9:22.
16   Ether 9:23.
17   Ether 9:26.
18   Ether 9:27.
19   Ether 10:30–31.

split community for four decades until he finally overthrew Amgid in battle "and obtained power over the remainder of the kingdom."[20] Things were looking up for Com and his family, yet just as peace and prosperity approached, so too did the secret combinations once again:

> And in the days of Com there began to be robbers in the land; and they adopted the old plans, and administered oaths after the manner of the ancients, and sought again to destroy the kingdom. Now Com did fight against them much; nevertheless, he did not prevail against them.[21]

Though Com tried to contain the robbers and defend his renewed kingdom, the "old plans" easily seduced those who wanted to embrace the Old World's ways. As prophets had long warned, once the seed of secret combinations took root, it would not be easily eradicated. Soon, the populace found itself embroiled yet again in brutal struggles for power, each usurper fueled by a sense of entitlement that viewed murder and intrigue as acceptable paths to the throne. And as each generation inherited the legacy of increasingly entrenched conspiracies, the slow stain of worldly ambition smothered the last flicker of faith in and obedience to God. Eventually, so many voices of righteousness were rejected—or even exterminated—that communal repentance became all but impossible.[22] This pattern would continue in waves until, in the final chapters of the Jaredite story, the entire civilization

---

20 Ether 10:32.
21 Ether 10:33–34.
22 Ether 11:5, 12.

would reap the harvest of devastation sown by centuries of corruption and apostasy.

Riplakish's Tyranny

Before the eventual collapse of Jaredite society, successive kings employed the Akish strategy to topple the throne and install themselves or their loved ones instead. Over several generations, each factional struggle for power further distanced the people from their original covenant with the Lord. By the time Riplakish arose as a prominent ruler, the notion that might made right—and that wealth and power took precedence over righteousness—had become deeply entrenched in Jaredite society.

What we read of Riplakish's polygamy, taxes, forced labor, and penal system makes clear how the Jaredites had degraded into the monarchical practices of the Old World from which their ancestors had escaped:

> And it came to pass that Riplakish did not do that which was right in the sight of the Lord, for he did have many wives and concubines, and did lay that upon men's shoulders which was grievous to be borne; yea, he did tax them with heavy taxes; and with the taxes he did build many spacious buildings.
>
> And he did erect him an exceedingly beautiful throne; and he did build many prisons, and whoso would not be subject unto taxes he did cast into prison; and whoso was not able to pay taxes he did cast into prison; and he did cause that they should labor continually for

their support; and whoso refused to labor he did cause to be put to death.

Wherefore he did obtain all his fine work, yea, even his fine gold he did cause to be refined in prison; and all manner of fine workmanship he did cause to be wrought in prison. And it came to pass that he did afflict the people with his whoredoms and abominations.[23]

A people once committed to a God-centered society had become subjugated under an exploitative system rooted in greed and self-indulgence. Rather than prioritizing justice or moral rectitude, Riplakish's administration reflected the values of a civilization undone by its appetite for worldly gain. The seeds planted by earlier conspirators reached full bloom in his regime, bearing the bitter fruit of spiritual decay and social upheaval. Despite being killed in another uprising years later and his descendants all being driven out of the land,[24] Riplakish's reign makes clear how many people—particularly those in power—embrace the slow stain and invite it to spread. Society disintegrates when power replaces principle.

In the final chapters of Ether, the slow stain of worldly influence reaches a brutal crescendo, plunging the Jaredites into ceaseless warfare.[25] Factions splinter and realign in pursuit of power until social order all but disintegrates. Prophets like Ether call for repentance, yet their warnings go unheeded; the

---

23 Ether 10:5–7.
24 Ether 10:8.
25 Ether 13–15.

people were long past the point of listening to God's messengers. And with each new generation inheriting the unresolved conflicts of the last, violence became the only real inheritance left. In the end, the Jaredites destroyed themselves entirely—a once-hopeful nation undone by relentless ambition, forsaken principles, and the unrelenting moral decay they refused to curb.

THE NEPHITES

Most who read King Mosiah's story come away with a superficial understanding of what was happening—not unlike my ignorance as a recently called missionary to what the olive tree allegory was really about. What we find, if we peel back a layer or two, is a direct connection to the Jaredite nation and an opportunity to stop the spread of pride and power lust that had caused that nation to implode.

Let's establish some context first. Mosiah was a monarch, one in a line of Nephite kings—a system that was less than ideal from the start. Like the Israelites rejecting God as their ruler and desiring kingly control,[1] Nephi explains that his people "would that I should be their king"—a proposal he rejected since he "was desirous that they should have *no* king."[2] But Nephi ultimately gave in to their demands in his old age and "anointed a man to be a king and a ruler over his people" just before his death.[3] This follows a similar turn of events centuries before when Jared and his brother's people "desired of them that they should anoint one of their sons to be a king over them." Jared's brother, considering the request "griev-

---

1   1 Samuel 8:7.
2   2 Nephi 5:18; emphasis added.
3   Jacob 1:9.

ous," explained: "Surely this thing leadeth to captivity"[4]—a prophecy that plays out throughout Ether's entire record.

Nephite kings fared better than their Jaredite counterparts, at least. In general, the Nephite kings were righteous and served a dual role as religious ministers to the people, more closely resembling a theocracy than a monarchy. For hundreds of years, this system of government was maintained until King Mosiah obtained and translated the Jaredite record,[5] which revealed the inherent dangers that come with centralized political power into a single ruler. Think of it: Mosiah was reading this historical record and learning of the absolute carnage that had destroyed an entire society. In his shoes, what lesson might you draw from this information? It is evident that the knowledge gained from the Jaredite record deeply impacted Mosiah, so much so that he suggested changing their system of government altogether. He, the king, argued that there should no longer be one. No doubt with the bloody Jaredite battles on his mind, he told his people, "I fear there would rise contentions among you... which would be the cause of shedding much blood and perverting the way of the Lord, yea, and destroy the souls of many people."[6] With ample evidence from his reading of the Jaredite record, he exclaimed, "how much iniquity doth one wicked king cause to be committed, yea, and what great destruction!"[7]

---

4   Ether 6:21-23; 7:5.
5   Mosiah 28:17.
6   Mosiah 29:7.
7   Mosiah 29:17.

Mosiah argued his point further: "because all men are not just it is not expedient that ye should have a king or kings to rule over you."[8] The system of mortals ruling over one another—something that dictators, presidents, governors, mayors, and kings all share in common to varying degrees—is rightly called into question because of man's fallible nature. Because positions of power attract "king-men"[9] who desire to control others, it becomes an unfortunate truism that "when the wicked rule, the people mourn."[10] And so, the king wisely pushed for a different path in order to "do that which will make for the peace of this people,"[11] introducing a decentralized system of judges who would interpret and apply God's law. Think of it like a stain remover to expunge the problem from his community. The king's about-face, borne of the warning from the Jaredite nation and lessons learned from King Noah, deserves to be quoted at length:

> And I command you to do these things [selecting judges] in the fear of the Lord; and I command you to do these things, and that ye have no king; that if these people commit sins and iniquities they shall be answered upon their own heads.
>
> For behold I say unto you, the sins of many people have been caused by the iniquities of their kings; therefore their iniquities are answered upon the heads of their kings.

---

8   Mosiah 29:16.
9   Alma 51:5-8.
10 D&C 98:9.
11 Mosiah 29:10.

And now I desire that this inequality should be no more in this land, especially among this my people; but I desire that this land be a land of liberty, and every man may enjoy his rights and privileges alike...

And he also unfolded unto them all the disadvantages they labored under, by having an unrighteous king to rule over them;

Yea, all his iniquities and abominations, and all the wars, and contentions, and bloodshed, and the stealing, and the plundering, and the committing of whoredoms, and all manner of iniquities which cannot be enumerated—telling them that these things ought not to be, that they were expressly repugnant to the commandments of God.[12]

It cannot get clearer than that: a God-fearing king came to recognize that substituting mortal rulers for God is "expressly repugnant" to God's will. He saw what the slow stain of worldly ambition had done to the Jaredites, and he recognized this was his opportunity to stop its advance within the Nephite nation. To his credit, Mosiah's people were "convinced of the truth of his words" and "relinquished their desires for a king."[13]

---

12   Mosiah 29:30-32, 35-36.
13   Mosiah 29:37-38.

Nephite Self-Rule

What's interesting about Mosiah's change in governance is that it actually accelerated the demise of Nephite society. (Damned if you do, damned if you don't?) What was before a relatively peaceful existence under Nephite monarchy devolved into a story of turbulence and violence. From the time that Mosiah instituted the "reign of the judges" until Christ's post-resurrection arrival, there are fifteen major war campaigns recorded. A common thread among *all fifteen* of them is that they were instigated and incited by dissenting Nephites who aspired for power, broke away from the group, and through various means incited the Lamanites to riot and war against the Nephites. The Lamanites were pawns in a war of propaganda, corraled and controlled by power-seeking authoritarians. The fifteen provocations are:

1. Amlici[14]
2. The People of Ammonihah[15]
3. Amalekites[16]
4. Zoramites[17]
5. Amalickiah[18]
6. Morianton[19]

---

14 Alma 2.
15 Alma 8:3, 9, 16; Alma 10:27-32; Alma 16:1-11; Alma 25:1-8; Alma 49:3.
16 Alma 21:3-6; Alma 23 7-14; Alma 24; Alma 27:1-3.
17 Alma 31:8; Alma 43:3-17.
18 Alma 46, 47, 48, 49; Alma 51:9-12, 22-37.
19 Alma 50:25-35.

7. Kingmen[20]
8. Ammoron[21]
9. Pachus[22]
10. Nephite Dissenters[23]
11. Coriantumr and Tubaloth[24]
12. Wealthy Nephites[25]
13. Gadianton Robbers[26]
14. Dissenters and Gadianton Robbers[27]
15. Giddianhi[28]

As important as was Mosiah's insight about monarchy, a decentralized political framework did not itself inoculate the Nephites from the same corrosive ambition that undermined the Jaredite system. Free from a single monarch's control, multiple aspiring rulers rose up to contend for power and riches. Time and again, a minor faction or disaffected clique recognized it could seize influence by inciting fear or by appealing to vanity. While these dissenters manipulated the Lamanites into open conflict against the Nephite nation, an even more insidious threat arose from their seductive promise of power and wealth, leading many Nephites to forsake their covenants

---

20 Alma 51:8, 15-21; Alma 60:14-18.
21 Alma 52:19-20, 33-36; Alma 59:7; Alma 62:33-36.
22 Alma 61:3-20; Alma 62:1-11.
23 Alma 63:10-15.
24 Helaman 1.
25 Helaman 4.
26 Helaman 10:18-19; Helaman 11:1-10.
27 Helaman 11:21-26.
28 3 Nephi 1:27; 3 Nephi 2, 3, 4.

for short-term gain—and ultimately trapping them through flattery, bribes, or hollow pledges.

Rather than eradicate the slow stain that the Jaredite record had so vividly warned about, the Nephites appeared to invite it through their growing appetite for luxury and status.[29] In their rush to distinguish themselves with finery or titles,[30] many lost sight of the God who had given them everything—creating the conditions where dissidents could repeatedly exploit the public's worldly inclinations and fuel one uprising after another.[31]

Where It All Began

The Nephite record begins with Nephi and his family's journey across the ocean to the promised land. His father, Lehi, had a vision of Jerusalem's imminent destruction and was commanded to leave with his children and a few others.[32] But Laman and Lemuel, two of his sons, held a deep-rooted attachment to the comforts and social status they had enjoyed in Jerusalem. Rather than seeing their father as a prophet delivering them from a doomed city, they fixated on the wealth and power they had forsaken, having "to leave the land of their inheritance, and their gold, and their silver, and their precious things," only "to perish in the wilderness," as they put it.[33] Their incessant complaints all shared this same tune:

---

29 Helaman 3:33–36; 4:12.
30 Alma 4:6–8; Alma 51:5–8, 21; Helaman 7:4–5.
31 3 Nephi 6:10–14.
32 1 Nephi 1:4, 13.
33 1 Nephi 2:11-12.

"these many years we have suffered in the wilderness, which time we might have enjoyed our possessions and the land of our inheritance; yea, and we might have been happy."[34] Like the wandering Israelites yearning for the fleshpots of Egypt, Laman and Lemuel wandered in misery, yearning for the worldly delights to which they had become accustomed.

In this sense, Laman and Lemuel carried the slow stain of Jerusalem with them, refusing to relinquish the worldview they had absorbed in an idolatrous community that prized riches, status, and self-interest.[35] Despite witnessing miracles—being guided by the Liahona,[36] the provision of food in the wilderness,[37] and even the power of God in saving Nephi when they bound him at sea[38]—they continued to resist Lehi's revelations. Their hearts grew hardened, and their complaints multiplied at every turn, revealing just how deeply Jerusalem's materialistic culture had permeated their souls. Though they had physically removed themselves from their homeland, they never fully abandoned the vain ambitions, pride, and distrust that characterized a society on the brink of destruction. In dragging the remnants of Jerusalem's corruption to the promised land, they set in motion a chain of dissension and downfall that would plague their descendants for generations.

---

34   1 Nephi 17:20–22.
35   1 Nephi 7:6–12; 16:1–3.
36   1 Nephi 16:10, 28.
37   1 Nephi 16:31.
38   1 Nephi 18:11–20.

King Noah's Debauchery

A once-prosperous colony founded by Zeniff deteriorated, within a single generation, into a glaring example of how worldly indulgence can undermine spiritual strength.[39] Zeniff was a righteous, albeit somewhat naïve, person of ambition who saw the good in the Lamanites[40] and was "over-zealous to inherit the land of [his] fathers."[41] He struck a disadvantageous deal with the Lamanite king, whose people began to rob and oppress this Nephite offshoot.[42] Later, approaching his own death, Zeniff conferred the tiny kingdom upon one of his sons, Noah, who "did not walk in the ways of his father."[43] (Understatement of the century?)

Noah embraced a hedonistic lifestyle, which he financed by burdening his subjects with exorbitant taxes, using the proceeds to commission opulent buildings and sponsor lavish gatherings.[44] His unrestrained displays of affluence demonstrated how the humble resolve once guiding Zeniff's settlers had given way to gratification and vanity. Meanwhile, the priests serving Noah—elevated for political loyalty rather than any meaningful spiritual qualifications—succumbed to the same slow stain. These "religious leaders" were more in-

---

39 Mosiah 11:1–19.
40 Mosiah 9:1.
41 Mosiah 9:3.
42 Mosiah 9:11–13.
43 Mosiah 11:1.
44 Mosiah 11:3–10.

terested in justifying their king's pleasures than discharging their role with fidelity to God.[45]

It was into this moral vacuum that Abinadi emerged—an outsider in both appearance and demeanor, who bluntly rebuked the people's drift into idolatry and called out their hypocrisy. He delivered a message from God, pointing out that their "abominations, and their wickedness, and their whoredoms"[46] had kindled God's anger against them. Naturally, Noah and his minions hated being told they were in the wrong and attempted to kill Abinadi to shut him up.[47] When that initially failed, Noah's priests tried to refute him through rhetorical traps,[48] only to expose their own ignorance of the very law they claimed to uphold.[49] Their spiritual blindness ran so deep that they misread Isaiah's prophecies and failed to recognize basic truths about the coming Messiah.[50]

This tension between Abinadi's heaven-sent message and the establishment's corrupt viewpoint typifies the "slow stain" pattern. As worldly greed and luxury took root, it eroded the people's ability—even among their supposed religious leaders—to discern truth. By condemning Abinadi to death,[51] Noah sealed the fate of a small society whose moral anchor was cut loose, resulting in political and military disaster not long thereafter.[52] The Zeniffite experiment offers a cautionary

45   Mosiah 12:25–27.
46   Mosiah 11:20.
47   Mosiah 11:26.
48   Mosiah 12:19–24.
49   Mosiah 12:27.
50   Mosiah 13:33–35.
51   Mosiah 17:1.
52   Mosiah 19.

tale: once a culture prizes materialism and embraces worldly ways, the path back to righteousness grows ever narrower—and without timely repentance, the results can be fatal.

Nehor's False Doctrine

It was a pivotal cultural moment for the Nephites when the new system of judges was established.[53] Perhaps as a result of this drastic and sudden change, some seemed eager to test the boundaries of individual freedom. Enter Nehor, who began promoting twisted religious ideas that deviated from the gospel taught among the Nephites. Nehor's version promised universal salvation regardless of obedience or righteousness.[54] Obviously, such flattery resonated with those who found the true church's doctrines demanding or uncomfortable. This was, after all, Lucifer's primary stratagem in the premortal realm, enticing a third of the host of heaven to follow him[55] by flattering them into feeling like they would be able to enjoy carnal pleasures without long-term spiritual consequences. Satan sought to "redeem all mankind"[56] just as he suggested Nehor should.[57]

Nehor's false doctrine was enticing on its face for offering to allow people to "eat, drink, and be merry, for tomorrow we die; and it shall be well with us."[58] Beyond this deception, Nehor elevated priests above the people and urged

---

53 Alma 1:1.
54 Alma 1:4.
55 D&C 29:36; Revelation 12:4; Moses 4:6.
56 Moses 4:1.
57 Alma 1:15.
58 2 Nephi 28:7.

them to be supported through wealth garnered from their congregations,[59] thus tapping into the carnal man's desire for power and prestige. His charismatic presence and seductive message spread quickly, appealing to the pride of those who yearned for status and ease; "many did believe on his words," the record states.[60]

The danger of Nehor's doctrine was that it offered a supposed shortcut to spirituality—exactly the sort of slow stain Israel and the Jaredites had before welcomed, to their inevitable undoing. By dismissing the need for repentance and moral purity, Nehor's philosophy justified the prioritization and pursuit of carnal desires. The swift growth of his following reveals how susceptible God's people can be when a persuasive voice appeals to their baser inclinations. If it worked on a third of God's children eons ago, it can work here on Earth in communities small and large. And these stains can be very difficult to remove from society. Even after Nehor openly killed Gideon and was punished according to the law,[61] the influence of his teachings continued. Many, having tasted the allure of easy grace and social privilege, clung to his ideas, setting the stage for later conflicts that would arise from combining religious trappings with pride and covetousness.

The People of Ammonihah

If Nehor planted a rotten seed, the people of Ammonihah eagerly fertilized it. While Nehor had popularized a comfort-

---

59   Alma 1:3.
60   Alma 1:5.
61   Alma 1:7–15.

able theology that emphasized prestige and convenience, the inhabitants of Ammonihah fashioned an entire civic culture around those same tenets.[62] Their city's judicial system—and the social norms that upheld it—became a breeding ground for arrogance and intellectual pride. Indeed, Alma's initial attempts to preach there were met with harsh dismissal, with many arguing that their wealth, learning, and social structures negated any influence he might have on them.[63]

When Alma later returned with Amulek, their warnings were shrugged off with indifference by a populace fully entrenched in the slow stain of worldly self-assurance.[64] The intellectual elite, particularly the lawyers and judges, twisted their laws to ensnare the two missionaries, rather than seeking any semblance of truth or justice.[65] They deliberately used rhetoric to frame these men of God as lawbreakers, showing how a society drunk with rationalization could corrupt an entire "justice" system. And in their contempt for repentance, the city's proud citizens not only rejected a prophet's message but also persecuted those who believed it, burning both scripture and new converts alike.[66] Nehor started a slow stain of his own, a drip by comparison, while the folks in Ammonihah were saturating anyone they could.

The city's inhabitants boasted of their economic and intellectual clout, yet they had abandoned any kind of moral foundation. Ultimately, they reaped the tragic consequence

---

62 Alma 8:8–10.
63 Alma 8:11–13.
64 Alma 8:14–32; 10:27–31.
65 Alma 14:2–5.
66 Alma 14:8–14.

of their obstinacy: a swift and devastating destruction at the hands of Lamanite invaders.[67] Having disqualified themselves from receiving God's protection, they stood defenseless when war arrived. In a single blow, all their vaunted logic, legal cunning, and civic pride proved utterly worthless. Their fate illustrates that once the stain of worldly ways becomes embedded in the cultural fabric, only sincere repentance can avert a self-inflicted collapse.

Zoramite Apostasy

The arrogance and self-assurance of Ammonihah were eerily similar to what Alma and Amulek later encountered in the Zoramite community, whose leader was "leading the hearts of the people to bow down to dumb idols."[68] Here Alma's small band of missionaries found a people that had constructed an elitist religion in which wealth and social standing defined spiritual worth.[69] The very act of worship became a performance—exemplified by the Rameumptom upon which they extolled their supposed superiority over every other group.[70] Their proud proclamations were more about affirming their social hierarchy rather than acknowledging God in any sincere way. Alma saw them for what they were: "a wicked and a perverse people; yea, he saw that their hearts were set upon gold, and upon silver, and upon all manner of fine goods."[71]

---

67 Alma 16:1–11.
68 Alma 31:1.
69 Alma 31:24–28.
70 Alma 31:12–23.
71 Alma 31:24.

The stain of pride had seemingly seeped into every facet of Zoramite life, dividing the people between a favored class and those deemed "poor" in both material and spiritual terms.[72] While the elite congratulated themselves for their prosperity, they neglected basic compassion and cast out those who did not conform to their vain rituals.[73] Of course, these were not heathen gentiles or idolatrous infidels lacking the light of the gospel to correct their prideful, pagan ways. These were "dissenters from the Nephites; therefore they had had the word of God preached unto them."[74] They knew better. And yet their faith had become corrupted—warped into a tool to justify their vanity and soothe their consciences as they chose power and wealth over a commitment to Christ. Once again, the lesson is clear: anyone who was once taught the truth is susceptible to abandoning or corrupting it when seduced by worldly aspirations; the elect, too, can be deceived.[75]

More than Nephites and Lamanites?

Before exploring additional examples of how the gradual spread of worldly influences corrupted the Nephite nation and led to its downfall, let's first consider the sources of these influences. Sure, Laman and Lemuel established the initial pattern of apostasy by prioritizing their desire for material wealth and secular pursuits over their faithfulness to the Lord and their loyalty to their father. This initial influence set off a

---

72 Alma 32:2–5.
73 Alma 32:5.
74 Alma 31:8.
75 Joseph Smith—Matthew 1:22.

chain of events throughout the generations, with their prideful posterity feeling like they were robbed of political power[76] and justifying conquest and control as a means of building material wealth. It became a generational tradition, teaching "their children that they should hate [the Nephites], and that they should murder them, and that they should rob and plunder them, and do all they could to destroy them."[77]

After fleeing with his loyal family members to leave Laman and Lemuel behind (and after resisting their desire that he be their king), Nephi shares a revelation from the Lord about the posterity of his wicked brothers: "They shall be a scourge unto thy seed, to stir them up in remembrance of me; and inasmuch as they will not remember me, and hearken unto my words, they shall scourge them even unto destruction."[78] And clearly, we see this play out through the pages of the Book of Mormon—again and again, the Lamanites (typically whipped into a frenzy by corrupt, dissenting Nephites) go to battle against the Nephites, which often humbles them into relying on the Lord for protection and deliverance.

But is that it? Is the sole source of worldly ways in the Nephite story their corrupt cousins? This is seemingly how most people understand the record—an empty, promised land that was peopled by the Jaredites (who died), the Mulekites (who left Jerusalem shortly after Lehi's group, sailed across the ocean, and later joined forces with the Nephites), and Lehi's posterity. That's it. Thus, if we read the record this way,

---

76 2 Nephi 5:3; Mosiah 10:12–16; Alma 54:17.

77 Mosiah 10:17.

78 2 Nephi 5:25.

the "slow stain" is all their own doing—factions of faithless dissenters embracing Satan's enticements and becoming, on their own accord, the divine scourge to keep the righteous in line.

Maybe there's more to the story. Consider the possibility that the Book of Mormon is not actually a history of all the people who have lived in North and South America. It only claims, rather, to be an account of a few groups of people who inhabited a particular portion of the promised land. And nowhere does it claim that the Jaredites were the first human beings on the continent. There were other people already present! As Hugh Nibley wrote:

> Just because Lehi's people had come from Jerusalem by special direction we are not to conclude that other men cannot have had the same experience. And by the same token the fact that the Jaredites were led to the land of promise at the time of the dispersion gives us no right to conclude that no one else was ever so led, either earlier or later than they. It is nowhere said or implied that even the Jaredites were the first to come here, any more than it is said or implied that they were the first or only people to be led from the tower....

> Now there is a great deal said in the Book of Mormon about the past and future of the promised land, but never is it described as an empty land. The descendants of Lehi were never the only people on the continent, and the Jaredites never claimed to be.[79]

79 Hugh Nibley, "The World of the Jaredites," *Improvement Era* 55, no. 5 (May 1952), 342.

This idea has lightly been tossed around in the past. For example, in the April 1929 general conference, a member of the First Presidency, Anthony W. Ivins, encouraged us to "be careful in the conclusions that we reach" regarding this precise topic. He continued:

> The Book of Mormon teaches the history of three distinct peoples, or two peoples and three different colonies of people, who came from the old world to this continent. It does not tell us that there was no one here before them. It does not tell us that people did not come after. And so if discoveries are made which suggest differences in race origins, it can very easily be accounted for, and reasonably, for we do believe that other people came to this continent.[80]

A decade later, Elder John A. Widstoe, an apostle, wrote about the three primary groups recorded and stated that "There may also have been others not recorded in the Book or not known to the ancient authors."[81] A few years later, another apostle published, with First Presidency approval, a statement that described the Book of Mormon as "part of a record, both sacred and secular, of prophets and peoples who (with supplementary groups) were among the ancestors of the American 'Indians.'"[82]

---

80 Anthony W. Ivins, *Conference Report*, April 1929, 15.
81 John A. Widtsoe and Franklin S. Harris Jr., *Seven Claims of the Book of Mormon: A Collection of Evidences* (Independence: Zion's Printing and Publishing, 1937), 87.
82 Richard L. Evans, "What Is a 'Mormon'?" *Religions of America*, edited by Leo Rosten (London: Heinemann, 1957), 94.

Suddenly the slow stain of the world makes far more sense in its pervasive influence in the New World if we realize that God's people were surrounded by competing cultures, each with their varied idolatrous influences. It wasn't just Laman and Lemuel's descendants becoming Satan's whipping boys: like their Israelite ancestors, each of these groups had to navigate operating in a society with people with wildly conflicting worldviews. The idea makes sense when reading about each group of people from this perspective. Think of the Jaredites whose group included several families cramming into small barges to journey across the sea.[83] Between when they settled in the promised land to when Coriantumr became the sole survivor of his people, over thirty generations had passed.[84] Frequent wars,[85] famines,[86] and poisonous serpents[87] decimated the population on many occasions. A likely high fertility rate was definitely tempered by a high mortality rate, suggesting the population would struggle to significantly grow. Yet the destruction Coriantumr witnessed in the final apocalyptic showdown resulted in the deaths of "two millions of mighty men, and also their wives and their children." Assuming just

---

83 Ether 3:1; Ether 2:16.
84 Ether's genealogy is outlined in Ether 1, tracing back to Jared. The record lists 30 generations, but in verse 6, it notes that Ether "was a descendant" of Coriantor, while for all other entries it explicitly states "was the son" of their respective fathers. This distinction suggests that Coriantor may not have been Ether's immediate father but rather a near-distant relative. Consequently, I speculate that the total number of generation slightly exceeds 30.
85 The citations are too many to list; nearly the entire book of Ether is a record of warfare and bloodshed.
86 Ether 9:30.
87 Ether 9:31.

half the men were married, each with on average, say, four children at the time, that's seven million people snuffed out in a horrifying genocide. With numbers that large, it seems wholly plausible that in over two millennia, the Jaredite society had grown through intermarriage and immigration to encompass a much broader group of people than their pure-blood relatives alone.

What about the Mulekites? Nibley observes that "The idea of other migrations to the New World is taken so completely for granted that the story of the Mulekites is dismissed in a few verses." Here they are:

> Behold, it came to pass that Mosiah discovered that the people of Zarahemla came out from Jerusalem at the time that Zedekiah, king of Judah, was carried away captive into Babylon. And they journeyed in the wilderness, and were brought by the hand of the Lord across the great waters, into the land where Mosiah discovered them; and they had dwelt there from that time forth.[88]

That's it. It's met with a shrug of casual indifference, not a mind-blowing exclamation at the realization that another group had been led to the same land. But what's more interesting still is the description that follows:

> And at the time that Mosiah discovered them, they had become exceedingly numerous. Nevertheless, they had had many wars and serious contentions, and had fallen by the sword from time to time; and their lan-

---

88   Omni 1:15–16.

guage had become corrupted; and they had brought no records with them; and they denied the being of their Creator; and Mosiah, nor the people of Mosiah, could understand them.[89]

Mulek's group left Jerusalem only a few years after Lehi's family fled, yet when they all joined up in Zarahemla, Mulek's group was observed to be "exceedingly numerous," suggesting, by contrast, that they were larger than the group of Nephites. Further, in the course of just over four centuries, this entire group was speaking a language unintelligible to the Nephites. One might conclude that the descriptions that follow were the cause of their linguistic corruption: "they had brought no records with them." The Nephites had records to reinforce culture and language among a tight-knit group. But plenty of people throughout world history have been entirely illiterate yet have retained their language, with only slight dialectical changes over a multicentury span of time. Consider Iceland, whose geographic isolation has led to a slow evolution of its language, which traces its origins to the ninth century when Norse Vikings settled the island, bringing with them a dialect of Old Norse. Due to limited contact with the outside world, the language developed independently, preserving many features of Old Norse that have been lost in other Scandinavian languages. The people of Zarahemla speaking a foreign language as a group of people is a strong indicator that they had embraced the culture and tongue of existing people, leading

89 Omni 1:17.

to a rapid evolution (or perhaps total abandonment) of their ancestral language.

Let's wrap up with the primary protagonists for a couple of final examples. Just after Nephi's death, his younger brother Jacob delivers a sermon to his people, denouncing their pride, vanity, and whoredoms. Recall who followed Nephi: his siblings—Sam, Jacob, Joseph, and his unnamed sisters—along with Zoram and each of their spouses. Assuming three sisters, that's eight couples total, and assuming two new generations at Nephi's death and an average of five children from each couple, we're looking at around 150 people total in Nephi's community. But by the time of Nephi's death, there had been numerous "wars and contentions and destructions"[90] in which he "wielded the sword of Laban in their defense,"[91] which would have surely reduced the number of men in the tiny Nephite population. Yet Jacob rebukes his people for lusting after "many wives and concubines," pursuing polygamous "whoredoms" that God considered "abominable."[92] This appears to suggest a much larger population of females than could have been the case from only the surviving posterity from eight couples two generations ago.

And then there's Sherem. Just a few years after Jacob's sermon, "there came a man among the people of Nephi, whose name was Sherem."[93] He told Jacob that he had "sought much opportunity that I might speak unto you; for I have heard and

---

90   1 Nephi 19:4.
91   Jacob 1:10.
92   Jacob 2:23–28.
93   Jacob 7:1.

also know that thou goest about much, preaching that which ye call the gospel, or the doctrine of Christ."[94] Again, if the population of their group at the time is some 100–150 people, that's a tiny village at most. Jacob, their spiritual leader, would have had regular contact with each person and had a visible presence in the fledgling community; everyone would know everyone else. Then how could Sherem never have seen Jacob, and why would he have persisted so long in trying to make contact with him? And where would Jacob "go about" preaching, as Sherem said, if his group was so small? Finally, from where did Sherem "[come]... among the people of Nephi?" One might wonder if he was a distant cousin from the Lamanite branch of the family, but that is unlikely as Sherem acknowledged that he believed in the scriptures (and thus the Law of Moses) when asked by Jacob.[95] This story makes much more sense if Nephi's people were surrounded by and had integrated to some degree with an existing populace, swelling their numbers sufficiently to produce a wider number of people literate in the language and theology of the Nephite community.[96]

There are other examples,[97] such as a passing, curious reference to "Lamanitish women."[98] And Nephi saying, after listing his family members fleeing with him, that his group

---

94 Jacob 7:6.

95 Jacob 7:10.

96 For more analysis and a differing perspective, see A. Keith Thompson, "Who Was Sherem?" *Interpreter: A Journal of Mormon Scripture*, vol. 14 (2015), 1–15.

97 Another I don't mention here is Nephi's choice of Isaiah's scripture, as documented in "Did Interactions with 'Others' Influence Nephi's Selection of Isaiah?" Scripture Central, March 24, 2020, https://scripturecentral.org/knowhy/did-interactions-with-others-influence-nephis-selection-of-isaiah.

98 Alma 19:16.

included "all those who would go with me," who were "those
who believed in the warnings and the revelations of God,"
suggesting a contingent of non-Lehite converts.[99] Another
is Nephi and his people building a massive temple structure
"like unto the temple of Solomon"[100]—the logistics for which,
including the acquisition of materials and the coordination of
labor, would be challenging in a population of merely several
dozen people. What's far more likely in all of this is that the
Jaredites, Mulekites, and Nephites were each minority groups
living among indigenous (and idolatrous) people who had
significant influence through intermarriage, immigration,
and other forms of societal integration. Think back to the
olive tree allegory: branches broken off the tame tree (historical Israel[101]) were grafted onto wild trees (non-Israelite
groups), with "young and tender branches"[102] joining into existing, wild trees "in the nethermost parts of the vineyard."[103]
With this understanding, we now realize how God's people
in the promised land faced the same difficulty presented to
Israel in the Old World—how to remain faithful to God and
maintain theological purity when surrounded and seduced by
idolatrous practices and the prevailing cultural influences of
neighboring societies. Laman and Lemuel's intergenerational
stains probably paled in comparison to the enticing influence
of the natives surrounding their descendants.

---

99   2 Nephi 5:5–6.
100 2 Nephi 5:16.
101 Jacob 5:3.
102 Jacob 5:8.
103 Jacob 5:14.

Secret Combinations

Toward the end of his record, Mormon identifies, with righteous passion, the primary problem that felled his civilization and that of the Jaredites.[104] These secret combinations, for the Nephites, began with the rise of Gadianton and his band of robbers whose activities demonstrate how deeply the slow stain of worldly power can penetrate. It began when Kishkumen assassinated Pahoran as he sat upon the judgment-seat,[105] fleeing into the protection of his co-conspirators who "all entered into a covenant, yea, swearing by their everlasting Maker, that they would tell no man that Kishkumen had murdered Pahoran."[106] The smooth-talking Gadianton soon became leader of this cabal,[107] and once the group had expanded its operations with astonishing success, the secret combination "did prove the overthrow, yea, almost the entire destruction of the people of Nephi."[108]

Like much of the idolatry and wickedness that God's people have embraced over time, many Nephites perceived this creeping tide of worldly influence not as a corrupting force but as an appealing mark of progress. After an about-face leading them to gospel conversion, the Lamanites made a concerted effort to expunge this stain from their community—whereas the Nephites became their lifeline:

---

104 Ether 8:18–21.
105 Helaman 1:9.
106 Helaman 1:11.
107 Helaman 2:4.
108 Helaman 2:13.

And it came to pass that the Lamanites did hunt the band of robbers of Gadianton; and they did preach the word of God among the more wicked part of them, insomuch that this band of robbers was utterly destroyed from among the Lamanites.

And it came to pass on the other hand, that the Nephites did build them up and support them, beginning at the more wicked part of them, until they had overspread all the land of the Nephites, and had seduced the more part of the righteous until they had come down to believe in their works and partake of their spoils, and to join with them in their secret murders and combinations.[109]

Seduced to partake of their spoils and share power with them—it's the original promise Satan made to Cain in persuading him to murder Abel. A secret plot, sanctioned murder, all to acquire wealth and power.[110] He's been making the same offer to people throughout world history, that through "secret plans [they might] obtain kingdoms and great glory."[111] During the Nephite era, these evil machinations took root precisely because so many Nephites valued prestige and comfort over righteousness—making it tragically easy for Gadianton's conspirators to infiltrate the upper echelons of society and gain access to the levers of power. Far from being a fringe rebellion, the Gadianton society embedded itself in commerce, courts, and councils. In many cases, those supposedly called

---

109 Helaman 6:37–38.
110 Moses 5:29–33.
111 Ether 8:9.

to uphold justice were little more than puppets in the employ of Gadianton's circle, revealing how treacherous the slow infiltration of greed and vanity can be when it meets a population willing to compromise its moral foundation. Isaiah's rebuke of those "that call evil good, and good evil; that put darkness for light, and light for darkness"[112] cuts to the heart of this mindset, exposing how greed and prestige can transform a poisonous stain into a coveted badge of honor.

A Zion Society Falls

The arrival of Jesus Christ among the Nephites ushered in a remarkable period of unity and holiness unlike any other in their history. His ministry healed centuries of conflict between the two principal factions, and for generations thereafter "there was no contention in the land."[113] With hearts knit together in charity,[114] the people became "one," holding "all things common among them" in Zion-like fashion.[115] By turning their attention firmly to the Savior's teachings, they appeared to have broken the recurring cycle of apostasy that had plagued their ancestors for centuries. For nearly 200 years, this flourishing era vindicated the Savior's promise that those who honored His commandments would enjoy peace, prosperity, and divine favor.[116]

Yet as time wore on and the first generation of steadfast believers passed away, subtle undercurrents of worldliness

---

112 Isaiah 5:20.
113 4 Nephi 1:2.
114 4 Nephi 1:15.
115 4 Nephi 1:3.
116 4 Nephi 1:22.

began to surface once more. A new generation grew up that had not personally witnessed the miracles of Christ's ministry; they inherited comfort and prosperity but lacked the firsthand sense of awe that bound their parents to the Lord.[117] Gradually, the Nephite community yielded to the allure of personal gain—coveting ornaments, riches, and the perceived prestige that comes with social standing. This was the slow stain reemerging: small concessions to pride and vanity cropping up in daily life, then quietly proliferating among merchants, officials, and families. Before long, "they began to be divided into classes,"[118] reinstituting the same social hierarchies that had spelled disaster for their ancestors.

As these fissures widened, the faithful remnant sounded the alarm, but many dismissed their concerns in favor of economic ambitions and material indulgence, denying "the more parts of [Christ's] gospel."[119] Factions formed, and the fleeting focus on shared worship and community gave way to renewed competition, wealth-building, and the kind of cultural splintering that inevitably ushers in deeper contention. It was, in essence, the same pattern: what started as small glimmers of pride soon escalated into overt self-promotion and social stratification. By the time the division was more widespread, the people had largely forgotten the unifying power of the Savior's personal visit, succumbing instead to internal rifts that would propel them toward final collapse.[120]

Thus, even the Nephite golden age—a near-Edenic moment when war and strife were unknown—eventually suc-

---

117 4 Nephi 1:20.
118 4 Nephi 1:26.
119 4 Nephi 1:24, 27.
120 4 Nephi 1:35–38.

cumbed to the slow infiltration of worldly attitudes. Their story suggests that no matter how strong a society's covenant ties may be, if its members gradually invite pride back into their hearts, peace and unity cannot endure. No man, despite how hard he tries, can serve two masters.[121]

The Book of Mormon is, of course, replete with countless other examples of corruption. King-men contending against freemen demonstrated how a thirst for power and titles could split a society, opening the door to external threats.[122] And the entire record is a tale of the "pride cycle" playing out—with periods of ease and prosperity that breed complacency, vanity, and eventually a return to conflict.[123] These and many other scriptural stories all emphasize the record's central point: failing to stay vigilant and resist the slow stain of the world means you will ultimately fall prey to its corroding influence.

---

121 Matthew 6:24.
122 Alma 51.
123 Helaman 3:33–36; 4:11–13; and 6:17.

.

THE EARLY CHRISTIANS

If the Lord's 'other sheep"[1] in the New World soon sought out worldly stains after His visit, how did the disciples in the Old World fare? Predictably, those in Jerusalem and surrounding regions grappled with much the same challenge. Despite the outpouring of spiritual gifts at Pentecost, the earnest teachings of the Twelve, and the expansion of the early Christian community, worldly influences soon found their way into Christ's fledgling Church.

Paul witnessed these struggles firsthand. To the Galatians, he wrote with urgency about "another gospel" that was leading members astray, promoted by those who "would pervert the gospel of Christ."[2] In Corinth, he warned against those preaching "another Jesus" or receiving "another spirit."[3] Luke's account reveals a similar pattern of creeping corruption: some believers insisted upon integrating former religious practices or philosophies into the Way of Christ, while others exploited the Church for wealth or influence.[4] With each epistle and missionary journey, Christ's apostles found

---

1   John 10:16.
2   Galatians 1:6–9.
3   2 Corinthians 11:3–4.
4   Acts 8:18–21; 15:1–5.

themselves striving to contain or correct these disruptive currents before they reached a tipping point.

The Rise of Gnosticism

The successful spread of Greek philosophy throughout the Hellenistic world became a powerful corroding force during Christianity's early days. By the mid-to-late first century AD, ideas such as Platonism and Stoicism had already shaped countless minds in cities like Alexandria, Ephesus, and Corinth. These ideas emphasized abstract notions of reality, dualistic worldviews, and the pursuit of specialized "higher knowledge." While early converts to Christianity found aspects of Greek philosophy intriguing—sometimes even harmonious with scriptural principles—others took it a step further, merging Christian doctrine with the esoteric concepts of their Greek heritage to create distinct theological movements. Chief among these were the Gnostic sects, whose name derived from the Greek word *gnosis*, or knowledge.

Gnosticism thrived on the promise that salvation could be found through hidden wisdom or secret teachings accessible only to an enlightened few. Its adherents often claimed that the material world was an inherently evil domain governed by lesser divine beings, in opposition to a perfect realm of spirit. This dualistic outlook brought them into tension with core Christian truths. Where the apostles stressed the tangible reality of Christ's resurrection[5] and the importance of bodily

---

5   John 20:27; Luke 24:39.

sanctity,[6] Gnostic believers instead portrayed a "distant" or "unknown" Father-god separate from physical creation—one who was considered utterly incomprehensible and removed from the material world. This warped version of Christianity reimagined Jesus not as God with a body who created our world[7] but as a teacher dispensing secret knowledge for spiritual liberation. In Paul's epistle to Timothy, he explicitly warned:

> O Timothy, keep that which is committed to thy trust, avoiding profane and vain babblings, and oppositions of [gnosis] falsely so called: Which some professing have erred concerning the faith.[8]

The slow stain of Greek philosophy, which Paul had warned was infiltrating the infant Church, advanced even more rapidly in early Christian hubs like Alexandria, where intellectual cross-pollination among Jews, Greeks, and Egyptians was already rife. It also spread through trade routes into Asia Minor and beyond, finding fertile ground wherever converts yearned for an advanced, mystical path to salvation. Instead of embracing and guarding the revealed truths proclaimed by Christ's apostles—namely His atoning sacrifice and bodily resurrection—these groups mixed tenets of the gospel with philosophical speculation. Over time, the appeal of "higher wisdom," the lure of insider status, and curiosity

---

6   1 Corinthians 6:19–20.
7   Moses 1:33; Moses 2:1; D&C 76:24; John 1:3.
8   1 Timothy 6:20–21; *gnosis* is the Greek word used, though the King James Version uses 'science' instead of 'knowledge.' Paul was clearly warning about the early forms of Gnostic teaching and false teachings masquerading as true knowledge.

about mysterious teachings led many believers to dilute the pure gospel. Gnosticism thus stands as one of the first great tests of the post-apostolic era, illustrating how the philosophies of men—when mingled with scripture—inevitably undermine the core claims of Christianity.

Mingling with Pagan Festivals

By the time Gnosticism and other esoteric movements began drawing converts away from apostolic Christianity, believers faced yet another challenge: reconciling the vibrant pagan cultures surrounding them with their newfound faith. In regions like Asia Minor, North Africa, and throughout the Roman Empire, recent converts often wished to retain the annual cycles and community celebrations they had known since childhood. Eager to make Christianity more accessible, local Church leaders sometimes permitted these festivals to be transformed—or "rebranded"—into Christian feasts. Though it seemed a pragmatic way to ease conversion, such adaptations carried a lingering strain of pre-Christian rituals and symbolism, ultimately enabling the slow stain of worldly practices to burrow deeper into Church life.

One prominent example emerged during the fourth century when the Roman Empire's official shift toward Christianity spurred a broader blending of civic festivities with sacred observances. Saturnalia, a popular midwinter Roman festival marked by gift-giving, revelry, and a temporary reversal of social roles, gradually evolved—along with the celebration of the sun god Sol Invictus—into elements of what would later be celebrated as Christmas. Similarly, the springtime rites honoring fertility goddesses—such as Eostre—were absorbed into Christian commemorations of Christ's resurrection, eventually contributing to the modern Easter tradition (including the use of eggs, seen as a symbol of fertility and rebirth). While these rebranded feasts did revolve around Christian narratives, many of their external customs, such as feasting and specific ceremonial acts, retained echoes of their pagan heritage. It was a fusion of a people's pagan past with their newly adopted Christian faith—albeit one that was not as pure as it initially was.

From an outside perspective, these newly "Christianized" festivals seemed popular and praiseworthy, drawing families and entire villages into Church-sponsored gatherings. Yet beneath the surface, the pagan DNA had not entirely vanished. Many converts had deep-seated cultural traditions that did not simply vanish upon baptism. As with Gnostic teachings, the mixing of pagan celebrations with Christian worship emphasized earthly preferences over revealed truth, ultimately requiring far more vigilance from leaders and believers alike if the faith was to remain anchored in the gospel of Jesus Christ rather than the philosophies and habits of men.

Political Alliances with Rome

At its inception, Christianity was a minor religion within the Roman Empire, with its followers frequently facing localized persecution from the pagan majority due to their unconventional religious beliefs. This persecution intensified in AD

249 with the implementation of a Roman law requiring citizens to perform a pagan sacrifice or burn incense to demonstrate loyalty to the emperor and Roman gods. The sacrifices had to take place in front of a Roman magistrate, who would then issue a signed and witnessed certificate to confirm the sacrifice—an effort on the empire's part to identify and isolate those who opposed their rule. The resulting social pressures and fear of punishment led many Christians to abandon their faith, while others, strengthened by their convictions, grew even more steadfast, often finding deeper meaning in their oppression.

That all changed in the early fourth century with the rise of Emperor Constantine. In AD 313, Constantine issued the Edict of Milan, officially recognizing Christianity and liberating its adherents from state-sponsored persecution. But with this recognition came the potential for political collaboration. Bishops suddenly found themselves courted by imperial officials, sought after for policy advice, and awarded privileges once reserved for the Roman elite. Church and state began to merge, and a gospel originating from one whose "kingdom is not of this world"[9] was distorted into one content with building an earthly kingdom instead.

Church influence was a tool for Constantine to further his dominance over Rome. But it was a deal that cut both ways; the Church by this point was eager to survive and extend its reach—even if it meant compromising its principles and selling its soul to the devil. Prior to this merger: The Church did

---

9   John 18:36.

not support the state; Jesus' disciples were frequently persecuted and excluded from state positions; members were largely pacifists and unwilling to be cannon fodder for the empire;
and the Church was taxed with no state subsidy to support it.
Afterward: The Church integrated with the state; persecution
stopped, and collusion followed; the Church now supported
the state and its wars, with conscientious objectors excommunicated from the faith,[10] and state funds were used to build
up the tax-free Church. Turns out, you can buy anything in
this world with money—including the political allegiance of
an entire religion.

By the time Theodosius I declared Christianity the official state religion in AD 380, the Church found itself interwo-
ven with the bureaucratic and military frameworks of Rome.
Grand basilicas rose with imperial funding, bishops sat on
councils discussing taxation and governance, and ecclesiastical positions provided pathways to worldly prestige. This fusion of the sacred with the secular reshaped the faith's ethos:
instead of defending the downtrodden and rejecting Caesar,
the supposed leaders of the Christian Church were now con-

---

10 This comes from the Council of Arlnes, held by Constantine
    one year after the Edict of Milan. One of the things the gath-
    ered assembly of church leaders decided was that "those who
    lay down their weapons in peacetime" should "be excluded
    from fellowship." During the persecutions of the previous
    decades, the military was tasked with enforcing imperial de-
    crees, which would cause problems for any Christians serving
    in its ranks. But with the legalization of Christianity, no such
    conflicts remained, eliminating the need for desertion (from
    the state's perspective). Thus the politically co-opted council
    of church leaders declared that Christians now had no justifica-
    tion for shirking their duty to serve in the military.

tending for episcopal appointments, administering vast land-holdings, and forging alliances with political rulers through-out the empire. Such closeness to temporal power fed vanity and corruption, revealing the slow stain that emerges when-ever discipleship and worldly politics try to share a throne.

The Council at Nicaea

In many ways, the stage for the Council of Nicaea was set the moment Constantine threw his imperial weight behind a once-marginalized Christian Church. While Christianity had existed for nearly three centuries within the Roman Empire—marked by sporadic and sometimes brutal persecution—its followers still made up only a small fraction of the population at the time of the Edict of Milan. Yet, less than a century later, nearly the entire empire nominally embraced the faith. This dizzying growth was widely interpreted by church authorities as a visible token of divine approval, spurring them to adopt practically any strategy that furthered their numerical expan-sion and influence. But what began as eagerness to share the gospel with pagan Romans soon became a willingness to ac-commodate every form of Roman custom and policy.

Constantine, meanwhile, had embraced Christianity pri-marily to weld together a fractured empire. He summoned bishops to the city of Nicaea in AD 325 with a single driving goal: to forge a consensus on doctrinal disputes that threat-ened the empire's fragile unity. Until then, competing theo-logical positions had flared across various Christian commu-nities, but no single authoritative structure existed to settle them. Now, under imperial sponsorship, the Church found itself in a kind of legislative council—a far cry from the modest, persecuted communities that marked the faith's earlier decades. Through this politically charged council of Church leaders, presided over by Constantine himself, the pervasive influence of Rome's worldliness was unmistakable. The doctrinal debates culminated in an official creed that established the theological platform of a politically co-opted Church. This creed incorporated elements of Greek philosophy, distorted the true nature of the Godhead, introduced profound confusion about Christ's identity, and was crafted without any trace of divine revelation.

In effect, Nicaea formalized the Church's new place within the Roman world. Having become a sanctioned branch of the state, the Church now shared in the very power structures that shaped that world. Imperially funded bishops arrived with entourages and political backers, entangling ecclesiastical decisions with matters of patronage and favor. By enforcing and endorsing the council's decrees as law throughout the empire—including using exile, excommunication, and state-sanctioned murder to punish dissenting Christian communities who didn't bend the knee to these doctrinal dictates—Constantine bound orthodoxy to imperial policy, making theological dissent tantamount to political disloyalty.[11] While Christianity rapidly multiplied converts and achieved unprec-

---

11 Arius and his followers asserted that Jesus Christ was not co-eternal or of the same divine essence as God the Father, but rather a created being who was subordinate to the Father. They were consequently excommunicated and exiled for refusing to submit to the doctrine of the Trinity.

edented growth—transforming from a persecuted minority to near-universal adoption—it lost its internal sense of identity. This was no longer the gospel of Christ, but something fundamentally altered, so deeply compromised and distorted that it became unrecognizable from the teachings Jesus gave to His disciples. The Church, now proclaiming its empire-wide ("catholic") dominion, achieved extraordinary power, though at the devastating cost of forsaking the original faith.

A few decades after Christ's death, Jude warned that "certain men crept in unawares ... ungodly men, turning the grace of our God into lasciviousness, and denying the only Lord God, and our Lord Jesus Christ."[12] Over the centuries, as apostles were martyred and revelation grew scarce, worldly ambitions infiltrated every corner of the faith. Splintered doctrine, political alliances, and the quest for influence turned a persecuted minority into a privileged state religion—yet at a steep cost. In place of the simple faith once so vital to Christian identity, vast clerical hierarchies emerged, wrestling more with each other and with governments than with matters of the soul. Far from quietly fading away, the worldly mindset Jude and the early apostles decried embedded itself in councils, ceremonies, and imperial decrees, leaving a faith outwardly oriented to Christ but inwardly polluted by the very forces His teachings intended to overcome.

---

12   Jude 1:4.

THE LATTER-DAY SAINTS

In the centuries following the early Christian apostasy, Europe plunged into the so-called Dark Ages—a prolonged period marked by political fragmentation, pervasive illiteracy, and limited religious freedom. Church and state remained effectively merged. Knowledge of Christ's teachings was guarded in Latin or Greek, out of reach for most believers. Over time, this spiritual deprivation left many people craving the direct, soul-changing faith that had characterized New Testament Christianity. Small movements emerged in response—thinkers and reformers calling for changes in worship, personal conversion, and access to the Bible in common tongues. Their efforts laid the groundwork for broader changes, culminating in the Reformation and the centuries of religious debate that followed. By the early nineteenth century, a new wave of religious fervor, dubbed the Second Great Awakening,[1] swept across parts of North America. Preachers traveled from town to town, urging listeners to follow their version of the gospel and steer clear of everyone else's. It was a choir of competing voices, each seemingly singing a different tune.

Into that Christian cacophony came the curious Joseph Smith, who was deeply confused by the differing voices all

---

1   The First Great Awakening took place decades earlier, in the 1730s and 1740s, in Britain and the thirteen colonies.

claiming ultimate truth. In response to the Lord's promise that "if any of you lack wisdom, let him ask of God,"[2] Joseph prayed for guidance and received an answer that would soon transform Christendom. In that first vision of God and Jesus Christ, Joseph learned that centuries of men's philosophies mingled with scripture had produced a tangle of creeds far removed from the Savior's original church:

> I was answered that I must join none of them, for they were all wrong; and the Personage who addressed me said that all their creeds were an abomination in his sight; that those professors were all corrupt; that: "they draw near to me with their lips, but their hearts are far from me, they teach for doctrines the commandments of men, having a form of godliness, but they deny the power thereof."[3]

So began the latter-day restoration—an unfolding process to restore gospel truths lost during the long night of apostasy. The Lord called apostles once again, and He provided priesthood power with direct revelations as in previous ages. Many converts embraced this restored gospel with its additional scripture and a reconnection to heaven. One of those new revelations, received on November 1, 1831, was given of God for the express purpose of serving as an introduction to the compiled book of previous revelations Joseph had already received. In it, God makes clear why He had begun "a marvelous work"[4] to address rampant corruption:

---

2   James 1:5.
3   Joseph Smith—History 1:19.
4   D&C 4:1.

And the arm of the Lord shall be revealed; and the day cometh that they who will not hear the voice of the Lord, neither the voice of his servants, neither give heed to the words of the prophets and apostles, shall be cut off from among the people;

For they have strayed from mine ordinances, and have broken mine everlasting covenant;

They seek not the Lord to establish his righteousness, but every man walketh in his own way, and after the image of his own god, whose image is in the likeness of the world, and whose substance is that of an idol, which waxeth old and shall perish in Babylon, even Babylon the great, which shall fall.[5]

Simply put, the whole of humanity is saturated in worldly ideas and practices, necessitating a new dispensation and a prophetic unfolding of the gospel truths that had long since been abandoned. Joseph Smith led a new generation of disciples who would learn about and attempt to live according to the commandments of God, straight from the mouth of a true prophet. One would hope that this time things would fare better. Yet the more things change, the more they seem to stay the same. Today's Church is no less susceptible to embracing the slow stain of the world than the ancient one.

In a pattern reminiscent of the Church's early post-Christ era, the fledgling Latter-day Saint community also faced relentless persecution—both testing and galvanizing its believ-

---

5   D&C 1:14–16.

ers as they weathered assaults and assassinations. These external pressures fortified loyalty and unity, urging the faithful to stand firm together. Yet, as is common across every generation, even this shared adversity could not entirely shield the Saints from the slow stain of the world.

The Failure to Establish Zion

Barely a year after the Saints officially organized the Church, the Lord provided a new revelation regarding "the land which I have appointed and consecrated for the gathering of the saints."[6] The chosen spot was in Independence, Missouri, and was envisioned as "the place for the city of Zion."[7] After Joseph Smith consecrated the land in that area just two weeks later, a new revelation from the Lord praised those "who have come up unto this land with an eye single to my glory, according to my commandments."[8] The faithful "who have obeyed my gospel"[9] would "receive a crown in the mansions of my Father."[10] The Saints were reminded to love God and serve Him, to love their neighbor, and to offer their prayers and sacraments regularly in order to "keep thyself unspotted from the world."[11] It was an exciting milestone in the much-anticipated path to the restoration of Zion, as Joseph Smith noted in an 1842 *Times and Seasons* editorial:

6   D&C 57:1.
7   D&C 57:2.
8   D&C 59:1.
9   D&C 59:3.
10   D&C 59:2.
11   D&C 59:5–9.

The building up of Zion is a cause that has interested the people of God in every age; it is a theme upon which prophets, priests and kings have dwelt with peculiar delight; they have looked forward with joyful anticipation to the day in which we live; and fired with heavenly and joyful anticipations they have sung and written and prophesied of this our day; but they died without the sight; we are the favored people that God has made choice of to bring about the Latter-day glory.[12]

Thirteen days after receiving a revelation directing them to Missouri,[13] Joseph Smith and other leaders started the 900-mile journey. They were followed by eager Saints who followed God's commandment to flee Babylon and build up Zion. One of the first to arrive expressed her joy, "praising God that she had lived to see the land of Zion."[14] But the effort failed within two years; by late 1833, the Saints had been persecuted so badly that they were driven out of their homes. The Zion experiment, it seemed, had failed. And here's why:

Behold, I say unto you, were it not for the transgressions of my people, speaking concerning the church and not individuals, they might have been redeemed even now. But behold, they have not learned to be obedient to the things which I required at their hands, but

---

12 Joseph Smith, *Times and Seasons*, May 2, 1842, https://www.josephsmithpapers.org/paper-summary/times-and-seasons-2-may-1842/10.

13 D&C 52, received on June 6, 1831, contains the Lord's direction that they depart for Missouri. They departed on June 19.

14 Polly Knight, as quoted in Newel Knight, *Autobiography and Journal*, ca. 1846, 32, 34.

are full of all manner of evil, and do not impart of their substance, as becometh saints, to the poor and afflict- ed among them; And are not united according to the union required by the law of the celestial kingdom.[15]

This community was far from being "of one heart and one mind."[16] According to the Lord, "there were jarrings, and con- tentions, and envyings, and strifes, and lustful and covetous desires among them"[17]—hardly a description befitting a Zion- like people. The promise of Zion had stalled because of the Saints' collective failures—wavering faith, hesitation to follow divine counsel, and foremost among them, pride, aptly called by Ezra Taft Benson the "great stumbling block to Zion."[18] In short, they hadn't first fled Babylon but were clinging to car- nal desires and temporal temptations. They had not cleansed themselves sufficiently from the stain of the world to rise above these base behaviors.

These worldly attitudes undercut the very purpose of the latter-day gathering. Instead of reflecting the harmony and mutual support that defines Zion, factions within the flock foreshadowed the many troubles to come. In hindsight, the Missouri period offered a critical lesson: external persecution, while severe, was not the ultimate reason why the Saints were driven from Independence. Internal strife played a significant role in undermining their attempts to build Zion and qualify for

---

15 D&C 105:2–4.
16 Moses 7:18.
17 D&C 101:6.
18 Ezra Taft Benson, "Beware of Pride," April 1989 General Con- ference, https://www.churchofjesuschrist.org/study/general- conference/1989/04/beware-of-pride.

the Lord's protection and deliverance. God called the Saints to create a city where they would live according to higher laws of love, sacrifice, and unity. Instead, they became mired in contention and disputes, demonstrating at the early outset of the latter-day dispensation how worldly influences can corrode even the most earnest and exciting spiritual endeavor.

The Book of Mormon

From its earliest mentions by Nephi—who saw a record of his descendants preserved for a future generation[19]—to Moroni's parting words centuries later,[20] the Book of Mormon was destined to play a transformative role among latter-day believers. The ancient prophets who wrote its pages and guarded its plates did so at great sacrifice, repeatedly testifying of Christ's mission, the covenant history of the Americas, and the critical lessons God intended for future readers. Moroni, in particular, went to extraordinary lengths: wandering alone for years to avoid capture, inscribing a final invitation for all to "come unto Christ,"[21] and sealing up the record with faith that it would one day bring souls to salvation by helping them understand gospel truths.

Undeniably, the record's foremost purpose is to serve as an additional witness of Jesus Christ, standing side by side with the Bible.[22] In doing so, it fulfills prophecies from Isaiah of a "marvelous work and a wonder," involving a sealed book that

---

19   1 Nephi 13:35–40.
20   Moroni 10:1–4.
21   Moroni 10:30–33.
22   2 Nephi 29:7–8.

would bring new knowledge,[23] and from Ezekiel of the stick of Judah and a stick from Ephraim joined "one to another into one stick."[24] The book powerfully talks of Christ, rejoices in Christ, and preaches and prophesies of Christ, "that our children may know to what source they may look for a remission of their sins."[25] Yet the Book of Mormon also carries a more cautionary function: to remind the Saints of the cyclical perils of apostasy, as illustrated by the Nephites and Jaredites. From the repeated cycles of pride[26] to the catastrophic collapse of two civilizations undone by conspiracy and greed,[27] this additional scripture is permeated with warnings of how worldly allurements can undermine God's people. As Elder L. Tom Perry said:

> Among the lessons we learn from the Book of Mormon are the cause and effect of war and under what conditions it is justified. It tells of evils and dangers of secret combinations, which are built up to get power and gain over the people. It tells of the reality of Satan and gives an indication of some of the methods he uses. It advises us on the proper use of wealth. It tells us of the plain and precious truths of the gospel and the reality and divinity of Jesus Christ and His atoning sacrifice for all mankind. It informs us of the gathering of the house of Israel in the last days. It tells us of the purpose and principles of missionary work. It warns us

23   Isaiah 29:11–19.
24   Ezekiel 37:16–17.
25   2 Nephi 25:26.
26   Helaman 3:33–36; 4:11–13; 6:17.
27   Ether 8; Mormon 2:10–15.

against pride, indifference, procrastination, the dangers of false traditions, hypocrisy, and unchastity.[28]

The Book of Mormon was provided to Latter-day Saints precisely so they might avoid repeating the mistakes of the past and recognize the slow stain of the world before it overtakes them. In other words, it's not enough to simply focus on the book's positive message of Christ while simultaneously ignoring its "negative" warnings of His chief adversary.

Yet that may be what the early Saints did. In the fall of 1832, Joseph Smith received a revelation—the first one that mentioned Zion since over a year prior when the Lord had first identified the location for the temple.[29] After explaining the significance of the prophesied New Jerusalem and the power of the priesthood, God then explains that the purpose of revealing His will is because "the whole world lieth in sin, and groaneth under darkness and under the bondage of sin."[30] And the Latter-day Saints were not excluded from this observation. In fact, quite the opposite:

> And your minds in times past have been darkened because of unbelief, and because you have treated lightly the things you have received—which vanity and unbelief have brought the whole church under condemnation.

---

28 L. Tom Perry, "Blessings Resulting from Reading the Book of Mormon," October 2005 General Conference, https://www.churchofjesuschrist.org/study/general-conference/2005/10/blessings-resulting-from-reading-the-book-of-mormon.

29 D&C 57 was the revelation in which the location was identified. D&C 84 was received over a year later.

30 D&C 84:49.

And this condemnation resteth upon the children of
Zion, even all. And they shall remain under this condemnation until they repent and remember the new
covenant, even the Book of Mormon and the former
commandments which I have given them, not only to
say, but to do according to that which I have written—
that they may bring forth fruit meet for their Father's
kingdom; otherwise there remaineth a scourge and
judgment to be poured out upon the children of Zion.[31]

Sure, the whole world was living in sin and darkness—but
here the Lord points out that the Church's own actions had
brought it under condemnation, a result that could only be
ameliorated by heeding the Book of Mormon's counsel. This
rebuke suggested that while they might have believed in the
record's divine origin, the Saints were failing to immerse
themselves in its revelations and apply its warnings to, among
other things, avoid pride and be watchful against secret combinations. The condemnation (which continues to this day)
reminds us that possessing sacred texts does little good if
those texts remain unheeded. The Saints' experience highlights a broader truth: revelation must be both cherished and
actively applied. Only then do covenant people stay aligned
with God's higher law and fortified against the creeping influence of the world that has repeatedly overthrown His societies in ages past.

---

31 D&C 84:54–58.

Polygamy

While most individuals marry monogamously, cross-cultural data reveals that polygamous marriage systems outnumber strictly monogamous ones worldwide. A mid-twentieth-century study of 1,231 societies found that only 15 percent were monogamous, while 48 percent practiced frequent polygamy, and 37 percent had occasional polygamy.[32] Polygamy was particularly widespread after the advent of agriculture in China, India, the Middle East, and parts of Western Europe. Rulers of ancient civilizations often maintained hundreds or thousands of wives, while common men typically had one or no wife. And despite the Puritan—and explicitly monogamous—heritage in America's early colonies, various societies of the day also embraced some form of polygamy.

One such community was "The Society of Free Brethren and Sisters," founded in 1817 in Saco, Maine. Adherents were known as "Cochranites" after the founder of the sect, Jacob Cochran, who gained notoriety for combining his Christian teachings with a form of so-called "spiritual wifery," a euphemism for polygamy. Two years into the social experiment, Cochran was convicted of adultery. One newspaper noted that "the notorious preacher and leader of a new party of reli-

---

32 George P. Murdock, "Ethnographic Atlas Codebook," 1998 World Cultures 10(1):86-136, https://web.archive.org/ web/20121118232413/http://eclectic.ss.uci.edu/~drwhite/ worldcul/Codebook4EthnoAtlas.pdf. My use of the term polygamy here refers to polygyny, or one man and multiple women. The study found that 0.3% of cultures practiced polyandry, or one woman and multiple men.

gious zealots in this country, has been sentenced... to 13 days solitary imprisonment, and four years hard labor in the state's prison, for the crime of adultery."[33] Despite Cochran's legal problems, the community continued to grow—later becoming a receptive audience for Latter-day Saint missionaries.

In 1832, Joseph Smith's younger brother Samuel arrived in this community while on a missionary journey to "the eastern countries,"[34] or states, which included Maine. Along with Orson Hyde, he held frequent meetings with Cochranite members and stayed in their homes. On one occasion, Smith notes that his meeting was interrupted "by a man and woman that taught the doctrine of the devil, such as abstaining from meat and having spiritual wives and so forth."[35] Hyde observed that the group had a "lustful spirit, because they believe in a 'plurality of wives' which they call spiritual wives, knowing them not after the flesh but after the spirit, but by the appearance they know one another after the flesh."[36] It was clear to these outsiders that polygamy, though wrapped in spiritual garb, was being practiced by this group.

Lustful spirit aside, the Cochranites turned out to become warm prospects for the missionaries, and hundreds joined the Church and went westward in subsequent years. One historian half a century later would write that "The Cochran craze paved the way for a Mormon invasion in the Saco valley. A full-blooded Cochranite made a first class Mormon saint. Jake

33 "From the Boston Patriot," *National Intelligencer*, November 13, 1819.
34 D&C 75:13.
35 Samuel Harrison Smith, Diary. July 1, 1832.
36 Orson Hyde, 1832 Mission Journal, October 11, 1832.

Cochran was a John the Baptist for the Mormon apostles, who appeared on his old battleground and gathered up the spoils."[37] Enough converts had joined that two Church conferences were held in Saco, in 1834 and 1835; the latter one was attended by seven of the newly ordained apostles, including Brigham Young, who would soon thereafter polygamously marry a woman who lived among the Cochranites, Augusta Adams Cobb (who, it should be noted, was still married to her first husband).

No contemporary evidence exists to confirm that the Cochranite polygamous practices are what later led the Mormon community to embrace the same. But just as the children of Israel physically left Egypt but carried with them their beliefs and practices, and just as the Jaredites and Nephites fled the Old World yet were unable to abandon their customs and traditions, it is quite reasonable to assume that, to whatever degree, the Cochranite influence was a factor leading many others to secretly begin engaging in "spiritual wifery" of their own. By the 1840s, there were tens of thousands of Mormon converts, all of whom had come from a variety of religious backgrounds. Everyone had theological baggage of one kind or another, and Joseph found himself repeatedly having to admonish the Saints to adhere to the gospel, untainted by these traditions and temptations.

That was certainly true of polygamy. Its practice in the early Church has largely been painted as a straightforward consensus: Joseph reluctantly and secretly engaged in and

---

37 Gideon T. Ridlon, *Saco Valley Settlements and Families* (Rutland: Charles E. Tuttle Company, 1895), 281.

taught others the practice. But searching for the truth on this issue leads one to realize that the issue is far more complex and uncertain than is typically taught. For example, despite claims from Church leaders and historians to the contrary, all contemporary evidence during Joseph's life shows he opposed plural marriage (or spiritual wifery or polygamy or adultery). There is zero evidence[38] of any sexual relationship between Joseph and any woman other than his wife, Emma.[39] There is no DNA evidence demonstrating that he fathered any children with anyone other than Emma, yet he had nine with her—so clearly he was quite fertile. There are no contempo-

---

38 Even historian Richard Bushman notes that there exists "no certain evidence that Joseph had sexual relations with any of the wives who were married to other men." See Richard Bushman, *Rough Stone Rolling* (New York: Vintage Books, 2005), 439. But the same holds true for the single sisters as well; the so-called "evidence" that does exist rests entirely upon claims made either by Joseph's enemies (which Joseph routinely refuted while alive) or decades later by some of the women— dubious testimony which falls apart under closer scrutiny. Often these claims are second or third-hand and nothing more than hearsay. Even historians who believe Joseph taught and practiced plural marriage, such as Todd Compton and Brian Hales, cannot agree among themselves about which couples were physically intimate. The equivocal position of historians like these and Bushman reveal how problematic the underlying theory is and how there is no evidence to actually support it.

39 Decades later, Joseph F. Smith and others would produce affidavits from women claiming to have been Joseph's wife ("sealed or married"), done in an attempt to defend the practice against the persecution by the federal government and the competing claims of the Reorganized Church of Jesus Christ of Latter-day Saints. These affidavits (which mainly used boilerplate text and were often unsigned by the women) conflicted with contemporary records, such as diaries. Again, no contemporary evidence (*i.e.*, prior to Joseph's death) exists to support the claim that he engaged in polygamous marital relationships.

rary records of any kind that would indicate Joseph had additional wives—no journal entries, no marriage certificates, no firsthand accounts, no indication of financial support, and no women taking his name. There is no credible contemporary evidence of his teaching plural marriage to anyone.[40] Yet throughout Nauvoo, in particular, many men, in order to solicit sex from women, were secretly claiming Joseph had authorized the practice. Joseph lashed out in an 1842 epistle against men who "say they have authority from Joseph, or the First Presidency," advising the sisters of the newly formed Relief Society not to "believe anything as coming from us, contrary to the established morals and virtues and scriptural laws."[41] The women were further advised to denounce these men as imposters and liars and to "shun them as the flying fiery serpent, whether they are prophets, seers, or revelators; Patriarchs, twelve apostles, elders, priests, mayors, generals, city councillors, aldermen, marshals, police, lord mayors or the Devil, are alike culpable and shall be damned for such evil practices."[42]

---

40 The primary argument against this claim is the content of the William Clayton journals which purport to reveal instances in which Joseph did engage in polygamous teachings and marriages. But the journal in question was not contemporaneously recorded as an authentic daily record; its provenance is unknown and thus questionable; and Clayton may not be a credible witness given how his own journal reveals his adulterous predilections while on his mission in England. The official narrative around polygamy rests upon the foundation of Clayton's journals—a foundation that is flimsy at best.

41 Nauvoo Relief Society Minute Book, p. 86, The Joseph Smith Papers, accessed January 4, 2025, https://www.josephsmithpapers.org/paper-summary/nauvoo-relief-society-minute-book/109.

42 Ibid.

The condemnation was primarily focused on furtive characters like John C. Bennett who, while serving as assistant president of the Church, was propositioning women and telling them it was religiously authorized. Interestingly, the March 31 epistle, which was later read to the sisters on September 28, was signed not only by Joseph and his brother Hyrum (both of whom vehemently opposed all things polygamy) but also by Brigham Young, Heber Kimball, and Willard Richards. Young took his first polygamous wife only weeks after signing; Kimball already had one; and Richards would secretly marry his first plural wife ten months after signing. Many of Joseph's colleagues were engaging in the same practices for which he (and they!) were excommunicating the likes of Bennett. Ten days after the epistle was signed, Joseph "preached in the grove, and pronounced a curse upon all adulterers and fornicators, and unvirtuous persons and those who have made use of my name to carry on their iniquitous designs."[43] More than merely claiming Joseph sanctioned it, these men would later claim—after Joseph's death, when he was no longer able to defend himself—that he had secretly taken additional wives of his own. (Joseph's wife Emma denied this claim throughout her life, including in a final interview she gave just prior to her death in 1879.[44]) But this ru-

---

43 History, 1838–1856, volume C-1, accessed January 4, 2025, https://www.josephsmithpapers.org/paper-summary/history-1838-1856-volume-c-1-2-november-1838-31-july-1842/490.
44 Emma Smith, interview with Joseph Smith III, *The Saints' Herald*, October 1, 1879. Here is the relevant portion:

Q. What about the revelation on Polygamy? Did Joseph Smith have anything like it? What of spiritual wifery?

mor was circulating while he was living as well, prompting him to observe, just a month before his death:

> I had not been married scarcely five minutes, and made one proclamation of the Gospel, before it was reported that I had seven wives... I am innocent of all these charges... What a thing it is for a man to be accused of committing adultery, and having seven wives, when I can only find one. I am the same man, and as

---

A. There was no revelation on either polygamy, or spiritual wives. There were some rumors of something of the sort, of which I asked my husband. He assured me that all there was of it was, that, in a chat about plural wives, he had said, "Well, such a system might possibly be, if everybody was agreed to it, and would behave as they should; but they would not; and besides, it was contrary to the will of heaven." No such thing as polygamy, or spiritual wifery, was taught, publicly or privately, before my husband's death, that I have now, or ever had any knowledge of.

Q. Did he not have other wives than yourself?
A. He had no other wife but me; nor did he to my knowledge ever have.

Q. Did he not hold marital relation with women other than yourself?
A. He did not have improper relations with any woman that ever came to my knowledge.

Q. Was there nothing about spiritual wives that you recollect?
A. At one time my husband came to me and asked me if I had heard certain rumors about spiritual marriages, or anything of the kind; and assured me that if I had, that they were without foundation; that there was no such doctrine, and never should be with his knowledge, or consent. I know that he had no other wife or wives than myself, in any sense, either spiritual or otherwise.

innocent as I was fourteen years ago; and I can prove them all perjurers.[45]

He wasn't being flippant when saying he could prove these claims to be lies. In the same address, he noted that he had been employing several clerks to keep "a record of all of my acts and proceedings" who had "accompanied [him] everywhere, and carefully kept [his] history, and they have written down what [he had] done, where [he had] been, and what [he had] said."[46] One of those clerks was the aforementioned Willard Richards, who wrote in the prophet's journal on October 5, 1843, that Joseph "Walked up and down the street with Scribe and gave instructions to try [or, bring charges against] those who were preaching, teaching, or practicing the doctrine of plurality of wives on this law. Joseph forbids it and the practice thereof. No man shall have but one wife." Setting aside the fact that Richards had already secretly taken another wife by this point, it is illuminating to look at the official history of the Church (compiled years later) compared to Joseph's journal. Here is a side-by-side comparison, showing the text that was removed from the original (strikethrough) and added (underline):

45 Discourse, 26 May 1844, as compiled by Leo Hawkins, accessed January 4, 2025, https://www.josephsmithpapers.org/paper-summary/discourse-26-may-1844-as-compiled-by-leo-hawkins/1.
46 Ibid.

Joseph's Journal	History of the Church
Walked up and down the street with Scribe and gave instructions to try those who were preaching, teaching, or practicing the doctrine of plurality of wives ~~on this Law. Joseph forbids it and the practice thereof~~. No man shall have but one wife.	Walked up and down the street with Scribe and gave instructions to try those persons who were preaching, teaching, or practicing the doctrine of plurality of wives; <u>for, according to the law, I hold the keys of this power in the last days; for there is never but one on earth at a time on whom the power and its keys are conferred; and I have constantly said</u> no man shall have but one wife at a time<u>, unless the Lord directs otherwise</u>.

These edits were made after Joseph's death, completely reversing what he had clearly said—and what his secretly-polygamous scribe had documented. After Joseph's death, the men who had embraced spiritual wifery orchestrated a veritable smear campaign against the murdered prophet, saying that Joseph had authorized it in secret—despite no evidence to support the claim and all contemporary evidence showing the exact opposite. After Joseph's death, Brigham Young and scribes set to work compiling the Church's history, and it is they who made edits like the one above. In fact, nearly a year after Joseph's death, Brigham records, "I commenced revising the history of Joseph Smith" along with Heber C. Kimball, in Willard Richards's office. Over and over, he says he "revised" the history: "Engaged at Elder Richards' office with Elders Kimball and [George A.] Smith revising Church History"; "With Elders Heber C. Kimball, W. Richards and George A. Smith reading and revising Church History"; "we read and revised history all day"; "We read and revised fifty-seven pages of History of Joseph Smith"; and many more.[47] As one Latter-day Saint historian put it, "The Twelve's nineteenth-century propaganda mill was so adroit that few outside Brigham Young's inner circle were aware of the behind-the-scenes alterations that were seamlessly stitched into church history."[48] Charles Wesley Wandell, an assistant historian working under Richards on this project, later wrote that "after Joseph's death his memoir was 'doctored' to suit the new order of things, and this, too, by the direct order of Brigham Young to Doctor Richards and systematically by Richards."[49] This charge seems supported by Wilford Woodruff, who recorded in his journal one such example he was involved in while working in the historian's office. Woodruff asked Young about a "piece of history... concerning Hyrum leading this church and trac-

47   These appear in Volume 7 of *History of the Church of Jesus Christ of Latter-day Saints* (Salt Lake City: Deseret News, 1932). See pages 389–390, 408, 411, 414, 427, 428, 514, 532, 533.

48   Richard S. Van Wagoner, *Sidney Rigdon: A Portrait of Religious Excess* (Salt Lake City: Signature Books, 1994), 322.

49   *Journal of History*, vol 3, no. 1 (Lamoni: Reorganized Church of Jesus Christ of Latter-day Saints), 456. See also "Changing LDS Church History," Hemlock Knots, January 18, 2022, https://hemlockknots.com/changing-lds-church-history-1/.

ing the Aaronic priesthood." Young's response? He said, "it is not essential to be inserted in the history and it had better be omitted."[50]

This "new order of things" is what plagued past societies—a deep stain of adulterous lust. Nephi's brother Jacob condemned these "grosser crimes" happening in his own day, revealing that the people were "committing whoredoms, because of the things which were written concerning David, and Solomon his son."[51] These two men "truly had many wives and concubines, which thing was abominable before me, saith the Lord."[52] (The Book of Mormon consistently condemns polygamy, describing it with words such as abomination, whoredom, wickedness, filthiness, or crime.[53]) Years after Joseph's death, Brigham Young produced a document he claimed to be a revelation received by the founding prophet, which had been kept private the entire time. It describes "the principle and doctrine of... many wives and concubines" (a phrase that appears four times in the Book of Mormon, each time condemned outright[54]) and, contradicting Jacob, argues

---

50 Wilford Woodruff journal entry, July 11, 1856, https://arts.wilfordwoodruffpapers.org/day-in-the-life/1856-07-11.

51 Jacob 2:23.

52 Jacob 2:24.

53 References include "abominations" (Jacob 2:10, 24, 28, 31; Mosiah 11: 2); "whoredoms" (Jacob 2:23, 28, 33; 3:5; Mosiah 11:2, 6); "wickedness" (Jacob 1:15; 2:6, 10, 31; Mosiah 11:2); "filthiness" (Jacob 3:9-10); and "crime" (Jacob 2:9; 2:22-23).

54 The references pertain to David and Solomon engaged in "wicked practices" (Jacob 1:15) which were "abominable" to God (Jacob 2:24), Riplakish whose polygamy was not "right in the sight of the Lord" (Ether 10:5), and King Noah whose "abominable" actions violated "the commandments of God" (Mosiah 11:2).

that "David's wives and concubines were given unto him of me, by the hand of Nathan."[55] Later codified as section 132 of the Doctrine and Covenants, this purported revelation—made public eight years after Joseph's death—directly contradicted scriptures established during his lifetime. First, there is the revelation Joseph referred to as "the law of the Church" which commands, "Thou shalt love thy wife with all thy heart, and shalt cleave unto her and none else."[56] Second, there is the 1835 statement on marriage, which explicitly declared:

> Inasmuch as this church of Christ has been reproached with the crime of fornication and polygamy, we declare that we believe that one man should have one wife; and one woman, but one husband, except in case of death, when either is at liberty to marry again.[57]

---

55 D&C 132:1, 39.
56 D&C 42:22.
57 Appendix 3: Statement on Marriage, circa August 1835, accessed January 4, 2025, https://www.josephsmithpapers. org/paper-summary/appendix-3-statement-on-marriage-circa-august-1835/2. Some apologists attempt to dismiss this issue by claiming that section 101 was not inspired or revelatory. The Faithful Saints group, for example, states that "the statement on marriage was NOT a revelation, was NOT written by Joseph Smith, and was also NOT authorized to be presented to the members of the Church the day it was voted on." (See "Altering The Revelation On Marriage?" Faithful Saints, https://faithfulsaints.com/altering-the-revelation-on-marriage/.) Setting aside the dubious claim that the officers of the Church were not authorized to propose it for inclusion in the Book of Commandments, the rest of their claims are equally true of section 134, the declaration of belief on government, which was not a revelation and was likely written by Oliver Cowdery—and which, like the section on marriage, was adopted into scriptural cannon via common consent of the members present at the conference, following established protocol precisely.

Adopted by the Church in 1835 through common consent
of all those present, this particular section of scripture was
quietly removed from the canon in 1876, without the common consent or awareness of Church members, and replaced
with its exact opposite, the new section 132. But the claim
in this alleged revelation about David and Solomon, directly
contradicting what Jacob and the Book of Mormon said, is
further undermined by reviewing Joseph's inspired translation of the Bible. Every doctrinal change he made to the Old
Testament that related to polygamy served to more strongly
condemn it; he made no changes that justified or supported
any kind of divine favor for "many wives and concubines."
Let's consider a few examples involving David, the first from
1 Kings 3:14, where the Lord communicates with Solomon in
a dream (strikethrough text showing what Joseph removed,
underlined text showing what he added):

King James Version	Joseph Smith Translation
And if thou wilt walk in my ways, to keep my statutes and my commandments, ~~as thy father David did walk,~~ then I will lengthen thy days.	And if thou wilt walk in my ways, to keep my statutes and my commandments, then I will lengthen thy days, <u>and thou shalt not walk in unrighteousness as did thy father David.</u>

The conventional translation states that David *did* walk in
God's ways, effectively sanctioning his polygamy. But Joseph

clarifies that David's polygamy was wicked. The same result happens in 2 Samuel 12:13—and remember that section 132 claims that "David's wives and concubines were given unto him of [God], by the hand of Nathan." Here's what Joseph fixed:

King James Version	Joseph Smith Translation
And David said unto Nathan, I have sinned against the Lord. And Nathan said unto David, The Lord also hath put away thy sin; thou shalt not die.	And David said unto Nathan, I have sinned against the Lord. And Nathan said unto David, The Lord also hath <u>not</u> put away thy sin; thou shalt not die.

It's a simple but substantive edit. In the original, Nathan dismisses David's sin; Joseph changes it to clarify the exact opposite. And as a final example, Solomon is not spared the same correction; note this change to 1 Kings 11:

King James Version	Joseph Smith Translation
4 For it came to pass, when Solomon was old, ~~that~~ his wives turned away his heart after other gods: and his heart was not perfect with the LORD his God, ~~as was~~ the heart of David his father.	4 For it came to pass, when Solomon was old, his wives turned away his heart after other gods; and his heart was not perfect with the Lord, his God, <u>and it became as</u> the heart of David, his father.

(cont'd.)

King James Version	Joseph Smith Translation
5 For Solomon went after Ashtoreth the goddess of the Zidonians, and after Milcom the abomination of the Ammonites.	5 For Solomon went after Ashtoreth the goddess of the Zidonians, and after Milcom the abomination of the Ammonites.
6 And Solomon did evil in the sight of the LORD, and went not fully after the LORD, ~~as did David his father~~.	6 And Solomon did evil in the sight of the Lord, <u>as David, his father</u>, and went not fully after the Lord.

Though Christ's gospel defines marriage as being between one man and one woman,[58] many felt the worldly practice of polygamy was justified by the Old Testament patriarchs. Yet Joseph would have none of it. Here is his position on the matter, defended by his brother Hyrum on May 14, 1843:

> There were many that had a great deal to say about the ancient order of things as Solomon and David having many wives and concubines but it is an abomination in the sight of God. If an angel from heaven should come and preach such doctrine, [you] would be sure to see his cloven foot and cloud of blackness over his head, though his garments might shine as white as snow. A man might have one wife but concubines he should have none.[59]

---

58   Matthew 19:4–6; 1 Timothy 3:2.
59   Levi Richards journal, May 14, 1843, accessed May 3, 2025, https://catalog.churchofjesuschrist.org/assets/e8d44719-6577-4503-86b8-1641367be6b9/0/0.

One possible explanation for the whole polygamy narrative is that Joseph Smith was misunderstood, intentionally or innocently, by individuals who wrongly connected eternal sealings to temporal, conjugal marital relationships. Joseph had the sealing power and taught about it to others. It was a generous, glorious doctrine—to connect the whole of humanity through an unbroken chain. Joseph wasn't secretly marrying (and sleeping with) women other than his wife, Emma; he was, it would appear, attempting to introduce a higher order of human connection that was quickly corrupted by those exploiting it as an opportunity to engage in spiritual wifery with its sexual implications. It seems that the founding prophet was trying to bridge the gap between heaven and earth and use his newfound sealing power to bless others' lives. Instead, it was twisted into a temporal system of plural marriage that the scriptures had decried as an abomination; as Joseph said days before his death, "the truth of God was transformed into a lie."[60] Evil had become sanctioned as good, and Joseph was no longer around to stop the "new order of things." The stain spread and pushed the Church into seclusion and persecution for decades.

---

60   Joseph Smith, in Revised Minutes, 17 June 1844, as published in *Nauvoo Neighbor*, https://www.josephsmithpapers.org/paper-summary/revised-minutes-17-june-1844-as-published-in-nauvoo-neighbor/2.

Kirtland Safety Society

Not long after the Saints retreated from Missouri's failed experiment at Zion, they hoped for a fresh start in Kirtland, Ohio. The community there showed promise: a commitment to build the Lord's house while Joseph Smith continued receiving revelations to guide them.[61] Yet even in this fertile spiritual environment, economic pressures and personal ambition began to seep into daily life. Many Saints viewed Kirtland as a chance to establish both the kingdom of God and a thriving economy—two goals they believed went hand in hand. Over time, however, it became readily apparent that a person who tries to serve two masters ends up in trouble.

One of the most striking examples of this mindset was the formation of the Kirtland Safety Society in 1836. For years, Joseph Smith and other leaders felt the "embarrassments of a pecuniary nature that were now pressing upon the heads of the Church."[62] The members were largely poor and, therefore, had little by way of offerings to support the Church, which relied upon the contributions of its members. And the Church, following God's commandment, had begun buying large tracts of land in the Kirtland area as well as beginning construction of the temple. Many leaders thus believed that a financial institution could help raise capital to remedy this problem. But they were unable to obtain a bank charter from the state of

---

61 D&C 88; 89; 95.
62 Joseph Smith, "Discourse, 6 April 1837," https://www.josephsmithpapers.org/paper-summary/discourse-6-april-1837/1.

Ohio, so instead they organized a joint stock company with the power to issue its own notes as currency. This "bank" was called the Kirtland Safety Society Anti-Banking Company; Joseph served as treasurer and signed the promissory notes.

Eager to fund a growing community, Church leaders and members alike poured funds into the fledgling institution; the land they owned, under mortgage, became the capital base to back the notes. While their hopes were grounded in real needs—purchasing land and providing loans for agricultural and commercial growth—the feverish pursuit of quick returns escalated dangerously. The Church's official history explains that "the spirit of speculation in lands and property of all kinds, which was so prevalent throughout the whole nation, was taking deep root in the Church. As the fruits of this spirit, evil surmisings, fault-finding, disunion, dissension, and apostasy followed in quick succession, and it seemed as though all the powers of earth and hell were combining their influence in an especial manner to overthrow the Church at once, and make a final end."[63] It certainly didn't help—and clearly compounded the Society's problems—that people hostile to the church were trying to encourage its failure.

As it turns out, it was very poor timing to start a financial venture of this nature. In the two years prior, the volume of paper banknotes per capita in circulation throughout the United States had increased by a whopping 40 percent, creating massive inflation and speculation.[64] Community banks across the

---

63 B.H. Roberts, ed., *History of the Church of Jesus Christ of Latter-day Saints* (Salt Lake City: Deseret News, 1904), 487.

64 Joseph L. Locke and Ben Wright, ed., *The American Yawp: A*

country had issued notes far in excess of their ability to pay
if the holders of those notes were to redeem them en masse.
That was the strategy of one Grandison Newell, a financier
who saw the Church's endeavor as a competitive threat and
sought to "run the Mormons out of the country."[65] One of
his employees revealed that Newell "used to drive about the
country and buy up all the Mormon money possible, and the
next morning go to the bank and obtain the specie."[66] But with
the Society's assets primarily in illiquid land holdings, it could
not sustain such a heavy demand on what little gold and silver
it possessed. The ultimate failure of the Society and the losses
incurred by its more than 200 investors[67]—including Joseph,
who incurred the greatest personal losses—was part of a much
broader wave of bank runs. They began in New York on May
4, 1837, as customers desperately tried to exchange their paper money for hard currency. Six days later, banks in the city
had depleted their gold and silver reserves and stopped re-
deeming notes, which triggered a nationwide banking crisis.
Five days later, the largest crowd in Pennsylvania history had
gathered outside Independence Hall in Philadelphia, chanting
that banks were part of a "system of fraud and oppression."[68]

Massively Collaborative Open U.S. History Textbook, volume 1
(Stanford: Stanford University Press, 2019), 240.

65 J. H. Kennedy, *Early Days of Mormonism* (Charles Scribner's
Sons, 1888), 168.

66 James Thompson, Statement, in *Naked Truths about Mormonism* (Oakland, Calif.: Deming, 1888), 3.

67 See Jeffrey N. Walker, "The Kirtland Safety Society and the
Fraud of Grandison Newell: A Legal Examination," *BYU Studies
Quarterly*: Vol. 54, 59.

68 *The American Yawp*, 241–2.

Hundreds of financial institutions across the country closed their doors—as did the Society.

Investors watched their fortunes disappear almost overnight, and waves of confusion and finger-pointing followed. Deeply disappointed, many members concluded that Joseph Smith had steered them astray, criticizing him for what they perceived as mismanagement. Yet underlying the financial collapse was a deeper issue: the Saints had often relied on the worldly allure of quick wealth over the Lord's directions to consecrate their property and focus on building up His kingdom instead of their own. The growing spirit of consecration that had earlier (and only temporarily) unified the Saints—demonstrated so powerfully in Kirtland's temple building—gave way to individual ambition. Zion-like ideals of mutual support and brotherly love fractured under the weight of rapidly accumulating debt, disputes over failed investments, and broader envy spurred by the promise of affluence. The aftermath ignited a wave of disillusionment and apostasy from those who saw in the whole affair Joseph's moral failings and lack of prophetic foresight. Around one-third of Church leadership—as one historian notes, "some of the elite, some of the well educated, some of the more prosperous" among them—turned against him, many leaving the Church.[69] In truth, their own embrace of speculation and trust in worldly expertise over divine direction had primed them for the collapse. Kirt-

---

69   Ronald K. Esplin, "Joseph Smith and the Kirtland Crisis," in *Joseph Smith, the Prophet and Seer*, ed. Richard Neitzel Holzapfel and Kent P. Jackson (Salt Lake City: Deseret Book, 2010), 262.

land's troubled economic experiment reminds us that nobody is immune from the stain of worldly pursuits and temporal desires for building wealth.

Joseph's Struggle with the Saints

On January 21, 1844, Joseph Smith preached before a large congregation gathered at the unfinished Nauvoo Temple on the subject of sealing. According to notes taken by Wilford Woodruff, Joseph said:

> The Saints have not too much time to save and redeem their dead, and gather together their living relatives that they may be saved also, before the earth will be smitten, and the consumption decreed falls upon the world. I would advise all the Saints to go to with their might and gather together all their living relatives to this place that they may be sealed and saved, that they may be prepared against the day that the destroying angel goes forth, and if the whole church should go to with all their might to save their dead, seal their posterity, and gather their living friends and spend none of their time in behalf of the world, they would hardly get through before night would come, when no man can work, and my only trouble at the present time is concerning ourselves that the Saints will be divided, broken up and scattered before we get our salvation secure.[70]

---

70   Joseph Smith, as reported by Wilford Woodruff, History, 1838–1856, volume E-1 [1 July 1843–30 April 1844], https://www.josephsmithpapers.org/paper-summary/history-1838-1856-volume-e-1-1-july-1843-30-april-1844/237.

The prophet clearly felt anxiety about the topic and felt that the protective sealing power needed to be implemented with great urgency in order to spare the growing flock. And perhaps with the corruption of this sealing practice in mind, Joseph lamented:

> There has been a great difficulty in getting anything into the heads of this generation; it has been like splitting hemlock knots [very dense knot of wood] with a corn dodger [piece of corn bread] for a wedge, and a pumpkin for a beetle [hammer]. Even the Saints are slow to understand. I have tried for a number of years to get the minds of the saints prepared to receive the things of God, but we frequently see some of them, after suffering all they have for the work of God will fly to pieces like glass, as soon as anything comes that is contrary to their traditions; they cannot stand the fire at all; how many will be able to abide a celestial law and go through, and receive their exaltation, I am unable to say; as many are called but few are chosen.[71]

It was a stinging rebuke of the Saints by the man God had chosen to teach and lead them. His metaphors underscored the fragility of even the most faithful, revealing how quickly some hearts fractured under the weight of unfamiliar or challenging doctrine. His concerns would be validated once more just three months later, on April 7, when he spoke to the largest gathering of Saints up to that point, assembled to honor Elder King Follett, who had died in a tragic accident. In this lecture, Joseph taught unexpected (and unconventional)

71 Ibid.

doctrines that God "was once a man like us," dwelling on an earth "the same as Jesus Christ himself did," and exhorted the faithful to "learn how to be Gods yourselves... the same as all Gods have done before you."[72] Such a bold theology brought delight to many believers who yearned for increased spiritual understanding; others, however, struggled to reconcile these revelations with their traditional viewpoints. The editor of the Church's *Millennial Star* predicted precisely that polarizing response: "We feel greatly the importance of the principles upon which it [the King Follett Discourse] treats, and are convinced they will have a mighty effect, generally upon the Saints, for good or evil... it may be that some may turn away, being unable to endure the everlasting truth of heaven."[73]

Among those who turned away was William Law, formerly Joseph's second counselor in the First Presidency. Having already been removed from that post in January over disagreements with Joseph, Law and his wife were excommunicated from the Church just eleven days after the King Follett discourse. He soon organized the so-called True Church of Jesus Christ of Latter-day Saints, styling himself its president and publicly declaring that Joseph had become a fallen prophet. These developments underscored the intensity of the doctrinal divide; bold, celestial teachings drew many hearts closer while simultaneously driving some members—or entire fac-

---

72   Joseph Smith, as documented in History, 1838–1856, volume E-1 [1 July 1843–30 April 1844], https://www.josephsmithpapers.org/paper-summary/history-1838-1856-volume-e-1-1-july-1843-30-april-1844/342.

73   Thomas Ward, ed. *The Latter-day Saints' Millennial Star*, volume 5 (Liverpool: Thomas Ward, 1845), 95.

tions—out of alignment with the prophet. Even as Joseph taught a grand vision of eternal progression, he found himself grappling with the sobering reality that not everyone would embrace those glorious concepts; some would bitterly fight against them.

Law and his like-minded band of detractors not only started their own sect—they launched the infamous *Nauvoo Expositor* whose destruction would build momentum for the murders of Joseph and Hyrum just weeks later. The single issue they published—a four-page document on June 7—decried "heretical and damnable" doctrines including those Joseph had recently shared. The relevant passage reads:

> Among the many items of false doctrine that are taught the Church, is the doctrine of many Gods, one of the most direful in its effects that has characterized the world for many centuries. We know not what to call it other than blasphemy, for it is most unquestionably, speaking of God in an impious and irreverent manner. It is contended that there are innumerable gods as much above the God that presides over this universe, as he is above us; and if he varies from the law unto which he is subjected, he, with all his creatures, will be cast down as was Lucifer: thus holding forth a doctrine which is effectually calculated to sap the very foundation of our faith, and now, O Lord! shall we set still and be silent, while thy name is thus blasphemed, and thine Honor, power and glory, brought into disrepute?[74]

---

74 See *Cultures In Conflict A Documentary History of the Mormon War in Illinois* (Logan: Utah State University Press, 1995), 145.

The scriptures, and especially the Book of Mormon, frequently warn us about clinging to the "traditions of our fathers." These traditions involved clinging to material wealth,[75] supporting war,[75] hatred of others,[77] and rejecting gospel truth.[78] Joseph rightly noted the tendency the Saints had—and that all humans have—of clinging to the traditions with which we were raised as opposed to embracing new truths that may conflict with them. Clearly, some Saints remained firmly anchored in familiar theological ground and had a reflexive urge to preserve longstanding religious beliefs—ones that felt secure and immutable. Their traditions proved more compelling than new revelation because they offered a sense of stability in times already fraught with social and political upheaval. Thomas Jefferson once observed that some people "prefer the calm of despotism to the tempestuous sea of liberty"[79]—a concession that embracing principle comes with uncertainty and danger, while the flaxen cord of security actually binds you down under an oppression you sadly welcomed in hopes of feeling safe. The same holds true of Joseph's commentary on the Saints: they preferred the stability of their existing understanding to the tempestuous sea of new gospel truths. Familiar chains often seem friendlier than uncharted waters.

In this instance, the world's influence was less about external wealth or power and more about inherited and incomplete religious traditions. Rather than being open to the re-

---

75   1 Peter 1:18.
76   Mosiah 10:12.
77   Alma 60:32.
78   D&C 93:39.
79   Letter to M. Mazzei, Minerva (New York: 1791).

velatory ideas Joseph introduced, many Saints clung to their familiar theological frameworks. These older beliefs ultimately hindered spiritual progress when they collided with loftier gospel truths. By resisting the new light being offered, some found themselves entangled in a past understanding that no longer served them—effectively illustrating how dearly held traditions can become a subtle but potent form of worldly corruption, hindering our heavenly journey.

From the early Israelites to the Latter-day Saints, God's chosen people have consistently struggled to avoid the slow stain of the world. Time and again, many of them have allowed false ideas and corrupt practices to combine with their faith, producing a syncretic substitute that deceives its practitioners into thinking they are like the wise virgins when in reality they are the foolish ones who will be denied admittance by the bridegroom. "I know you not," was His stinging rebuke.[80] The early Saints, although often willing to sacrifice enormously for the gospel's cause, were not immune to this recurring pattern. They learned by sad experience that attempting to merge God's revelations with their own ingrained assumptions frequently led to disappointment and discord. In each stumbling episode, however, Joseph Smith hoped to elevate their gaze to heavenly ideals—reminding them that only by setting aside inherited traditions and worldly cravings can we wholeheartedly embrace heaven's far-reaching truths.

---

80   Matthew 25:10–12.

But what about the even more "latter" Latter-day Saints—those of us who have now inherited two centuries of Church culture and tradition on top of the original teachings of the restored gospel? In a society layered with toxic sludge from social media, gender ideology, cultural Marxism, celebrity worship, materialism, and much more—in this type of environment, how can we avoid the world's slow stain to remain pure before the Lord? Later in the book, we'll explore some of the threats we face today that deserve our attention and action. First, however, let's pause to review these historical examples and determine what lessons we can extract from them to apply to ourselves.

PART TWO

APPLYING THE SCRIPTURES

There is perhaps no truer adage than this one: those who do not learn from the mistakes of the past are condemned to repeat them.[1] (And, sadly, those who *do* learn from them are still condemned to suffer through their repetition since most everyone else didn't learn the lesson.) This is ultimately the purpose of history: to inform its students about what went wrong in the past so they can build a better future. And yet too many people reactively meander throughout their lives without heeding the warning signs of the past, written "as the voice of one crying from the dust."[2] We reap what we sow—and society has sown a whole lot of intentional ignorance. Thus comes the whirlwind.[3]

The prophetic admonition to *remember* (and apply) God's teachings pervades scripture. The Israelites were instructed to wear "fringes in the borders of their garments" to help them "remember all the commandments of the Lord, and do them."[4] God told them to "remember that thou wast a bondman in the land of Egypt, and the Lord thy God redeemed thee."[5] The Israelites "went a whoring" after other Gods because they "remembered not the Lord their God, who had delivered them."[6] Paul told his Gentile converts to "remember,

---

1   George Santayana's original quote is "Those who cannot remember the past are condemned to repeat it." See "Quote Origin: Those Who Cannot Remember the Past Are Condemned To Repeat It," Quote Investigator, March 4, 2024, https://quoteinvestigator.com/2024/03/04/past-repeat/.

2   2 Nephi 33:13. See also Isaiah 29:4; 2 Nephi 26:15–16; Moroni 10:27.

3   Mosiah 7:29–31.

4   Numbers 15:38–39.

5   Deuteronomy 15:15.

6   Judges 8:33–34.

that ye being in time past Gentiles... now in Christ Jesus ye who sometimes were far off are made nigh by the blood of Christ."[7]

Over and over again, we're told to remember—and nowhere is this more striking than in the Book of Mormon, where the word or its variants are used 227 times.[8] On his deathbed, Lehi urged his youngest son to "Remember the words of thy dying father"[9] regarding the gospel. Nephi rebuked his wayward brothers who were "swift to do iniquity but slow to remember the Lord your God."[10] The righteous Nephites who humbled themselves "did remember how great things the Lord had done for them."[11] Moroni explained that "it is wisdom in God" that the Jaredite and Nephite records regarding secret combinations "should be shown unto you, that thereby ye may repent of your sins, and suffer not that these murderous combinations shall get above you."[12] Helaman urged his sons to "remember... the words which king Benjamin spake"[13] regarding the atonement of Jesus Christ. Those sons "did remember his words; and therefore they went forth, keeping the commandments of God."[14]

And that's the point of remembering—to *act*. Prophets, ancient and modern, don't reveal God's word as a passive in-

7   Ephesians 2:11–13.
8   "Remembering and Forgetting," By Study and By Faith, April 17, 2022, https //bystudyandfaith.net/2022/04/remembering-and-forgetting/.
9   2 Nephi 3:25.
10   1 Nephi 17:45.
11   Alma 62:49–50.
12   Ether 8:23.
13   Helaman 5:9.
14   Helaman 5:14.

tellectual exercise for us to become proficient at superficial scriptural trivia but remain content to continue our present course. No—the purpose of reviewing God's dealings with His people is to observe trends, discern lessons, and apply this new knowledge to our own life. Yet how often have believers throughout history neglected that principle? We see it in Israel's failure to purge Canaanite rites from their worship, in the Church's early acceptance of post-apostolic philosophical ideas, and in the Latter-day Saints' struggles to commit to the heavenly standard being revealed to them. Each episode offers a cautionary tale that "remembering" means more than intellectual recall; it involves changing behavior in real, tangible ways. Our goal is not to read these examples and marvel at the foolishness of those who came before, but rather to recognize the same pitfalls in ourselves—and act.

Recall that the Latter-day Saints brought condemnation upon themselves for treating lightly the revelations God had given—hence the warning that "they shall remain under this condemnation until they repent and remember the new covenant, even the Book of Mormon and the former commandments which I have given them, *not only to say, but to do* according to that which I have written."[15] Simply stockpiling scriptural knowledge isn't enough; as Nephi admonished, we must "liken all scriptures unto us, that it might be for our profit and learning."[16] Failing to learn from the mistakes of the past inevitably dooms us to repeat them, especially when the Book of Mormon so clearly outlines how worldly corruption

---

15   D&C 84:54–58; emphasis added.
16   1 Nephi 19:23.

has undone countless groups of people. If we do not actively guard ourselves—applying the lessons and heeding the warnings within those sacred pages—we risk being overcome by the same slow stain that seeped into and ultimately destroyed so many civilizations in the past.

What, then, are the lessons we must learn? The previous part of the book highlighted several instances of the slow stain of the world in the past. Before we explore the modern versions that threaten us today, let's liken these scriptural accounts to ourselves and extract from them several valuable lessons to consider for our own profit and learning.

COMPLACENCY INVITES CORRUPTION

John, like his apostolic peers, suffered for the faith. For his rebellious preaching of the gospel, Roman authorities exiled him to Patmos—a small, rocky island in the Aegean Sea that was a dumping ground for criminals and political prisoners under Roman rule. While in captivity, John received a revelation about the last days, laced with allegorical imagery and prophetic warnings. Among these, John relayed a message from the Savior to the church in Laodicea, rebuking them for their spiritual lukewarmness: "I know thy works, that thou art neither cold nor hot: I would thou wert cold or hot. So then because thou art lukewarm, and neither cold nor hot, I will spue thee out of my mouth."[1] It is not enough to profess faith in name only or to be halfhearted in our devotion. To be lukewarm is to dwell in a state of compromise—neither fervent in righteousness nor fully consumed by rebellion, but somewhere in a dangerous middle ground. The Laodiceans, situated in a wealthy and self-sufficient city, had allowed the comforts and distractions of the world to dilute their commitment to the gospel. They became blind to their spiritual

---

1   Revelation 3:15-16.

poverty, believing they had no need of the Lord's sustaining grace. They had grown complacent.

Complacency often begins as a subtle shift. Instead of conscious rebellion or overt disobedience, a once-committed people gradually let go of daily disciplines that would keep them on the strait and narrow.[2] In the Old Testament, the Israelites left Egypt through a series of dramatic miracles—plagues, parting seas, and divine manifestations.[3] Yet barely had they completed their celebration of deliverance when complaints began to surface.[4] Their reliance on God's power degraded into a worldly desire to be "like all the nations" around them.[5] Though called to remain a peculiar people by a jealous God,[6] they grew lax and embraced the slow infiltration of pagan customs and beliefs. The Nephites had tasted profound spiritual blessings: visions, ministering angels, and even the personal ministry of the resurrected Savior.[7] Yet over generations, they relaxed in their prosperity, letting pride and material ambition overshadow the unity Christ had established.[8] And any spiritual vigilance the Jaredite community once had gave way to wresting political control through deceit and murder.[9]

Early Christianity followed much the same pattern. With the outpouring of the Holy Ghost at Pentecost[10] and the fervor

2   1 Nephi 8:20.
3   Exodus 7–14.
4   Numbers 11:4–6; Exodus 16:2–3.
5   1 Samuel 8:5.
6   Deuteronomy 14:2; 5:9.
7   3 Nephi 11.
8   4 Nephi 1:24–26.
9   Ether 8:9–26.
10 Acts 2:1–4.

of apostolic missionary work, the faith spread quickly. Over time, however, new converts brought with them old ideas, attempting to reconcile God's ways with the world's. Perhaps prioritizing the growth of the Church community over its theological purity, leaders began to tolerate more and more corruption to the Christian way. And Latter-day Saints are by no means immune from this trend. The Book of Mormon admonishes its latter-day readers to remain on guard against the deceptive overtures of the adversary. Nephi prophecies of our day, warning of profound corruption including false doctrine, denial of God's power, pride vanity, class division, and more.[11] He then pinpoints why complacency can invite such corruption:

> For behold, at that day shall he rage in the hearts of the children of men, and stir them up to anger against that which is good. And others will he pacify, and lull them away into carnal security, that they will say: All is well in Zion; yea, Zion prospereth, all is well—and thus the devil cheateth their souls, and leadeth them away carefully down to hell.[12]

Like a dam slowly eroded by persistent trickles of water, our spiritual fortifications are hollowed out by repeated neglect. Maintaining those fortifications can be tiresome and boring, like the virgins who slept while the bridegroom tarried.[13] And because the trickle of water seems insignificant in comparison to the mighty dam, we might delude ourselves

---

11 2 Nephi 28:5–15.
12 2 Nephi 28:20–21.
13 Matthew 25:5.

into thinking, like the people of Ammonihah thought about their great city, that it could never be destroyed[14]—that our neglect is tolerable and won't have any meaningful or significant long-term consequences. History is littered with people who were similarly deceived. By small and simple things, of course, are great (and terrible[15]) things brought to pass.[16]

The scriptures we've examined reveal how often people prefer carnal security—the calm of despotism, as Jefferson called it—and are often willing to trade their spiritual birthright for a temporal mess of pottage.[17] Like the spirits who followed Lucifer, they yearn to escape the consequences of their actions, desiring to "eat, drink, and be merry"[18] while expecting to be saved in their sins. To them, Christ's commandments appear as unreasonable impositions—a paternalistic list of "thou shalt nots" that hinders their pursuit of pleasure. Determined to avoid these perceived obstacles, they attempt to sail smoothly through life, no matter the cost. Life is filled with challenges and trials, placed there for a divine purpose: to strengthen and refine us. As the Stoic philosopher (and Roman emperor) Marcus Aurelius observed, "The impediment to action advances action. What stands in the way *becomes* the way."[19] These obstacles are not curses but opportunities for growth. Just as physical muscles grow through the exer-

---

14 Alma 9:4-5; 16:9.
15 Joel 2:31; 1 Nephi 12:5; 2 Nephi 26:3.
16 Alma 37:6.
17 Genesis 25:29–34.
18 2 Nephi 28:7–8.
19 Marcus Aurelius, as quoted in Ryan Holiday, *The Obstacle is the Way* (New York: Portfolio, 2014), xiv.

tion and microscopic tears caused by resistance, our spiritual muscles are built by consistently moving forward on the strait and narrow path as life's difficulties try to divert our course.

Imagine a person trying to move a boulder blocking their path. Day after day, their efforts strain and strengthen their muscles until, at last, they possess the power to dislodge the obstacle. In the process, they emerge stronger and better prepared for future challenges. Similarly, when we confront life's obstacles with faith and determination—seeking to make all well in Zion by addressing what is not—we develop greater spiritual fortitude. This is why the Lord "chastens [us] because he loveth [us]."[20] For those who embrace His correction, the end result is a deeper commitment to Christ and a more resilient faith. The "opposition in all things"[21] we experience compels us to make a choice: to be on the Lord's side, building up His kingdom; or to serve our own interests, following the path of least resistance. God wants us to be cold or hot—not lukewarm. Choosing to be complacent makes us "complicit with the consequences."[22]

How can we liken these ideas to ourselves? First, we must understand what we're up against. Studying the adversary's tactics enables us to recognize and reject them, just as a skilled soldier learns the enemy's strategy to prepare for battle. Knowing that the false promise of carnal security leads to complacency can help us reframe the challenges we face,

20 Helaman 15:3; Revelation 3:19.
21 2 Nephi 2:11.
22 Gary B. Sabin, "Stand Up Inside and Be All In," April 2017 General Conference, https://www.churchofjesuschrist.org/study/general-conference/2017/04/stand-up-inside-and-be-all-in.

seeing them as opportunities to fortify ourselves spiritually rather than as burdens to avoid. The obstacle is the way; it is through facing opposition that we grow in faith, strength, and resilience.

Second, we must prioritize the "small and simple things" that build our spiritual fortifications. Daily prayer, scripture study, meaningful worship, and finding practical ways to demonstrate our love of God and our fellow man may seem simple and repetitive, but they are powerful tools that keep us grounded in the gospel and resistant to the adversary's subtle intrusions. Conversely, allowing spiritually harmful influences into our lives, even if they seem minor or insignificant at first, can wear us down over time, eroding our defenses and leading to disastrous consequences.

Finally, we must cultivate spiritual vigilance, recognizing that the journey of discipleship requires constant effort and renewal. Complacency often creeps in when we convince ourselves that we have "arrived," believing our faith is strong enough or our current efforts are sufficient to sustain us indefinitely. This illusion of safety is one of the adversary's most effective traps, as it lulls us into a false sense of security, leaving us unprepared for future challenges. Like a soldier who lays down his armor, believing the battle is over, we risk leaving ourselves vulnerable to spiritual harm when we stop actively striving. Vigilance means staying alert to the small signs of complacency—neglecting prayer, embracing worldly ideas, letting scripture study become rote, or allowing pride to enter our heart.

Complacency is the enemy of discipleship—a silent invitation for corruption to take root and weaken our resolve. Yet, through vigilant effort and with the Savior as our constant guide, we can turn obstacles into opportunities for growth, fortifying our spirits against the relentless storms of a world intent on eroding faith.

POWERFUL POSITIONS INVITE TEMPTATION

After His baptism, Jesus spent forty days in the wilderness "to be with God."[1] Led up to a high mountain, He was shown "all the kingdoms of the world and the glory of them."[2] Surely such a spectacular review of God's creations would be edifying and inspiring—a much-needed spiritual boost for the Son of God before He began His ministry. In interruption, Satan arrived with a temptation: "All this power will I give thee, and the glory of them: for that is delivered unto me; and to whomsoever I will I give it. If thou therefore wilt worship me, all shall be thine."[3]

Cast down to this earthly domain, Lucifer sees earthly possessions as "delivered unto" him—and uses worldly treasures to finance efforts to reign on the earth. Adam's son Cain was the first to fall prey to Satan's promise that one can "murder and get gain,"[4] and then get away with it. Countless others throughout world history have similarly "entered into a covenant with Satan, after the manner of Cain."[5] This was Satan's

---

1   Joseph Smith Translation, Matthew 4:1.
2   Matthew 4:8.
3   Luke 4:6–7.
4   Moses 5:31.
5   Moses 5:49. See also Ether 8:22–23 and 11:15.

offer to Jesus as well: "If thou therefore wilt worship me, all shall be thine." It is interesting to note that Jesus did not indicate that Satan was making an offer he could not fulfill; it was, perhaps, not an empty promise. In other words, it is within Satan's ability to influence those who desire and use power and wealth, and their allegiance can lead to action that Satan desires. Jesus did not call out his fallen brother for lying. He simply stated: "Get thee behind me, Satan: for it is written, Thou shalt worship the Lord thy God, and him only shalt thou serve."[6]

The devil understands something crucial about our mortal condition: influence, authority, and power can open the door to pride and spiritual downfall. Worldly power and glory are among the adversary's most enticing currencies. Jesus rightly refused—but for many of God's children throughout history, the pursuit of status or control proved far harder to resist. Solomon's lavish reign remains one of the most striking reminders of this pitfall.[7] Called to lead God's people, he was blessed with gifts of discernment and wisdom. Yet the lure of political alliances and personal prestige weakened his spiritual resolve, leading him to accommodate idolatrous ideas—ultimately "turning away" his heart from God's covenant.[8] Power here was the accelerant for an already-simmering pride. Once enthroned and praised for his splendor, Solomon no longer exercised the humility that had initially defined his relation-

---

6   Luke 4:8.
7   1 Kings 10–11.
8   1 Kings 11:4.

ship with the Lord.[9] Similar scenarios permeate the scriptural record. King Noah's high seat among the Nephites turned him into a tyrant, squeezing his people for taxes and indulging the basest desires.[10] To support his polygamous harem and personal vanity, Riplakish "did lay that upon men's shoulders which was grievous to be borne; yea, he did tax them with heavy taxes; and with the taxes he did build many spacious buildings."[11] Those who wielded power and abused it are the rule, not the exception.

Power, in short, can be a strong intoxicant—dulling spiritual sensitivity and inflating one's sense of self-importance. No wonder the heavens withdraw themselves "when we undertake to cover our sins, or to gratify our pride, our vain ambition."[12] Satan expertly exploits these vulnerabilities. The scriptures paint him as "the prince of this world,"[13] suggesting he has a wide berth to grant or withhold earthly honors for a price[14]—using the treasures of the earth, he buys the loyalty of false priests and tyrants to do his bidding. Once the bargain is sealed—earthly treasure for allegiance—the corruption is immediate, for Nephi declared that every church (or effort, more broadly) "built up to get gain" already belongs to the devil's kingdom.[15] Power corrupts, and absolute power corrupts absolutely.

---

9   1 Kings 3:5–13.
10   Mosiah 11:3–10.
11   Ether 10:5–7.
12   D&C 121:37.
13   John 14:30.
14   Luke 4:6–7.
15   1 Nephi 22:23.

This pattern of power leading to spiritual downfall is, of course, not limited to kings and rulers of ancient times. It is a recurring theme that threads through history and continues into our modern era. Those who are entrusted with authority often begin with noble intentions but can gradually succumb to the intoxicating allure of control, wealth, and influence—such as King David, whose moral lapse led him to orchestrate the death of Uriah to try and conceal his adulterous sin. This is why Joseph Smith's observation is so strikingly relevant: "We have learned by sad experience that it is the nature and disposition of almost all men, as soon as they get a little authority, as they suppose, they will immediately begin to exercise unrighteous dominion."[16] The phrase "as they suppose" underscores the self-deception that often accompanies the misuse of power—believing that one's actions are justified or even righteous when, in reality, they are rooted in pride and selfish ambition. Power corrupts, but it also deceives.

How can we liken these ideas to ourselves? First, we must recognize how easily we can be drawn toward worldly markers of influence—what the scriptures repeatedly warn against as the arm of flesh.[17] Placing our trust in mortal leaders, powerful institutions, or societal systems can lead to disillusionment when they prove fallible and corrupt. Worse, these entities often entice others to follow them, much like the Nephites were seduced to join secret combinations, lured by the promise of power and wealth.[18] The arm of flesh may

16   D&C 121:39.
17   2 Nephi 28:31.
18   Helaman 6:38.

initially appear welcoming and reassuring, outstretched as if to lift us up, but its true nature is far more insidious. Like flaxen cords, these enticements seem harmless at first, but they gradually tighten until they bind us down, making it harder to break free from their grip.[19] Recognizing these dangers early allows us to avoid their traps and place our faith where it truly belongs—in God.

Second, we should consciously cultivate humility—the antidote to pride and vanity. Pride often sprouts up in small ways: a dismissive remark toward a coworker, the refusal to admit a mistake, or the subtle delight we take when recognized for our talents. Over time, these seeds of self-importance can grow into the same corrupt impulses that toppled the likes of David and Solomon. The applause that trails fame and fortune insulates the heart from correction, giving pride far more frequent—and socially rewarded—opportunities than the quiet envy that can trouble the poor. After all, God despises "the wise, and the learned, and they that are rich, who are puffed up because of their learning, and their wisdom, and their riches."[20] By contrast, He operates true power "by persuasion, by long-suffering, by gentleness and meekness, and by love unfeigned"[21]—a stark contrast to the coercive means used by Satan's minions on earth. But the sin of pride is not reserved only for those who have amassed worldly power and made deals with the devil. It can also quietly infect the lives of ordinary individuals—parents who become authoritarian in their

---

19   2 Nephi 26:22.
20   2 Nephi 9:42.
21   D&C 121:41.

homes, community members who hoard their riches and neglect to care for the poor, or even Church members who pride themselves on their callings or perceived righteousness. Pride is a universal temptation, no matter our station in life, because it appeals to the natural man within each of us. As C.S. Lewis aptly observed, pride is "the essential vice, the utmost evil," for it "leads to every other vice" and turns our focus inward instead of upward toward God.[22] It blinds us to our dependence on Him, convincing us that our successes are solely the result of our own merits. In contrast, a humble heart is fertile ground for the Lord's guidance. Every time we kneel in prayer, we are reminded that our abilities—and any power we actually have—come from God, not from our own merit. Confessing our faults to Him and to others—whether it's apologizing for a harsh word or correcting a misunderstanding—carves out space for the Spirit to operate. This day-to-day discipline keeps our hearts soft and malleable, resilient against the high-mindedness that so often sneaks in when we feel we've arrived at a position of influence.

Third, we can remember and try to follow the example of Jesus Christ, who "came not to be ministered unto, but to minister"[23]—an instruction confirmed by His act of washing the disciples' feet on the eve of His own betrayal.[24] If God Himself can stoop to serve the least, how much more should we seek opportunities to do likewise? We can emulate Christ's

22 C.S. Lewis, *Mere Christianity* (New York: HarperOne, 2001), 121-2.
23 Matthew 20:28.
24 John 13:4–17.

example in simple yet meaningful ways. Consider a modern example: A father who, despite his busy schedule, quietly arrives early to set up chairs for a ward activity without fanfare or acknowledgment. Or a mother, overwhelmed with her own responsibilities, who makes time to patiently listen to her teenager's struggles, setting aside her own exhaustion to be fully present. Such small, selfless acts remind us that genuine influence—and the right kind we should cultivate, as opposed to the world's corrupt counterfeit—comes not from titles or acclaim but from the quiet power of love and service. King Benjamin, one of the great examples of righteous leadership in scripture, described his approach: "I, myself, have labored with mine own hands that I might serve you, and that ye should not be laden with taxes, and that there should nothing come upon you which was grievous to be borne."[25] By keeping his focus on service and accountability before God, Benjamin avoided the snares of pride and selfish ambition, leaving a legacy of peace and righteousness for his people—and one that we can try to emulate. Our goal must be to protect ourselves from the slow poison of self-importance—the very temptation that led to widespread wickedness and war among both major peoples of the Book of Mormon. By consistently striving to serve rather than be served, we make the Savior's model our own and ensure that whatever influence we hold remains a holy stewardship rather than a stumbling block.

The pull of power, pride, and self-importance is a universal and timeless challenge, but the antidote is clear: humil-

---

25 Mosiah 2:14.

ity, service, and a steadfast reliance on God. By rejecting the world's corrosive influence and embracing Christ's model of servant leadership—a model of true, godly power—we not only safeguard our souls but also magnify our ability to bless others. True greatness lies not in being exalted by the world but in being a faithful steward of the Lord's work.

PROSPERITY'S CURSE

The Promised Land was regularly described by the Lord to be a land "flowing with milk and honey,"[1] one that could support the migrant population with great abundance. When Moses sent spies to investigate the area and "bring of the fruit of the land," they later returned—bringing evidence of the bounteous harvest available—with a cluster of grapes so large that two of them had to carry it together.[2] Longing for the fleshpots of Egypt and having grown tired of the heaven-sent manna, the wandering Israelites were ready for a feast. But God, perfectly knowing how prone mankind is to become conditioned to prosperity, cautioned them not to forget Him in the moment of plenty:

> Beware that thou forget not the Lord thy God, in not keeping his commandments, and his judgments, and his statutes, which I command thee this day: Lest when thou hast eaten and art full, and hast built goodly houses, and dwelt therein; And when thy herds and thy flocks multiply, and thy silver and thy gold is multiplied, and all that thou hast is multiplied; Then thine heart be lifted up, and thou forget the Lord thy God,

1   Exodus 3:8; Numbers 14:8; Deuteronomy 31:20; Ezekiel 20:15.
2   Numbers 13:17–23.

which brought thee forth out of the land of Egypt, from the house of bondage;[3]

It's a universal pattern: as resources increase, reliance on heaven often decreases. With greater affluence comes an ease of living that can dull our spiritual senses. Bounty that should inspire praise and righteous stewardship instead becomes a catalyst for vanity and covetousness. And instead of seeking God's counsel and relying on Him daily, people come to lean on their stored wealth or earthly security, trusting instead in the arm of flesh. The "exceedingly great riches and... prosperity in the land"[4] enjoyed by God's people is a great blessing that too easily and too often becomes their curse. Nephi lays it out plainly:

> Yea, and we may see at the very time when he doth prosper his people, yea, in the increase of their fields, their flocks and their herds, and in gold, and in silver, and in all manner of precious things of every kind and art; sparing their lives, and delivering them out of the hands of their enemies; softening the hearts of their enemies that they should not declare wars against them; yea, and in fine, doing all things for the welfare and happiness of his people; yea, then is the time that they do harden their hearts, and do forget the Lord their God, and do trample under their feet the Holy One—yea, and this because of their ease, and their exceedingly great prosperity.[5]

---

3   Deuteronomy 8:11–14.
4   Helaman 3:36.
5   Helaman 12:2.

Curiously, the Book of Mormon mentions how the pride in people's hearts, resulting from their prosperity, "did grow upon them from day to day"[6]—a slow stain seeping into their attitudes and actions that eventually led to their downfall. This gradual corruption reveals the insidious nature of pride—it rarely appears in dramatic, recognizable ways at first. Instead, it begins subtly, manifesting in attitudes of entitlement, ingratitude, and a desire for self-exaltation. God said that we can't serve both Him and Mammon for a reason[7]—the earth's resources can't build both God's kingdom and our own. No man can serve two masters.[8]

Remaining righteous while experiencing prosperity is not impossible; we shouldn't assume that prosperity inherently and always leads to wickedness. True, it typically does—we have an abundance of examples to confirm this unfortunate reality. But there are exceptions—important ones we ought to scrutinize in order to see if we might replicate them. Consider one example from the Nephite nation after the "wars, and bloodsheds, and famine, and affliction," which lasted "for the space of many years"[9]—decades, actually. As the dust settled and people began to rebuild, they began to prosper again and became "exceedingly rich."[10]

> But notwithstanding their riches, or their strength, or their prosperity, they were not lifted up in the pride of their eyes; neither were they slow to remember the

---

6   Helaman 3:36.
7   Matthew 6:24.
8   Ibid.
9   Alma 62:39.
10   Alma 62:48.

Lord their God; but they did humble themselves exceedingly before him.

Yea, they did remember how great things the Lord had done for them, that he had delivered them from death, and from bonds, and from prisons, and from all manner of afflictions, and he had delivered them out of the hands of their enemies.

And they did pray unto the Lord their God continually, insomuch that the Lord did bless them, according to his word, so that they did wax strong and prosper in the land.[11]

Perhaps most important to note from this example is the double reference to remembering. First, the Nephites made sure to frequently remember God, presumably keeping their eye single to His glory[12] rather than their own, despite their accumulation of material wealth along the way. Second, they specifically remembered the wonderful blessings God had given them—His protection and deliverance from harm and death. They prayed often and, in righteousness, "did wax strong and prosper in the land." They figured out a way to not fall into the trap of past generations,[13] which inevitably grew forgetful of past blessings and the Lord's hand in their lives.

---

11 Alma 62:49–51.
12 D&C 4:5.
13 Until about 25 years later, that is, because of the next generation's "pride of their hearts, because of their exceeding riches, yea, it was because of their oppression to the poor, withholding their food from the hungry, withholding their clothing from the naked, and smiting their humble brethren upon the cheek,

An even better example comes later, after Christ's visit to the New World. Those who survived the great destruction were so astonished by this experience—or, for those not present, the testimony of those who were—that "the people were all converted unto the Lord, upon all the face of the land, both Nephites and Lamanites, and there were no contentions and disputations among them, and every man did deal justly one with another."[14] In response, "the Lord did prosper them exceedingly in the land."[15] There was no contention or significant wickedness, as previous generations had experienced so often, "because of the love of God which did dwell in the hearts of the people."[16] In summarizing their records, Mormon observes how "blessed and prospered" they were:

> And now I, Mormon, would that ye should know that the people had multiplied, insomuch that they were spread upon all the face of the land, and that they had become exceedingly rich, because of their prosperity in Christ.[17]

The narrator really wants our attention focused on this point; only one other time in Mormon's record does he write that he "would that [we] should know" something.[18] Perhaps he, more than anyone, understood how important an anomaly this situation was in contrast to the constant conflict and destruction he had been reading and writing about up until this

---

making a mock of that which was sacred ..." Helaman 4:12.

14 4 Nephi 1:2.

15 4 Nephi 1:7.

16 4 Nephi 1:15–17.

17 4 Nephi 1:23.

18 Helaman 8:19.

point. It deserves special attention; it deserves reflection and replication. This wasn't just material wealth—it was "prosperity in Christ," alongside being "exceedingly rich"—no doubt using the earth's resources as righteous stewards to bless others and create a tight-knit, Christ-centered community. Nearly 170 years of this pattern of prosperity in righteousness continued without interruption—a remarkable achievement no doubt made possible because of the strong influence of Christ's teachings and the recency of His having directly taught them to the people.

But people are often forgetful and sometimes stupid. Thus, "there began to be among them those who were lifted up in pride, such as the wearing of costly apparel, and all manner of fine pearls, and of the fine things of the world."[19] Class division crept in, as did material inequality. Generations had passed since Christ's visit, and memories faded—distracted by the shiny allure of the world's wealth and the status and power that claims to come with it. Yet despite the example having a sad conclusion, the decades-long durability of this society suggests that it's not impossible for others to achieve as well. The Wright Brothers proved that human flight was achievable, even if their inaugural flight lasted only twelve seconds. Others built on their success and expanded what was possible. A Zion-like community can produce the same results and reap the same heavenly rewards.

How can we liken these ideas to ourselves? First, we need a way to routinely check ourselves to guard against creeping

---

19   4 Nephi 1:24–26.

pride. After Alma organized a church in Sidom to support the newly converted exiles from Ammonihah, he observed "a great check, yea, seeing that the people were checked as to the pride of their hearts, and began to humble themselves before God, and began tc assemble themselves together at their sanctuaries to worship God before the altar, watching and praying continually, that they might be delivered from Satan..."[20] Their daily practices served as a "check" to guard against inconsistent actions. The slow stain that incrementally advances is difficult to detect, as scriptural history makes all too clear. How much better to have, say, a daily or weekly ritual of self-analysis and spiritual focus to measure ourselves, assess our behaviors, repent as necessary, and purge from our life anything that may be allowing the stain to spread? We need a way to consistently and habitually check ourselves—and help check our loved ones—to ensure that we do not embrace ideas and practices that are inconsistent with the gospel.

Second, we need to reject ownership and control. We do not possess resources; we are stewards of them. All things belong to[21] and are beneath[22] God. We are mere stewards of what is actually God's.[23] Thus, the material wealth we accumulate in this life serves a higher purpose than we might typically perceive. The Lord has provided ample resources—"there is

---

20 Alma 15:17.
21 Leviticus 25:23; Deuteronomy 10:14; 1 Corinthians 10:26; Psalm 24:1; D&C 104:14–15; 38:39.
22 1 Chronicles 29:12–16; Psalm 47:2; 2 Chronicles 20:6; John 17:2; D&C 63:59.
23 D&C 104:55–56; 78:22; 136:27.

enough and to spare" for His children.[24] The "fulness of the earth is [ours]" and all things upon the earth "are made for the benefit and the use of man."[25] These resources are meant for ourselves and our families to prosper, "with thanksgiving"[26] in recognition of Him who provided us with them. But we are also meant to use them to benefit others. Recall that the prosperous people in the Book of Mormon faltered precisely when they began "turning their backs upon the needy and the naked and those who were hungry, and those who were athirst, and those who were sick and afflicted."[27] The scriptures call upon us to "think of your brethren like unto yourselves, and be familiar with all and free with your substance."[28] And they condemn those who withhold temporal support from others out of some prideful prioritization of one's self. God's resources are meant to benefit His children—certainly ourselves and our families primarily, but, importantly, those within our broader stewardship as well. Only when we view our wealth as God's can we escape the pride that poisons prosperity. By using His resources to bless the lives of others, we fulfill the divine mandate to be His stewards and secure treasures in heaven that will never corrupt.[29]

Third, we can deliberately cultivate an attitude of gratitude, remembering that every good thing ultimately comes from the Lord. Too often, the Nephites' prosperity led them

---

24   D&C 104:17.
25   D&C 59:16–20.
26   D&C 59:15.
27   Alma 4:12.
28   Jacob 2:17.
29   Matthew 6:19–21.

to instead adopt an attitude of self-congratulation that "lifted [them] up in pride."[30] Had they paused to recognize the divine hand behind their success—like the post-war group who "did remember how great things the Lord had done for them"[31]— they might have stayed anchored. This principle applies just as much to us: making gratitude a deliberate habit—whether by reflecting on daily mercies, offering sincere and detailed prayers of gratitude, or communicating our gratitude to others in our life for their support and love—transforms prosperity into an opportunity for spiritual growth rather than a catalyst for arrogance. In acknowledging the true source of our abundance, we emulate those rare exceptions in scripture who thrived in their wealth precisely because they knew it came from God.

Prosperity per se is not the enemy; it is our attitude toward and actions resulting from prosperity that either sanctify us or sow the seeds of our downfall. By remembering that every good thing originates from a loving Father and that the resources in our stewardship are meant to be used with thanksgiving and freely shared with others in need, we can create a "great check" to guard against the slow stain of pride in our lives and ensure that abundance remains a blessing rather than the beginning of spiritual decline.

---

30 Helaman 3:33–36.
31 Alma 62:49–50.

CULTURE IS PERVASIVE AND PERSUASIVE

If ever there were a single thread binding humanity across ages and kingdoms, it is the desire to fit in—a social tug that can be as invisible as gravity yet just as powerful. In his research on influence, psychologist Robert Cialdini labels this inclination "social proof," describing how "one means we use to determine what is correct is to find out what other people think is correct."[1] He continues:

> We view a behavior as more correct in a given situation to the degree that we see others performing it. Whether the question is what to do with an empty popcorn box in a movie theater, how fast to drive on a certain stretch of highway, or how to eat the chicken at a dinner party, the actions of those around us will be important in defining the answer.[2]

The peer pressures and pointers we absorb affect benign behaviors like Cialdini describes. But they also acclimate us to far more sinister actions—even murder. In response to hearing Nazi officials argue in court that they were "just fol-

---

1   Robert Cialdini, *Influence: The Psychology of Persuasion* (New York: HarperCollins, 2009), 88.
2   Ibid.

lowing orders" to carry out their butchery, Stanley Milgram, a social psychologist at Yale, created an experiment to understand why people go along with what they are expected to do. In this study, participants were instructed to perform an act that violated their conscience: the administration of a series of electric shocks upon a person in another room whom they could hear but not see. Each shock, participants were told, would be more powerful and painful than the last, leading to a final, fatal voltage being delivered. Of course, no pain was actually inflicted upon the unseen person, because they were actors pretending to be shocked—but participants did not know this and could only hear the unseen person's screams of agony. As participants protested throughout the process, they were instructed by the authority figure to continue—that the experiment was important and required completion. Reluctantly, but compliantly, most participants subordinated their concerns and did as instructed, to the point of (in their minds) administering death to another. The Milgram experiment has been consistently replicated, with results showing that over 60 percent of participants will inflict the fatal voltage upon the other person when instructed to do so by the authority figure.[3] We are so prone to adopting others' behaviors and following social cues that two-thirds of us are willing to kill others.

In view of this alarming data, we can better understand and appreciate the difficulty God's children have had through-

---

3   Thomas Blass, "The Man Who Shocked The World," Psychology Today, March 2002, https://www.psychologytoday.com/intl/articles/200203/the-man-who-shocked-the-world.

out history in resisting cultural pressures and remaining a peculiar people. It's difficult to act against the natural man's psychological wiring. Ancient Israel's desire to be "like all the nations"[4] in having a mortal king wasn't raw rebellion in their eyes—rather, they wished to blend comfortably with neighboring kingdoms, hoping to replicate the success and stability they perceived in outsiders. By seeking to conform to worldly standards, they set aside direct divine guidance, revealing how cultural norms can overpower whatever spiritual goals we might conceptually value.

The Israelites were a monotheistic island floating in a sea of pagan idolatry. The cultural waves of surrounding communities crashed against their shores repeatedly, constantly drawing their gaze and inviting their participation. And despite being commanded to worship only the Lord, they emulated and embraced the practices of idolatrous neighbors, representing a capitulation to cultural norms that promised prosperity and security. These religious rites claimed to offer immediate, tangible benefits in exchange for forsaking the intangible God who had delivered them from bondage. But that was the past; in their daily present, Israel was far more intoxicated by the apparent benefits of the exciting cultures around them. Other scriptural societies were no less immune to these trends. It's a problem for all people, both ancient and modern. (As we'll later see, cultural forces are even more pervasive and persuasive today.)

---

4   1 Samuel 8:5.

God's people have always struggled to maintain a cohesive identity, and fidelity to God, while surrounded by idolatrous cults. Time and again "they went a whoring after other gods, and bowed themselves unto them: they turned quickly out of the way which their fathers walked in."[5] But Christ's kingdom is essentially counter-*cult*ural—the true religion contrasted against the imposter cult and its would-be gods. For example, the Romans proclaimed their emperor as savior of the world and the prince of peace;[6] the disciples of Jesus appropriated these terms and applied them to the true Savior, for which Caesar was a mere counterfeit. Ultimately, we must decide which God we worship—the one true God or the imposter one represented by a thousand faces and names and belief systems. We are either members of His Church or its counterfeit, for "there are save two churches only; the one is the church of the Lamb of God, and the other is the church of the devil; wherefore, whoso belongeth not to the church of the Lamb of God belongeth to that great church, which is the mother of abominations; and she is the whore of all the earth."[7]

External pressures of surrounding cultures are certainly a threat, though one insight we gain from the scriptures is that the greater threat is from within. "Ye hear of wars in far countries," the Lord says, "and you say that there will soon be great wars in far countries, but ye know not the hearts of men in

5   Judges 2:17.
6   The imperial cult of Rome treated the emperor as a divine being—one to be worshiped and honored by his subjects. Caesar was showered with such titles as Savior of the World, Bringer of Peace, and Son of God.
7   1 Nephi 14:10.

your own land."[8] The Nephite and Jaredite experiences teach us that whatever corrupting influences they faced from surrounding cultures from people spread across the New World, secret combinations, internal dissension, and wickedness are what made them most vulnerable to God's wrath. Not all cultural influences come from outside pressures; many are deeply rooted in the "traditions of our fathers." These inherited ideas, practices, and beliefs—passed down through generations—carry a unique and often invisible weight. As Mormon observed, some of the people's false traditions and ideas were "a cause of all their destruction."[9] These deeply ingrained patterns blinded entire generations to the truth, creating a cycle of rebellion and ignorance that was difficult to break. Too often, it broke them.

The culture created through the compounding traditions of our fathers can act as a millstone around our necks, weighing us down with attitudes and practices that conflict with the gospel. This might include inherited prejudices, family patterns of behavior, or societal norms that subtly violate God's commandments. Consider the Pharisees, whose strict adherence to man-made traditions often obscured the higher law Christ came to teach. Their unwillingness to let go of their cultural and religious assumptions kept them from recognizing the Savior Himself. Culture, in their case, had deadly and eternal consequences. Modern disciples face similar challenges. We may inherit attitudes or habits from our families or communities that, while familiar, are not in harmony with

8   D&C 38:29.
9   Alma 51:16.

the Lord's will. Perhaps it's an emphasis on material success at the expense of spiritual priorities, a reluctance to forgive due to familial grudges, or cultural narratives that define worth by appearance or status. Traditions such as these may feel natural, even comfortable, but they can prevent us from fully embracing the Savior's teachings.

How can we liken these ideas to ourselves? First, we ought to take inventory of our own cultural attitudes and actions. Culture itself is inescapable; as social creatures, our environment and the people within it influence us imperceptibly. If we aren't consciously navigating culture, we become unconsciously controlled by it, "blinded by the subtle craftiness of men."[10] We might evaluate our daily routines, entertainment choices, or political views through the lens of Paul's counsel: "Prove all things; hold fast that which is good."[11] Reflecting on how we are influenced by others can awaken us to hidden pressures that, if unacknowledged, can nudge us to act or think in ways we'd otherwise reject. The story of the rich young ruler offers a poignant example. Though he had kept the commandments from his youth, he could not part with his great possessions when Christ invited him to follow.[12] His cultural attachment to wealth and status was so strong that it overpowered his desire for eternal life. This story compels us to ask: What cultural attachments might we be holding on to that prevent us from fully following the Savior?

---

10 D&C 123:12.
11 1 Thessalonians 5:21
12 Matthew 19:16–22.

Second, we should realize how deeply we are affected by those in power over us—and take steps to mitigate their potentially harmful influence. After reading the Jaredite record and learning of its tales of carnage, Mosiah—himself still the king—lamented, "How much iniquity doth one wicked king cause to be committed, yea, and what great destruction!"[13] Mormon observed, regarding the smooth-talking Amalickiah, "the great wickedness one very wicked man can cause to take place."[14] The lesson is clear: those in positions of power wield enormous influence, not only through their direct actions but also by shaping the beliefs, priorities, and behaviors of those they lead. As Milgram's experiment demonstrates, the natural man is highly susceptible to authority figures—often to the point of suppressing moral concerns in favor of compliance. This human weakness can lead to devastating consequences when exploited by unrighteous leaders, such as the evil King Noah, whose actions led the people to become "idolatrous, because they were deceived by the vain and flattering words of the king."[15] Recognizing this inherent vulnerability should compel us to approach authority with skepticism and vigilance. This doesn't mean rejecting all leaders outright but rather holding them accountable and evaluating their actions against eternal truths. As disciples of Christ, our ultimate loyalty must be to Him, not to any earthly authority. The Savior Himself modeled this principle when confronted by Pilate,

---

13 Mosiah 29:17.
14 Alma 46:9.
15 Mosiah 11:7.

declaring, "My kingdom is not of this world."[16] His words remind us that no mortal leader, regardless of their position or power, should dictate our moral or spiritual compass.

Third, we need to embrace and reinforce our peculiarity—the distinct differences God's people are called to live by in order to be counted as His. Today the word means "weird" or "strange," but the version used in scripture derives from the Latin *peculium*, meaning "property" or "possession." When God calls His people a "peculiar treasure,"[17] He is claiming them as His own, set apart from the world to fulfill His purposes. Throughout scripture, God's people are repeatedly commanded to be different from the world around them. Israel was given dietary restrictions, clothing regulations, and laws governing daily life—not merely to create arbitrary rules but to help them remain holy and distinct in the midst of surrounding pagan cultures. "And ye shall be holy unto me: for I the Lord am holy, and have severed you from other people, that ye should be mine."[18] Peter echoes this theme, calling disciples of Christ "a chosen generation, a royal priesthood, an holy nation, a peculiar people."[19] Embracing our peculiarity often means resisting the cultural pull to conform. Trying to fit in with worldly norms—whether in fashion, entertainment, sexual relationships, or political views—can lead us to surrender the very qualities that set us apart as God's people. If we instead embrace these differences and resist the lure of

---

16   John 18:36.
17   Exodus 19:5.
18   Leviticus 20:26.
19   1 Peter 2:9.

surrounding culture, we signal our willingness to follow God's path, no matter how countercultural it may appear.

Ultimately, culture exerts a powerful and often imperceptible influence, shaping our values, priorities, and desires in ways we may not fully recognize. The scriptures vividly illustrate how swiftly a faithful community can falter when seduced by the allure of conforming to the beliefs and practices of the world. As social creatures, we are deeply influenced by those around us, often more than we care to admit. To assume that we are immune to the cultural pressures that led past peoples astray is both dangerous and naive. Their stories are not relics of a bygone era but cautionary tales for us today, urging us to examine whether we, too, have unknowingly absorbed idolatrous attitudes and practices.

FALSE DOCTRINES BLEND EASILY WITH TRUTH

When Joseph Smith was visited by God the Father and Jesus Christ, he was told how sinful people throughout the world had become. "They have turned aside from the gospel and keep not my commandments," God told him. "They draw near to me with their lips while their hearts are far from me."[1] It was a clear condemnation of how twisted Christ's gospel had become. Of course, this has been a problem since the beginning of mankind's earthly existence; believers have long wrestled with (and become spiritual victims of) the infiltration of untrue philosophies that masquerade as doctrine. The Bible is effectively one long tale of habitual apostasy, with sporadic attempts from prophets and Christ Himself to recalibrate God's people and keep their worship fixed on truth. In the Old Testament, God describes a false prophet as one who "shall presume to speak a word in my name, which I have not commanded him to speak, or that shall speak in the name of other gods."[2] These deceivers share "a false vision and divina-

---

1   "Circa Summer 1832 History," The Church of Jesus Christ of Latter-day Saints, https://www.churchofjesuschrist.org/study/manual/first-vision-accounts/1832-account.
2   Deuteronomy 18:20.

tion, and a thing of nought, and the deceit of their heart."[3] In the New Testament, Jesus warned his followers of false prophets who could "deceive the very elect."[4]

These teachings are augmented dramatically by those offered in the Book of Mormon on the subject of false doctrine. As Ezra Taft Benson explained, the book "confounds false doctrines" and exposes "the evil designs, strategies, and doctrines of the devil in our day."[5] This scriptural record, in particular, empowers us to "know how to combat false educational, political, religious, and philosophical concepts of our time."[6] No wonder the early Latter-day Saints were condemned for treating lightly the potent warnings it offered them.[7]

The Book of Mormon highlights the story of several anti-Christs who spread false doctrine, such as Sherem,[8] who denied Christ's coming, and Nehor,[9] who introduced priestcraft and claimed repentance for sin was unnecessary. Chief among the examples offered is Korihor, who claimed that God didn't exist, that there was no life after this mortal experience, and that, therefore, sin did not exist.[10] He used rational arguments to assert that one could not know that God exists[11] or anything that one cannot see with one's own eyes.[12] The

3   Jeremiah 14:14.
4   Matthew 24:24.
5   Ezra Taft Benson, "The Book of Mormon Is the Word of God," *Ensign*, Jan. 1988, 3.
6   Ibid.
7   D&C 84:54–58.
8   Jacob 7.
9   Alma 1.
10 Alma 30.
11 Alma 30:13.
12 Alma 30:15.

belief system of the people he sought to persuade was, in his view, "the effect of a frenzied mind; and this derangement of your minds comes because of the traditions of your fathers, which lead you away into a belief of things which are not so."[13] Korihor effectively bullied believers into abandoning the gospel since it could not be proven with temporal means to his satisfaction. His cunning language and flattery led away "the hearts of many, causing them to lift up their heads in their wickedness, yea, leading away many women, and also men, to commit whoredoms—telling them that when a man was dead, that was the end thereof."[14]

A frontal assault on faith can clearly make an impact, but false doctrines do not always appear as strident, oppositional arguments by hostile speakers. More often, like a slow stain, they spread subtly, carefully, and incrementally. They appear harmless, masking themselves so closely to the truth that the sinister subtleties are difficult to detect. How else could Lucifer, for example, lead away so many of God's children—permanently consigning them to eternal condemnation? He promised them guaranteed salvation, regardless of their actions.[15] In effect, he was proposing that everybody would be able to "eat, drink and be merry,"[16] then at the judgment bar receive an unconditional stamp of approval. Talk about a persuasive proposal! Who wouldn't be enticed by a guaranteed positive outcome? Hence the Lord rightly called him "subtle"[17]—after

13 Alma 30:16.
14 Alma 30:18.
15 Moses 4:1.
16 2 Nephi 28:7–8.
17 Moses 4:5.

all, wouldn't a loving Father in Heaven want all of His children to return after their mortal journey? Wasn't this, Lucifer's pitch, a demonstration of love and inclusion? Wouldn't anything less be hateful and exclusionary? This wasn't a frontal assault—it was a cunning subversion, disguised as a moral high ground, appealing to the natural man's desire for ease and comfort over obedience and sacrifice. It was the ultimate distortion of divine love, twisted into a tool for rebellion. It was a false doctrine pitched as the fullest expression of God's love for His children.

The incremental adoption of false doctrines is accelerated by the sheer number of people who proclaim truth without possessing it. Joseph Smith's own experience is reflective of what God's people have long confronted—a cacophony of voices competing for truth claims. Large numbers of people "united themselves to the different religious parties" in his community, "which created no small stir and division among the people, some crying, 'Lo, here!' and others, 'Lo, there!'"[18] Opinions are as abundant as are the varied interpretations of God's word—everyone seems to think that *theirs* is the correct one. But the end result is spiritual confusion, where people "lose their way"[19] because they "seek not the Lord to establish his righteousness, but every man walketh in his own way, and after the image of his own god, whose image is in the likeness of the world, and whose substance is that of an idol..."[20] The false prophets, as well as those who emulate them, "set them-

18   Joseph Smith—History 1:5.
19   1 Nephi 8:23.
20   D&C 1:16.

selves up for a light unto the world, that they may get gain and praise of the world; but they seek not the welfare of Zion."[21] False doctrines often blend so easily with truth that without constant vigilance and reliance on revelation, even the faithful risk mistaking counterfeit light for divine guidance.

We also learn from scripture that spiritually weak people invite this doctrinal confusion in order to satiate their carnal desires. The Apostle Paul referred to people who do "not endure sound doctrine; but after their own lusts shall they heap to themselves teachers, having itching ears; And they shall turn away their ears from the truth."[22] This pattern is deeply evident in Korihor's teachings, which justified wickedness by dismissing eternal consequences.[23] Yet this attraction to false doctrines does not always appear as open rebellion as in his case. Often, individuals latch on to ideas and beliefs that permit them to "justify [themselves] in committing a little sin."[24] By embracing a false gospel that tolerates their sin, these people continue in wrongdoing while appearing devout. The net effect is a superficial piety masking deeper moral decay—a potent illustration of how cunningly error can disguise itself beneath a veneer of religiosity.

How can we liken these ideas to ourselves? First, we should recognize how frequently flattery is connected to the spread of falsehoods. Over half of the Book of Mormon's examples of wickedness use flattering speech and charisma to

---

21 2 Nephi 26:29.
22 2 Timothy 4:3–4.
23 Alma 30:17.
24 2 Nephi 28:8.

advance their agenda. Sherem "had a perfect knowledge of the language of the people; wherefore, he could use much flattery, and much power of speech, according to the power of the devil."[25] King Noah's idolatrous priests used "vain and flattering words"[26] to promote their false doctrines. Korihor's charisma enabled him to "[lead] away the hearts of many."[27] Amalickiah and Gadianton both used flattery to entice thousands of people to serve as their pawns.[28] None of this was the result of mere chance; flattery is an integral element in Satan's spreading of lies. It focuses on style over substance. It is, in George Orwell's words, "designed to make lies sound truthful and murder respectable, and to give an appearance of solidity to pure wind."[29] It is the language used by Satan himself—an "appealing, intriguing voice with dulcet tones."[30] After all, who would listen to and be persuaded by a rage-filled voice of anger and hostility? No wonder Jesus warned us of circumstances in which "all men shall speak well of you."[31] Flattery is false doctrine's delivery system. Like a Trojan horse, flattery cloaks falsehood in a facade of charm and credibility, allowing destructive ideas to enter unnoticed and corrupt the hearts of those who fail to discern its deceit.

---

25 Jacob 7:4.
26 Mosiah 11:7.
27 Alma 30:18.
28 Alma 46:10; Helaman 2:4.
29 George Orwell, "Politics and the English Language," https://www.orwellfoundation.com/the-orwell-foundation/orwell/essays-and-other-works/politics-and-the-english-language/.
30 James E. Faust, "The Forces That Will Save Us," Liahona, Jan. 2007, 4.
31 Luke 6:26.

Second, we should use the Savior's litmus test to assess doctrinal ideas. Good trees bring forth good fruit, and a corrupt tree brings forth evil fruit. "Wherefore by their fruits ye shall know them."[32] Of course, fruit takes time to develop and ripen—and so do the consequences of ideas. What may seem enticing and harmless at first may, with time, show its true colors and reveal its harm. By waiting for the fruit—to see the type of behavior certain ideas produce over time—we allow ourselves to patiently evaluate differing doctrinal concepts to determine their truthfulness. If a doctrine or idea produces pride and alienation from God, we can discern its source and reject it. Conversely, doctrines that lead to increased humility, faith, and a closer relationship with God are likely rooted in truth. To apply this test, we must also consider the personal impact of doctrines. Do they lead us to greater light and truth, as the Savior promised, or do they distract us with worldly pursuits and philosophies? True doctrine inspires us to follow Christ more closely, to love others more fully, and to grow in righteousness. False doctrines, by contrast, often justify sin, promote selfishness, or shift focus away from eternal truths to temporal concerns. This principle also underscores the importance of spiritual discernment. Just as fruit can sometimes appear outwardly appealing but be rotten inside, false doctrines can be disguised as virtuous or praiseworthy ideas. The adversary often packages his lies in ways that appear attractive and harmless, emphasizing superficial benefits while hiding long-term spiritual consequences. By regularly testing

---

32 Matthew 7:17–20.

the "fruit" of what we believe and follow, we can guard against deception and ensure that we remain anchored in truth.

Third, we should be extremely cautious of societal trends, ideologies, or popular opinions as a default position. Throughout scripture, we witness how insidiously worldly ideas can infiltrate God's people, at first creeping in slowly, almost imperceptibly, before eventually overtaking their host and leading to widespread spiritual decay. Consider the Israelites' desire for a king. What began as a seemingly innocuous desire to "be like all the nations"[33] led to a dramatic shift in their society, resulting in periods of tyranny, idolatry, and eventual captivity. This pattern—adopting worldly ideas under the guise of progress or conformity—repeats itself throughout scripture. The Nephites, for example, embraced secret combinations in pursuit of wealth and power, leading to their societal downfall.[34] Similarly, early Christians began incorporating elements of pagan philosophy into their worship practices, diluting the gospel and paving the way for the Great Apostasy. These examples remind us that societal trends, no matter how appealing or popular, often stand in opposition to God's laws. Worldly ideologies frequently emphasize convenience, self-gratification, or personal autonomy—values that are incompatible with the gospel's call to obedience, self-sacrifice, and reliance on God. Just as Israel's adoption of surrounding nations' practices led them away from their covenant relationship with God, embracing modern cultural norms without scrutiny can subtly and completely erode our

---

33 1 Samuel 8:5.
34 Helaman 6:38–40.

spiritual foundation. Standing against societal trends may make us unpopular or misunderstood. Christ warned His disciples that "the world hateth you" because they were "not of the world."[35] Embracing gospel principles over popular opinion requires courage and conviction, but it is essential if we are to remain true to our covenants and preserve the integrity of God's kingdom in a world that often seeks to erode it.

In a world awash with competing voices and evolving ideals, the gospel's purity can be obscured by even subtle insertions of error. When flattery, cultural "progress," or partially-true theologies tempt us to rationalize sin or minimize divinely established principles, we risk losing our spiritual footing. Only by constant vigilance, sincere self-reflection, and a steadfast commitment to revealed doctrine can we keep our faith undefiled—ensuring that we cling to Christ's true gospel amid the shifting sands of human opinion.

35　John 15:19.

SECRET COMBINATIONS LURK IN ANY ERA

The first recorded murder in scripture is between two of Adam and Eve's sons, Cain and Abel. This grievous sin was the result of the original secret combination—a literal pact with the devil. It began when Satan said to Cain, "Swear unto me by thy throat, and if thou tell it thou shalt die; and swear thy brethren by their heads, and by the living God, that they tell it not; for if they tell it, they shall surely die; and this that thy father may not know it; and this day I will deliver thy brother Abel into thine hands."[1] The record continues:

> And Satan sware unto Cain that he would do according to his commands. And all these things were done in secret. And Cain said: Truly I am Mahan, the master of this great secret, that I may murder and get gain. Wherefore Cain was called Master Mahan, and he gloried in his wickedness. And Cain went into the field, and Cain talked with Abel, his brother. And it came to pass that while they were in the field, Cain rose up against Abel, his brother, and slew him. And Cain gloried in that which he had done, saying: I am free; surely the flocks of my brother falleth into my hands.[2]

---

1   Moses 5:29.
2   Moses 5:30–33.

Here we learn the motive—the *why* behind the evil *what*. Cain's interest was in the world's resources, and Satan leveraged that desire to introduce a ghastly plan: "murder and get gain." Ironically, Cain believed that his actions brought him not only prosperity but also freedom—an illusion that perfectly encapsulates the deceptive, dark promise secret combinations so often sell. From the beginning, then, secret combinations have hinged on the delusion that illicit power and unrighteous possessions can bring happiness—an echo of the adversary's premortal strategy to "carefully" lead souls into ruin.[3]

Only a few generations after Cain, the pattern of secret murder for profit and protection resurfaces in the life of Lamech. Scripture records that Lamech killed a man in conjunction with the same twisted pacts first introduced by Satan to Cain.[4] Though fewer details are provided, Lamech's example underscores how these dark alliances evolve. They no longer aimed purely at personal gain—like Cain's appropriation of Abel's flocks—but also created a network of intimidation that shielded perpetrators from justice. Lamech's murder was "not like unto Cain... for the sake of getting gain, but he slew him for the oath's sake."[5] He killed a person who threatened to expose the conspiracy, telling his wives that if Cain, the original murderer, was protected, then his own life "shall be seventy and seven fold" more secure.[6] Membership in the secret order

3   2 Nephi 28:21.
4   Moses 5:44–49.
5   Moses 5:50.
6   Moses 5:48.

guarantees untouchable status. In other words, once a secret combination gains enough participants, they can ensure that anyone who tries to bring wrongdoers to light will face collective reprisal. Unlike ordinary wrongdoing, which might occur spontaneously, these conspiracies have a built-in mechanism for self-preservation. Members swear oaths—under penalty of death—to never reveal each other's crimes. This cloak of silence gives conspirators an edge: if a victim or witness dares speak out, they have not just one enemy but an entire group mobilized to silence or eliminate them.

Unfortunately, the Bible no longer contains—if it ever did—a detailed record about secret combinations and their influence from the time of Adam down through the millennia. Though the term itself is not used, the Bible does mention several conspiracies.[7] But the Book of Mormon effectively confirms their existence throughout biblical history, despite not being named so directly in the record we have today. For example, how did the daughter of Jared think up her conspiracy that ignited a wave of secret combinations? She mentioned to her father "the record which our fathers brought across the great deep"[8]—a record "which speaks concerning the creation of the world, and also of Adam, and an account from that time even to the great tower, and whatsoever things transpired among the children of men until that time..."[9] This historical record contained "an account concerning them of

---

7   Jeremiah 11:9; 1 Kings 16:9–10; 2 Kings 9:14–15; 2 Chronicles 33:24–25; Ezekiel 22:25.
8   Ether 8:9.
9   Ether 1:3.

old, that they by their secret plans did obtain kingdoms and great glory."[10] It was evidence enough that she and her father could replicate what past people had successfully done, thereby achieving the same rewards that they had.

The Jaredite record—the twenty-four gold plates—was passed down through the Nephite prophets as part of the overall records they maintained about their history. When it came time for Alma to pass them to Helaman, he mentioned "the mysteries and the works of darkness" written in the record.[11] "I command you," he told his son, "that ye retain all their oaths, and their covenants, and their agreements in their secret abominations; yea, and all their signs and their wonders ye shall keep from this people, that they know them not, lest peradventure they should fall into darkness also and be destroyed."[12] Helaman and his posterity did as instructed, withholding from public access the details about how secret combinations operated.[13] But despite their best efforts to stop the spread of these ideas, Satan himself shared the "secret signs, and... secret words"[14] directly with his new recruits:

> Now behold, those secret oaths and covenants did not come forth unto Gadianton from the records which were delivered unto Helaman; but behold, they were put into the heart of Gadianton by that same being who did entice our first parents to partake of the forbidden fruit—Yea, that same being who did plot with Cain,

10 Ether 8:9.
11 Alma 37:21.
12 Alma 37:27.
13 Alma 63:12.
14 Helaman 6:22.

that if he would murder his brother Abel it should not be known unto the world. And he did plot with Cain and his followers from that time forth.[15]

We learn from these examples that Satan "doth carry on his works of darkness and secret murder, and doth hand down their plots, and their oaths, and their covenants, and their plans of awful wickedness, from generation to generation according as he can get hold upon the hearts of the children of men."[16] Consider if you were a Jaredite or Nephite during these periods of pervasive influence by secret combinations. Would you have been aware of their existence, let alone the Satanic source of their power? Or would you have accepted any number of excuses and explanations given, such as chalking it up to political disagreement or concluding it was just an economic slump made worse by rivals in government? Maybe certain officials dismissed the growing chaos as the work of a fringe faction, claiming the rumors about murder and conspiracy were "overblown speculation" or "political propaganda." Others might have argued that infighting is just how nations operate—pointing to "internal disagreements" or "family feuds" rather than seeing them as methodical power grabs. Many individuals might have rationalized away any sense of impending disaster, confident in the official assurances or content to keep their eyes on short-term comforts. A similar dynamic can play out in our own day. It's far more comfortable to accept polished explanations or to wave off

---

15 Helaman 6:26–27.
16 Helaman 6:30.

troubling patterns as random or coincidental than to consider the possibility that intentional, morally bankrupt alliances may be operating behind the scenes. By ignoring the scriptural pattern of secret works—how they require complicity, silence, and a willingness among the people to settle for easy answers—we risk repeating the same fate of those who once brushed aside mounting signs until it was too late.

How can we liken these ideas to ourselves? First, we need to read between the lines to understand how pervasive secret combinations can be, even if their actions are explained away as something less controversial. Moroni, having reviewed their impact on two societies, shares a commandment from God regarding secret combinations: "when ye shall see these things come among you... ye shall awake to a sense of your awful situation."[17] We can't afford to be distracted by lies and allow the enemy to spread throughout society. We need to see evil for what it is, recognize its source, and expose its designs—as Joseph Smith wrote, "we should waste and wear out our lives in bringing to light all the hidden things of darkness, wherein we know them; and they are truly manifest from heaven."[18] We need to appreciate the widespread nature of these conspiracies. Remember, for example, how the Word of Wisdom was given "in consequence of evils and designs which do and will exist in the hearts of conspiring men in the last days."[19] Wicked people conspire in all sorts of industries and power centers; any who wish to do evil and "get away

---

17   Ether 8:24.
18   D&C 123:13.
19   D&C 89:4.

with it" are potential recruits for the adversary to offer his oaths and covenants.

Second, remember how the secret combinations "seduced the more part of the righteous until they had come down to believe in their works and partake of their spoils, and to join with them in their secret murders and combinations."[20] These wicked Nephites "did build them up and support them"[21] until they spread throughout the once godly society. By contrast, remember how "the Lamanites did hunt the band of robbers of Gadianton; and they did preach the word of God among the more wicked part of them, insomuch that this band of robbers was utterly destroyed from among the Lamanites."[22] Here we learn that "the preaching of the word had a great tendency to lead the people to do that which was just—yea, it had had more powerful effect upon the minds of the people than the sword, or anything else."[23] Fighting evil simply requires living and sharing the gospel of Jesus Christ. Jesus said to "let your light so shine before men, that they may see your good works, and glorify your Father which is in heaven."[24] Satan works in the shadows; we need to eradicate these shadows by spreading more light.

Third, we should refuse to justify means because of the ends. Cain felt free to murder because he believed the outcome—personal wealth—excused the method. Evil people often justify their wicked actions based on their perception of

---

20 Helaman 6:38.
21 Ibid.
22 Helaman 6:36.
23 Alma 31:5.
24 Matthew 5:14–16.

the goodness of the end result they seek. For example, Amalickiah manipulated political factions and lied about his intentions in order to acquire and consolidate power. His newfound
followers justified aligning with him despite the clear deception and betrayal he employed.[25] Each step along the way, the
conspirators rationalized underhanded acts as small sacrifices
for the greater cause of putting "the right man" on the throne.
No matter how praiseworthy the end might appear, a tactic
that discards the commandment to "do justly"[26] ultimately
sets a society on a trajectory toward greater corruption. We
must refuse to rationalize sin.

The scriptures command us to embrace truth and reject
evil—and the Book of Mormon, in particular, is emphatically
clear about the need to reject secret combinations and impede
their influence in our society. While it can be tempting for
many to dismiss such issues as "conspiracy theories," the truth
is that scripture reveals them to be conspiracy *facts*—coupled
with a warning and commandment from God directly to ar-
rest their spread throughout society in our own day.

25   Alma 46–47.
26   Micah 6:8.

SLOW STAINS SOON
SPREAD QUICKLY

When Nephi had a vision of latter-day wickedness, he observed how secret combinations were still a part of society, inspired by "the devil, for he is the founder of all these things."[1] And then Nephi revealed Satan's strategy: "he leadeth them by the neck with a flaxen cord, until he bindeth them with his strong cords forever."[2] Flax has been cultivated for thousands of years as both a food and fiber crop. Its fibers work well for producing linen, paper, and rope. To make rope, one must spin the individual fibers into thread—strands that themselves are thin and flimsy. Combining the threads together allows one to make thick, durable rope. Thus, Satan leads people with a barely noticeable restraint—one that still allows the individual to act as they please and feel in total control. The threads are added slowly, and only over time does their control compound such that the other person can be bound with now-strong cords. Nephi further explained that Satan will pacify and lull people into carnal security and lead them carefully down to hell—and "thus he whispereth in their ears, until he grasps them with his awful chains, from whence

---

1   2 Nephi 26:22.
2   Ibid.

there is no deliverance."[3] What starts slowly and simply soon accelerates into a seemingly inescapable outcome.

This strategy is employed by all who do Satan's bidding, including the respective Caesars of the world who wield temporal power over God's children.[4] In 1784, the Virginia Assembly considered imposing a mandatory tax to provide state support for the Christian Protestant religion. James Madison would have none of it, arguing that "it is proper to take alarm at the first experiment on our liberties."[5] He continued:

> We hold this prudent jealousy to be the first duty of citizens, and one of the noblest characteristics of the late Revolution. The freemen of America did not wait till usurped power had strengthened itself by exercise, and entangled the question in precedents. They saw all the consequences in the principle, and they avoided the consequences by denying the principle. We revere this lesson too much soon to forget it.[6]

Madison's quote emphasizes the importance of challenging violations of rights at their first appearance, rather than waiting until the violation becomes entrenched through precedent and practice. He was worried that a tax to support one church could later become a tax to support another and that churches relying on tax dollars would not be independent nor their people free. He was right to object at the outset before

---

3   2 Nephi 28:21–22.
4   For a full analysis, see Connor Boyack, *Christ versus Caesar: Two Masters, One Choice* (Lehi: Social Harmony, 2021).
5   James Madison, *Memorial and Remonstrance Against Religious Assessments*, 1785.
6   Ibid.

allowing this proposal to become established and entrenched. Consider a sad contrast with the introduction of the personal income tax in 1913. It was justified by proponents as a tiny tax primarily imposed upon wealthy Americans; anyone making over $3,000 (around $100,000 in today's dollars) paid a one percent tax, and those earning over $500,000 (over $16 million today) would have a 6 percent tax. It's laughable how much worse it is today: those making under $100,000 pay between 10 to 22 percent in taxes, with higher earners being forced to give the federal government around one-third of their income. Too bad more people didn't "take alarm at the first experiment on [their] liberties" when Congress passed the first income tax.

Fortunately, we can fight the adversary using the same strategy—beginning simply and slowly. After all, "by small and simple things are great things brought to pass."[7] Jesus taught this strategy in His parable of the leaven (or yeast). "The kingdom of heaven is like leaven," He taught, "which a woman took and hid in three measures of flour, till it was all leavened."[8] Here, a mere pinch of leaven—insignificant on its own—is capable of permeating and transforming an entire batch of dough. Even in small amounts, the leaven had a massive impact—just like a little bit of light can overtake darkness.[9] Worldly corruption spreads slowly until it is seemingly everywhere, but the same is true of righteousness. Abinadi was one man discharging his duty to God—and speaking to

---

7   Alma 37:6.
8   Matthew 13:33.
9   Matthew 5:14–16.

a hostile audience. By all measures, his words failed to have an impact... until they did. Alma repented, began teaching Abinadi's words, attracted a number of followers, and became an influential prophet impacting countless lives.[10] If the slow stain of the world starts slowly and increases in effect over time as it spreads, then so does its counteragent. We would be foolish not to employ so successful a strategy.

How can we liken these ideas to ourselves? First, we can be better guardians against initial encroachments as Madison suggested, intervening to stop any stain we see. Even if it's small and barely noticeable, we recognize that if ignored (or assisted), it will spread more quickly. Just as it would be prudent to take decisive action upon detecting a tiny clump of cancer cells in our body, we must likewise address even the slightest encroachments in our spiritual lives. By promptly recognizing and repenting of even a minor lapse, we prevent that stain from growing and affecting our entire character. Regular self-examination—through prayer, scripture study, and honest reflection—acts as our spiritual checkup, ensuring that no small compromise is allowed to spread unchecked. This vigilant care will enable us to resist the gradual infiltration of worldly values.

Second, we can slowly spread righteousness. We can be the leaven Jesus called us to be. Small, simple acts of obedience to God—especially the countercultural ones at odds with Babylonian tradition—become the catalyst for transformation in our families, communities, and beyond. Each sincere

---

10 Mosiah 11–18.

prayer, every act of service, and the consistent sharing of gospel truths contribute to a ripple effect that gradually changes hearts and minds. Christ called upon us to be "anxiously engaged in a good cause, and do many things of [our] own free will, and bring to pass much righteousness."[11] It's not enough to simply stop the spread of the slow stain of the world—we must cleanse it entirely through proactive righteousness. Our intentional promotion of the gospel of Jesus Christ paves the way for others to experience its transforming power. Over time, these individual contributions accumulate into a profound, collective impact that can change the course of civilization. It starts with us, today and each day.

Third, we need to remember that the slow stain of the world will not always remain slow. Wickedness compounds as it spreads, much like a tiny snowball rolling down a steep hill on a cold winter's day. At first, the snowball is barely noticeable—a small clump of snow that seems harmless. However, as it begins to roll, it picks up more snow with each rotation, and its surface area expands, allowing it to accumulate even more mass. Before long, that once-insignificant snowball has grown into a powerful force capable of triggering an avalanche and crushing anyone in its path. This is all the more reason why early intervention is critical—just as it's easier to break free of a flimsy, flaxen cord before Satan is able to bind us. "Therefore, wo be unto him that is at ease in Zion!" Nephi warns. "Wo be unto him that crieth: All is well! Yea, wo be unto him that hearkeneth unto the precepts of men..."[12] So

---

11   D&C 58:27.
12   2 Nephi 28:24–26.

many followers of God have lost their way and become over-whelmed by a tidal wave of idolatrous culture. If we want to avoid a similar fate, we need to recognize that all is *not* well in Zion—and that God wants us to "cheerfully do all things that lie in our power" as His agents on earth.[13] There's a spiritual war happening, and failing to fight on the Lord's side allows the enemy to advance.

As we'll see in the next part of the book, the slow stain of the world is a pernicious, pervasive influence that increases its influence as it grows—compounding its control as more and more become affected by it. To that end, calling it 'slow' is perhaps misleading, for it is only slow at the start. Entire societies have been overtaken by wickedness and have collapsed under its consequences—a result that was certainly not slow to those who observed how saturated people had become. As Mormon wrote, "Thus we see how quick the children of men do forget the Lord their God, yea, how quick to do iniquity, and to be led away by the evil one."[14] What starts slowly soon spreads quickly—a sad reality about Satan's strategy, but one that we can also employ in spreading the light of the gospel as a cleansing counteragent.

---

13   D&C 123:13–17.
14   Alma 46:8.

THE COST OF NEGLECTED SCRIPTURE

Josiah became king in Judah at the young age of eight. He succeeded his father, Amon, who presided over a wicked, idolatrous people that had forsaken the Lord. We are told, by contrast, that Josiah "did that which was right in the sight of the Lord."[1] And eighteen years into his reign, he commissioned a restoration project to repair the temple. As a result of that project, the high priest allegedly discovered "the book of the law in the house of the Lord"[2]—scripture that had been lost to Judah for some time. When Josiah read the book, "he rent his clothes" in despair, realizing how far his people had fallen. To the high priest, King Josiah commanded:

> Go ye, inquire of the Lord for me, and for the people, and for all Judah, concerning the words of this book that is found: for great is the wrath of the Lord that is kindled against us, because our fathers have not hearkened unto the words of this book, to do according unto all that which is written concerning us.[3]

---

1   2 Kings 22:2.
2   2 Kings 22:8.
3   2 Kings 22:13.

The record states that Josiah subsequently organized a public reading of the book, requiring attendance of "all the men of Judah and all the inhabitants of Jerusalem with him, and the priests, and the prophets, and all the people, both small and great."[4] Once the scripture was read, Josiah "made a covenant before the Lord, to walk after the Lord, and to keep his commandments and his testimonies and his statutes with all their heart and all their soul, to perform the words of this covenant that were written in this book."[5] He then followed through by ordering all the idolatrous objects in the temple be removed and burned;[6] he fired the idolatrous priests;[7] he "defiled the high places where the priests had burned incense" and burned the groves that served as their sites of idolatrous worship;[8] and he destroyed the various idolatrous sites established by Solomon.[9] The discovered scriptures certainly had an effect on him, leading him to use them as a tool to shape religious thought and action throughout his kingdom.[10]

---

4   2 Kings 23:2.
5   2 Kings 23:3.
6   2 Kings 23:4.
7   2 Kings 23:5.
8   2 Kings 23:6, 8.
9   2 Kings 23:13.
10   There is an alternative interpretation of this episode I'm quite intrigued by: that Josiah was not a righteous reformer stamping out idolatry but rather one who basically banned the original temple order, branding visionary men (like Jeremiah, Lehi, and others) as heretical false prophets. In this view, the Deuteronomists produced propaganda to justify his actions, centralizing and controlling worship under strict regulations. For purposes of this book we'll stick with the conventional view as an illustrative example, but for the other perspective see Margaret Barker, "What Did King Josiah Reform?" in *Glimpses of Lehi's Jerusalem* (Provo: Brigham Young University, 2004) 523–542.

This is the potential power of scripture—and the effect of ignoring it. Nephi knew the importance of obtaining the brass plates for his posterity because, otherwise, they would "dwindle and perish in unbelief."[11] Generations later, King Benjamin recognized this truth and taught it to his sons:

> And he also taught them concerning the records which were engraven on the plates of brass, saying: My sons, I would that ye should remember that were it not for these plates, which contain these records and these commandments, we must have suffered in ignorance, even at this present time, not knowing the mysteries of God.
>
> For it were not possible that our father, Lehi, could have remembered all these things, to have taught them to his children, except it were for the help of these plates; for he having been taught in the language of the Egyptians therefore he could read these engravings, and teach them to his children, that thereby they could teach them to their children, and so fulfilling the commandments of God, even down to this present time.
>
> I say unto you, my sons, were it not for these things, which have been kept and preserved by the hand of God, that we might read and understand of his mysteries, and have his commandments always before our eyes, that even our fathers would have dwindled in unbelief, and we should have been like unto our brethren, the Lamanites, who know nothing concern-

---

11   1 Nephi 4:13.

ing these things, or even do not believe them when they are taught them, because of the traditions of their fathers, which are not correct.[12]

Later in the record, Alma reminded his son Helaman that the records of the Nephite people had "enlarged the memory of this people, yea, and convinced many of the error of their ways, and brought them to the knowledge of their God unto the salvation of their souls."[13] And without the records, Ammon and his missionary companions could not have persuaded so many Lamanites to abandon their incorrect traditions. "These records and their words brought them unto repentance," he observed.[14] One of those Lamanites, Samuel, shared that "as many of them as are brought to the knowledge of the truth, and to know of the wicked and abominable traditions of their fathers, and are led to believe the holy scriptures, yea, the prophecies of the holy prophets, which are written," become "firm and steadfast in the faith."[15] It was exactly as Nephi said: "whoso would hearken unto the word of God, and would hold fast unto it, they would never perish; neither could the temptations and the fiery darts of the adversary overpower them unto blindness, to lead them away to destruction."[16] The word of God is how we stop the slow stain of the world. Without its guidance and teachings, people are more susceptible to walk "in [their] own way, and after the image of [their]

---

12   Mosiah 1:3–5.
13   Alma 37:8.
14   Alma 37:9.
15   Helaman 15:7–8.
16   1 Nephi 15:24.

own god, whose image is in the likeness of the world,"[17] embracing "false and vain and foolish doctrines"[18] taught by "the precepts of men."[19] Whether it's the people of Judah before Josiah's reforms, the Mulekites who "brought no records with them," which led to their language becoming corrupted and their abandonment of the gospel,[20] or any number of other scriptural examples, we see repeatedly how neglecting scripture causes spiritual decay.

How can we liken these ideas to ourselves? First, we should appreciate and seriously study what we have received. Is there any functional difference between the people of Judah, who perished in ignorance because of a lack of scripture, and ourselves today, if we don't actually read and adhere to what's in the scriptures we have? Simply possessing or periodically skimming scripture is insufficient; someone who casually ignores a warning manual is ill-prepared for the threats it warns about. Recall that the early Latter-day Saints were condemned for treating lightly the new scripture they had received[21]—and among the many consequences is the withholding of additional scripture, particularly the sealed portion of the golden plates.[22]

Second, we must act upon what we've read. The Lord said that the Saints would remain condemned until they would not merely say, "but to *do* according to that which I

---

17 D&C 1:16.
18 2 Nephi 28:9.
19 2 Nephi 28:14.
20 Omni 1:17.
21 D&C 84:54–58.
22 3 Nephi 26:7–10.

have written—that they may bring forth fruit meet for their Father's kingdom."[23] There are plenty of people who pay lip service to the Lord's teachings. These people "profess that they know God; but in works they deny him."[24] They "draw near [God] with their mouth, and with their lips do honor [Him], but have removed their heart far from [Him]."[25] Jesus had few nice things to say about such hypocrites who "reject the commandment of God, that [they] may keep [their] own tradition"[26]—or, in other words, keep the comfortable status quo instead of changing their behavior. The scriptures require more than a mere intellectual engagement with their theological ideas. They require change. They demand action. Josiah openly covenanted with God, promised change, then made it happen by destroying idolatrous sites and symbols.[27] We should similarly scrutinize the traditions of our fathers—the cultural beliefs and behaviors we've inherited—to determine which are inconsistent with the gospel. We need to embrace God's teachings and let them impact not only our religious belief system but also our decisions and actions in an economic, political, and social context as well. The gospel is more than a Sunday service and a list of faith positions. It's an instruction manual for daily living and how we interact with one another in every facet of life.

---

23 D&C 84:58; emphasis added.
24 Titus 1:16.
25 Isaiah 29:13.
26 Mark 7:9.
27 Again, this is the conventional view which may in fact be wrong. For additional perspective see D. John Butler, *In the Language of Adam* (Plain and Precious Publishing, 2024).

Third, we should share the scripture's messages and meaning with others. God requires "every man who hath been warned to warn his neighbor."[28] One person can't stop the slow stain of the world from spreading alone—we need many people to be "anxiously engaged in a good cause, and do many things of their own free will, and bring to pass much righteousness."[29] Fighting Satan's army of devilish minions is a team sport. Like Joseph Smith, we must recognize that "there are many yet on the earth among all sects, parties, and denominations, who are blinded by the subtle craftiness of men, whereby they lie in wait to deceive, and who are only kept from the truth because they know not where to find it."[30] We best use scripture when we make it part of our collective discourse and outreach efforts instead of relegating it primarily to private study.

The gospel of Jesus Christ, found in scripture, is the cleansing agent that will stop the slow stain of the world and reverse its progress. Failing to apply it allows the stain to spread, as evidenced in countless examples of people losing their faith, embracing idolatry, and embracing worldly teachings and traditions after being deprived of access to scripture. With daily, consistent use, we can ensure that no stain ever gains the upper hand on us.

---

28 D&C 88:81.
29 D&C 58:27.
30 D&C 123:12.

PART THREE

MODERN STAINS

Think of your average Sunday School class where the class reads about the idolatrous Israelites, the implosion of the Jaredite and Nephite societies, the apostasy of the early Christians, or the struggles of the early Latter-day Saints. In what percentage of those class discussions would you anticipate that participants are sincerely seeking ways to apply the lessons to themselves? In other words, how often do we truly consider that we are as guilty—or even more so—than the misguided folks we casually mention in class? The question sadly answers itself; we are just as prone to falling into spiritual traps as our forebears, yet somehow we frequently delude ourselves into thinking that we are more enlightened and advanced than they were. We shake our heads at the foibles of fallen people, then move on to the next lesson topic. After all, we can't be as bad as the children of Israel—they worshiped a *golden calf*! We do nothing like that. Right?

Wrong. Our apostasy and idolatry may look different, but I believe it is just as pervasive as it was with past peoples. It's more spiritual than physical, more sophisticated than simple. Sure, we're monotheistic and don't go "whoring after other gods"[1]—and yet, we do. We may not use altars and objects for direct worship, but our heart is just as seduced by competing loyalties, corrupt culture, and worldly ways. And there's an argument to be made that because today's slow stains of the world are more spiritual in nature, they're more difficult to detect and therefore more easily embraced by those who still outwardly profess their Christianity. It was one thing for

---

1   Judges 2:17.

a Jew to physically visit one of the worship sites set up for a pagan god and thereby risk detection. It's another for us to embrace these slow stains in the comfort and privacy of our private lives and digital worlds—where our devices are our constant companions. In the quiet of our homes, away from prying eyes, we are bombarded with endless streams of information and subtle cultural cues that, over time, can reshape our beliefs and priorities without our even noticing. Unlike the overt idolatry of ancient times, our struggles occur deep within our minds and hearts, often manifesting as quietly adopted opinions or preferences that we never fully scrutinize. If we're not careful, we can become like the whited sepulchers Jesus decried, "which indeed appear beautiful outward, but are within full of dead men's bones, and of all uncleanness."[2]

These private, individual shifts are insidious because they happen behind the screens of our everyday lives—through curated news feeds, echo chambers, and the pervasive influence of social media. We may inadvertently internalize ideas that conflict with gospel principles, all while believing that our external lives remain unchanged. This makes it all the more difficult for others, or even for ourselves in moments of self-reflection, to detect the gradual erosion of our fidelity to God. In our modern era, the battle for our souls is fought not in the open but in the quiet, private recesses of our personal devices and inner thoughts, where the slow stain of worldly influence can take hold before we even realize it.

---

2   Matthew 23:27.

Even worse, prophecies suggest that many of us in this latter-day dispensation will succumb to the slow stains of the world we've been warned about. Nephi said that "there shall be many which shall teach after this manner, false and vain and foolish doctrines, and shall be puffed up in their hearts, and shall seek deep to hide their counsels from the Lord."[3] He continued:

> Yea, they have all gone out of the way; they have become corrupted. Because of pride, and because of false teachers, and false doctrine, their churches have become corrupted, and their churches are lifted up; because of pride they are puffed up. They rob the poor because of their fine sanctuaries; they rob the poor because of their fine clothing; and they persecute the meek and the poor in heart, because in their pride they are puffed up.

> They wear stiff necks and high heads; yea, and because of pride, and wickedness, and abominations, and whoredoms, they have all gone astray save it be a few, who are the humble followers of Christ; nevertheless, they are led, that in many instances they do err because they are taught by the precepts of men.[4]

The conventional interpretation of this passage is that it applies to *others*—not us. Nephi is lamenting the corruption and pride of every other church, but not *ours*... We have the truth! The gospel has been restored! There's no way the

---

3   2 Nephi 28:10.
4   2 Nephi 28:11–14.

Church today can be what Nephi is referring to! But what
if that interpretation is wrong? What if we are among the
"guilty [who] taketh the truth to be hard, for it cutteth [us] to
the very center?"[5] That truth may very well be that we are as
susceptible to the slow stains of the modern world as were our
predecessors in the ancient world—that we are not immune
from idolatry and apostasy and embracing worldly ways while
thinking ourselves to be sufficiently righteous. We, too, can
fall—and most of us will, "save it be a few, who are the humble
followers of Christ."[6] Remember that the foolish virgins "took
their lamps, and went forth to meet the bridegroom"[7]—they
thought they were righteous and waiting for the Lord, like
good and faithful Saints going through the superficial motions. Asking to be let into the marriage celebration, the Lord
rebuked them: "I know you not."[8] Ouch. This stuff stings:

> Not every one that saith unto me, Lord, Lord, shall en-
> ter into the kingdom of heaven; but he that doeth the
> will of my Father who is in heaven. Many will say to
> me in that day: Lord, Lord, have we not prophesied in
> thy name, and in thy name have cast out devils, and in
> thy name done many wonderful works? And then will
> I profess unto them: I never knew you; depart from
> me, ye that work iniquity.[9]

So we're not immune, and despite thinking we're prepared
for the Bridegroom, He might deny even knowing us—a sure

5 1 Nephi 16:2.
6 2 Nephi 28:14.
7 Matthew 25:1.
8 Matthew 25:12.
9 3 Nephi 14:21–23.

sign of condemnation. Too many are hearers only and not do-ers of the word.[10] Perhaps the fact that so many Latter-day Saints will embrace worldly ways in this dispensation is why the Lord's vengeance will focus first on the Church:

> Behold, vengeance cometh speedily upon the inhab-itants of the earth, a day of wrath, a day of burning, a day of desolation, of weeping, of mourning, and of lamentation; and as a whirlwind it shall come upon all the face of the earth, saith the Lord.

> And upon my house shall it begin, and from my house shall it go forth, saith the Lord; First among those among you, saith the Lord, who have professed to know my name and have not known me, and have blas-phemed against me in the midst of my house, saith the Lord.[11]

The Lord has been very clear on this point. "For of him unto whom much is given much is required; and he who sins against the greater light shall receive the greater condemnation."[12] We who are beneficiaries of the restoration of the gospel of Jesus Christ are called to live a higher standard and reject the world's ways. Earlier Saints treated lightly the additional truth they had been given, resulting in their condemnation.[13] If we want to escape that condemnation and commit to Christ, then we need to be very aware of—and avoid—the modern stains of the world that are saturating our society. This part of the

10   James 1:22–25.
11   D&C 112:24–26.
12   D&C 82:3.
13   D&C 84:54–58.

book will review many of them. We'll first start with family-oriented topics relevant to the proclamation that President Hinckley read immediately after warning of the prevailing "allurement and enticement to take on the slow stain of the world."[14] Then we'll expand our view to additional threats we face in order to understand how bedeviled God's people are today. As we review them, keep in mind the lessons learned from scriptural stories and how we ought to apply them to ourselves today.

---

14   Hinckley, "Stand Strong against the Wiles of the World."

THE DECLINE OF MARRIAGE AND CHILDBEARING

"Have ye not read," Jesus asked the Pharisees, "that he which made them at the beginning made them male and female, And said, For this cause shall a man leave father and mother, and shall cleave to his wife: and they twain shall be one flesh? Wherefore they are no more twain, but one flesh."[1] From the union of Adam and Eve in the Garden of Eden—when they were commanded to "be fruitful, and multiply, and replenish the earth,"[2] marriage has been ordained of God. As stated in the Proclamation, "Marriage between man and woman is essential to His eternal plan."[3] Until very recently, this sacred union was widely upheld as the social standard, encompassing not only the joining of a man and a woman in covenant but also the natural process of sexual relations and the blessing of childbearing.

Multiple millennia of opposite-gender, monogamous marital practice have certainly had their deviations along the way—whether the abomination of polygamy or the counterfeit unions of same-sex couples. However, the modern threat

1   Matthew 19:4–6.
2   Genesis 1:28.
3   Hinckley, "Stand Strong against the Wiles of the World."

to marriage is not so much the emergence of alternative forms but rather its gradual abandonment. Today, we witness an erosion of commitment and an indifference toward the arrangement, with marriage increasingly seen as an outdated or optional institution rather than the divinely ordained covenant it is meant to be. The reasons are varied and voluminous; online respondents, when asked why marriage is on the decline, share a wide range of arguments: "Can't get divorced if you're never married!"; "Women no longer need a husband to have income and financial security. We've evolved beyond needing men, like it or not."; "Marriage is just a piece of paper. It isn't essential to happiness, fulfillment, or having children."; "The concept of marriage is incredibly outdated and unnecessary, and complicates healthy relationships."[4]

Whatever the reasons, the data clearly illustrate a decline. Married-couple households comprised 47 percent of all households in the United States in 2022, down from 71 percent in 1970.[5] The US marriage rate peaked in 1920 at a rate that is almost triple today's rate.[6] In 1980, 6 percent of forty-year-olds in the US had never married; today that number ex-

4   "What is your honest opinion on the declining marriage rates in America?" Reddit, accessed February 9, 2025, https://www.reddit.com/r/AskOldPeople/comments/1930g1j/what_is_your_honest_opinion_on_the_declining/.
5   "Census Bureau Releases New Estimates on Families and Living Arrangements," United States Census Bureau, May 30, 2024, https://www.census.gov/newsroom/press-releases/2024/families-living-arrangements.html.
6   "Marriage: More than a Century of Change, 1900-2022," Bowling Green State University, accessed February 9, 2025, https://www.bgsu.edu/ncfmr/resources/data/family-profiles/FP-24-10.html.

ceeds 25 percent.[7] One demographic projection suggests that a third of young adults will not marry by age forty-five and maybe never marry.[8] A social relationship deemed "essential" to God's plan is increasingly considered nonessential by many of His children.

This decrease in marital relationships has occurred alongside a corresponding increase in cohabitation. Whereas previously a surprise pregnancy would often lead to a shotgun wedding, now premarital sex and childbearing out of wedlock are culturally accepted. A century ago, half of all unmarried pregnant women in the US married before giving birth, but in recent years this rate has precipitously plummeted to only 6 percent.[9] The share of adults in the US age eighteen to forty-four who have cohabited with a romantic partner (59 percent) is now higher than the share who have ever been married (50 percent).[10] Young adults aged 18 to 29 are especially supportive, with 78 percent saying cohabitation is acceptable.[11] Twelve percent of this age bracket lives with an unmarried

---

7   "A record-high share of 40-year-olds in the U.S. have never been married," Pew Research Center, June 28, 2023, https://www.pewresearch.org/short-reads/2023/06/28/a-record-high-share-of-40-year-olds-in-the-us-have-never-been-married/.

8   "The closing of the American heart," *Deseret News*, April 30, 2024, https://www.deseret.com/family/2024/04/30/marriage-benefits-for-adults/.

9   "Is Shotgun Marriage Dead?" Duke University, November 1, 2016, https://today.duke.edu/2016/11/shotgun-marriage-dead.

10   "Marriage and Cohabitation in the U.S.," Pew Research Center, November 6, 2019, https://www.pewresearch.org/social-trends/2019/11/06/marriage-and-cohabitation-in-the-u-s/.

11   Ibid.

partner, compared with 5 percent in 1995.[12] This obviously means there are a larger number of children being born out of wedlock. In the US, 40 percent of children are now born to unmarried mothers—double the rate from 1980.[13] What used to be called illegitimacy is now the new normal.

The consequences of children being born out of wedlock run far deeper, of course, than shifting social labels. Numerous studies have shown that children raised in single-parent households—especially those without a present father—are more likely to encounter poverty, diminished educational opportunities, and emotional instability.[14] For example, in 1960, 17.5 percent of children lived apart from their fathers.[15] Today, that number has surged to over one-third of all children—over 25 million kids growing up without their biological father.[16] And while there are clearly justifiable exceptions to maintaining a two-parent household—as in the case of

---

12 "The landscape of marriage and cohabitation in the U.S.," Pew Research Center, November 6, 2019, https://www. pewresearch.org/social-trends/2019/11/06/the-landscape-of-marriage-and-cohabitation-in-the-u-s/.

13 "Unmarried Childbearing," National Center for Health Statistics, accessed February 10, 2025, https://www.cdc.gov/nchs/fastats/unmarried-childbearing.htm.

14 "The Consequences of Fatherlessness," Fathers.com, accessed February 11, 2025, https://fathers.com/the-consequences-of-fatherlessness/.

15 David Blakenhorn, *Fatherless America: Confronting Our Most Urgent Social Problem* (New York: HarperCollins, 1995), 18–19.

16 U.S. Census Bureau, Current Population Survey, "Living Arrangements of Children under 18 Years/1 and Marital Status of Parents by Age, Sex, Race, and Hispanic Origin/2 and Selected Characteristics of the Child for all Children 2010," Table C3, November, 2010.

abuse, abandonment, or an affair—what's clear is that the exception has transformed into a trend. This alarming absenteeism of fathers contributes to a cascade of downstream social degeneracy: fatherless children experience poverty at four times the rate of kids with married parents;[17] children without a present father are far more likely to abuse drugs and alcohol;[18] fatherless daughters are four times more likely to get pregnant as teenagers;[19] and kids raised in families without a father are more than twice as likely to commit suicide.[20] Dozens more data points validate the wisdom in the Proclamation: "Children are entitled to birth within the bonds of matrimony, and to be reared by a father and a mother who honor marital vows with complete fidelity." This familial stability, founded upon the commitment and covenant of a marital relationship, is on shaky ground. The lack of a committed, dual-parent unit deprives children of the balanced guidance, accountability, and shared responsibility that are essential to developing strong character and resilience.

---

17 U.S. Department of Health and Human Services, "ASEP Issue Brief: Information on Poverty and Income Statistics," September 12, 2012 http://aspe.hhs.gov/hsp/12/ PovertyAndIncomeEst/ib.shtml.

18 John Hoffmann, "The Community Context of Family Structure and Adolescent Drug Use," *Journal of Marriage and Family* 64 (May 2002), 314-330.

19 J.D. Teachman, "The Childhood Living Arrangements of Children and the Characteristics of Their Marriages," *Journal of Family Issues*, 25(1), 86-111, https://doi.org/10.1177/0192513X03255346.

20 "Absent Parent Doubles Child Suicide Risk," WebMD, January 23, 2003, http://www.webmd.com/baby/news/20030123/absent-parent-doubles-child-suicide-risk.

Add onto all of this the declining fertility rate in the US and across the world. In 1905, President Theodore Roosevelt famously said that women without children were "one of the most unpleasant and unwholesome features of modern life" and worthy of "contempt as hearty as any visited upon the soldier who runs away in battle."[21] At the time, the fertility rate in the US was nearly four children per woman—a decline from eight per woman a century prior.[22] Today, the rate is at a historic low, with 1.62 children per woman in 2023.[23] Global fertility rates have halved since 1950, while the number of women in the reproductive age bracket has tripled.[24] Secularized societies that discourage the formation of families and childbearing have all seen their fertility rates plummet below the population replacement rate of 2.1 children per woman—the rate required for a society to sustain its population numbers. The largest fifteen countries by GDP all now have a fertility rate below the replacement rate.[25] In the aggregate, the global population is expected to peak in 2084 at 10.29 billion and then decline year

21 Theodore Roosevelt, "Remarks Before the Mothers' Congress," March 13, 1905, https://www.presidency.ucsb.edu/documents/remarks-before-the-mothers-congress.

22 Michael R. Haines, "American Fertility in Transition: New Estimates of Birth Rates in the United States, 1900–1910," Demography 26 (February 1989):137–148.

23 "Births: Provisional Data for 2023," National Center for Health Statistics, accessed February 11, 2025, https://www.cdc.gov/nchs/data/vsrr/vsrr035.pdf.

24 "The Problem with 'Too Few,'" United Nations Population Fund, accessed February 11, 2025, https://www.unfpa.org/swp2023/too-few.

25 "Global fertility has collapsed, with profound economic consequences," *The Economist*, June 1, 2023, https://www.economist.com/leaders/2023/06/01/global-fertility-has-collapsed-with-profound-economic-consequences.

over year due to low fertility rates.[26] So why are couples having so few children in the modern era? According to one report:

> Changing norms regarding the intensity of parenting might change prospective parents' decisions on how many children to have or whether to have children at all. Such changes are particularly relevant in an era where parents, including mothers, work longer hours outside the home, clashing with career aspirations or a desire for more leisure time. This idea may incorporate choice in the context of trading off how many children parents want to have with how much they want to 'invest' in those children.[27]

Those changing norms are perpetuated by parents as well. Young adults today feel less pressure to marry and start families than ever. In the US, 80 percent of single individuals report feeling no pressure from their family to get married.[28] It's clear that the culture has shifted, and the expectations and attitudes once prevalent and taken for granted have been set aside as irrelevant to a modern world. Whether due to a focus on career and leisure, or climate anxiety, financial concerns,

---

26   "Peak global population and other key findings from the 2024 UN World Population Prospects," Our World in Data, July 11, 2024, https://ourworldindata.org/un-population-2024-revision.

27   "The Causes and Consequences of Declining US Fertility," Aspen Economic Strategy Group, December 2022, https://www.economicstrategygroup.org/wp-content/uploads/2022/08/Kearney_Levine_081222.pdf.

28   "Emerging Trends and Enduring Patterns in American Family Life," American Enterprise Institute, February 9, 2022, https://www.americansurveycenter.org/research/emerging-trends-and-enduring-patterns-in-american-family-life/.

apathy, or any number of other reasons, the data bears out this simple fact: family formation is nowhere near the priority it once was for young adults. The world's egocentric elevation of the self has driven a narcissistic prioritization of personal comfort and immediate gratification over the sacred call to family formation and childrearing. More people invest more time in cultivating their careers, leisure pursuits, and digital personas than in nurturing the familial relationships that sustain both their souls and society at large. In this self-centered culture, the idea of sacrificing personal desires for the greater good of raising a family is increasingly seen as antiquated—a relic of a bygone era rather than a vital component of eternal progress. Material success matters more to the world than marital success.

This outcome is clearly at odds with God's commandment to marry and bear children—to further His glory by enabling more of His children to obtain a body and mortal experience as part of their eternal progression. God's desire to "bring to pass the immortality and eternal life of man"[29] obviously requires man to form families and bear children. Married couples uniting together to create a family is a divine imperative, "that the earth might answer the end of its creation."[30] Those who therefore embrace worldly ways of premarital sex, cohabitation, and few or no children are at odds with God's commandments and have allowed themselves to be seduced by the popular allures and anxieties of counter-Christian culture. "What therefore God hath joined together," Jesus said, "let not man put asunder."

---

29   Moses 1:39.
30   D&C 49:16.

SEXUAL IDENTITY AND THE WAR ON TRUTH

Here's a startling set of statistics: As of 2022, 2.7 percent of Baby Boomers (born 1946–64) identify as lesbian, gay, bisexual, or transgender (LGBT); 3.3 percent of Gen X (1965–80) have embraced the identity; for Millennials (1981–96) it's 11.2 percent; and with Gen Z (1997–2004) it has skyrocketed to 19.7 percent.[1] These numbers have increased in recent years; Gen Z just two years prior was about 16 percent, and Millennials were around 9 percent.[2] This shift in sexual identity has affected society at large, including Latter-day Saints; only 78 percent of eighteen to twenty-five-year-old Saints say they are straight.[3] A second study confirmed the data, finding that about one in five Millennial or Gen Z Latter-day Saints identifies as LGBT.[4]

---

1   "7.2 Percent of U.S. Adults Identify as LGBT," Statista, February 28, 2023, https://www.statista.com/chart/18228/share-of-americans-identifying-as-lgbt/.

2   Ibid.

3   Ryan Burge, "Gender, Sexual Orientation and Religion Among American College Students," Graphs About Religion, September 18, 2023, https://www.graphsaboutreligion.com/p/gender-sexual-orientation-and-religion.

4   "Rising numbers of young adult Mormons in the US are gay, lesbian or bisexual," Religion News, June 21, 2021, https://religionnews.com/2021/06/21/rising-number-of-adult-mormons-in-the-us-are-gay-lesbian-or-bisexual/.

This alarming deviation has left many people—especially parents of these young identity-changing individuals—befuddled as to why the shift has been so pervasive. Certainly, there is a contingent of the population who have the innate challenges of same-gender attraction, whether caused by biological, environmental, or other factors. Worldwide, 11 percent of people are lesbian, gay, or bisexual (LGB without the T)—with younger age cohorts reporting much higher numbers.[5] Homosexual relationships and behavior are, of course, a choice; though difficult to ignore or act counter to one's desires, it is not impossible. Yet the decision to indulge these desires is often encouraged and praised in modern culture, which heaps rewards upon those who "come out" and join this celebrated tribe of people. Sexual identity is a powerful social currency, and awkward or unpopular teens can find it very tempting to "identify" in a way that will reward them with praise from peers. This is especially true for girls, who are three times more likely than boys to identify as bisexual.[6] Maybe—just maybe—this results in part from the cultural environment in which they're raised, where Katy Perry told us all in her #1 hit single, "I kissed a girl and I liked it," or where Megan Fox, Lindsay Lohan, Lady Gaga, Angelina Jolie, Drew Barrymore, and countless other women have publicly shared

---

5   "Share of adults attracted to the same sex worldwide in 2021," Statista, July 5, 2024, https://www.statista.com/ statistics/1270134/distribution-sexual-attraction-worldwide/.

6   "Women are more likely to become bisexual than men, say scientists," Daily Record, August 25, 2015, https://www. dailyrecord.co.uk/news/science-technology/women-more-likely-become-bisexual-6313595.

their bisexuality. There is, by contrast, no comparable crowd of popular men broadcasting their own bisexuality.

The mainstreaming of homosexuality in recent decades prompted endless questions about whether it was due to nature vs. nurture. "It's really hard to come up with any definite statement about the situation," concedes Richard Pillard, a prominent gay psychiatrist who has focused on studying the biological basis for sexual orientation. "I think some sort of genetic influence seems very likely, but beyond that, what really can we say? And the answer is: not a lot."[7] Despite the lack of scientific evidence, most people would presume that some part of one's sexual preferences is innate. But there's no question that, beyond biology, cultural forces (nurture) hold significant sway. The skyrocketing percentage of younger people embracing alternative sexual identities is itself evidence of what's commonly called social contagion—the idea that beliefs and behavior can spread through society like an infectious disease would. "Simple exposure sometimes appears to be a sufficient condition for social transmission to occur," says research psychologist Paul Marsden. "This is the social contagion thesis; that sociocultural phenomena can spread through, and leap between, populations more like outbreaks of measles or chicken pox than through a process of rational choice."[8]

---

7   "Nature vs. Nurture: The Biology of Sexuality," Boston University, November 16, 2010, https://www.bu.edu/articles/2010/nature-vs-nurture-the-biology-of-sexuality.

8   Paul Marsden, "Memetics & Social Contagion: Two Sides of the Same Coin?," *The Journal of Memetics: Evolutionary Models of Information Transmission*, 1998 Vol 2, https://web.archive.org/web/20200221015517/https://web.stanford.edu/~kcarmel/CC_BehavChange_Course/readings/Additional%20Resources/social%20contagion/Social%20Contagion.htm.

It's one thing to be influenced by your peers regarding the clothing you wear, the music you listen to, or the foods you eat. It's another thing entirely to engage in sexual behavior that you feel is encouraged or embraced by others. Far worse, however, is claiming to be something you're not—and expecting others to go along with the act. As the Proclamation states, "All human beings—male and female—are created in the image of God... Gender is an essential characteristic of individual premortal, mortal, and eternal identity and purpose."[9] Such a simple statement is sacrilege to a secular society that has swallowed the false idea that one's chosen identity creates one's reality—that a man who thinks he is a woman actually is. This mental illness has long existed and was recognized as such—but now everyone is pressured and badgered into buying into the delusions of those who change their identity; modern society demands affirming what others claim to be true. Orwell once wrote in his dystopian novel *1984* that the oppressive Party told people "to reject the evidence of your eyes and ears. It was their final, most essential command."[10] Or as Jordan Peterson once wrote, "There is literally no bigger lie than a man can be a woman. If you'll swallow that, no future camel will choke you."[11]

The reason is simple: gender ideology is a frontal assault on objective reality. Its proponents believe that people can

9   Hinckley, "Stand Strong against the Wiles of the World."
10   George Orwell, *1984*, accessed February 18, 2025, https://george-orwell.org/1984/6.html.
11   Dr. Jordan B. Peterson, "There is literally no bigger lie..." X (formerly Twitter), January 20, 2024, https://x.com/jordanbpeterson/status/1748939403479663026.

"speak their truth," disrupting the notion of an absolute, immutable reality—objective truth. They prefer subjective morality, where each person is their own judge. They define their own gender and expect you to affirm their self-proclaimed truth; there is no longer any right or wrong—only personal preferences and choices. "Truth is knowledge of things as they are," the Lord said—not as one wishes things to be. "And whatsoever is more or less than this is the spirit of that wicked one who was a liar from the beginning."[12] That's what we're really dealing with here: lies. It's a lie that a boy can change into a girl. It's a lie that cutting off your genitalia and sterilizing yourself with heavy hormone changes will improve your feelings of self-worth or resolve your gender dysphoria. It's a lie that God got anyone's gender—their eternal identity—wrong. Modern culture reinforces these lies upon impressionable young people, and everyone else is expected to be an affirming ally—to embrace the delusion and live by lies. In his powerful essay "Live Not By Lies," Soviet dissident and author Aleksandr Solzhenitsyn shared that the solution to this pervasive problem requires renouncing these lies outright, at which point they "simply cease to exist. Like parasites, they can only survive when attached to a person."[13] God's creations, including us, live in an objective reality with truths that do not change depending on the person or their preferences. Truth requires us to reject falsehood.

---

12 D&C 93:24–25.

13 Aleksandr Solzhenitsyn, "Live Not By Lies," The Aleksandr Solzhenitsyn Center, accessed February 18, 2025, https://www.solzhenitsyncenter.org/live-not-by-lies.

This cultural stain has seeped into the Church as well. Lauren Harrigian is a male convert who, for several years, experienced an eating disorder, depression, gender dysphoria, and panic attacks.[14] Amid this mental illness, he decided to transition from male to female and adopted the name Lauren. He was taught by sister missionaries and, with apparent permission of the First Presidency, was baptized.[15] According to Lauren, his membership record even lists him as a female.[16] In an interview with a Latter-day Saint "ally" Richard Ostler, Lauren said that he doesn't want to be called a "trans woman"—just a woman. "That's who I am," he said. "A really fun girl."[17] And Ostler went along with the lie, suggesting that we all ought to do the same:

> I think that's one of the things we can do as members of the Church is see you as a daughter of God, because that's how *you* see you. And I'm going to see you the way you see you. I'm not going to define you based on anything but how you're defining you. That just seems

---

14 "Trans long-distance runner finds freedom as she lives her life fearlessly," Outsports, November 18, 2020, https://www.outsports.com/2020/11/18/21572823/lauren-harrigian-running-trans-coming-out/.

15 "Lauren Harrigian, New Convert, Transgender Latter-day Saint," Listen, Learn, and Love, July 4, 2022, https://podcasts.apple.com/us/podcast/episode-540-lauren-harrigian-new-convert-transgender/id1347971725.

16 "Lauren Harrigian, New Covert, Transgender Latter-day Saint, Part 2," Listen, Learn, and Love, July 19, 2022, https://podcasts.apple.com/br/podcast/episode-545-lauren-harrigian-new-covert-transgender/id1347971725.

17 Ibid.

like the gospel of grace, or the gospel of kindness, or the gospel of love.[18]

Imagine how difficult it is for young people to navigate today's world, where so many accept these lies as truth and where social expectations are such that you feel pressured to agree with a person who has constructed a fantasy for themselves. No wonder social contagion spreads so quickly among the rising generation, whose brains spur them to seek attention and approval from peers as a method to determine correct behavior.[19] It is difficult for many people to seek the signal amid the noise—to sift fact from fiction and fantasy. This challenge is made more difficult by the fact that so few are willing to stand up against the cultural tide of conformity and risk alienation and persecution. How can we expect young people to embrace and defend the truth if we are unwilling to demonstrate how it's done?

God loves all His children—whether they face homosexual temptations, gender dysphoria, or social conditioning. But God does not affirm falsehoods; He does not condone sexual relations outside of a male/female marital union. His love does not include tolerance for sin nor requires believing lies. God's standard for sexuality and gender identity is eternal and unchanging. It calls us to uphold objective truth even when modern society celebrates its opposite. We must resist the seductive lure of cultural trends that promote subjective

---

18 Ibid.
19 "Why young brains are especially vulnerable to social media," American Psychological Association, August 3, 2023, https://www.apa.org/news/apa/2022/social-media-children-teens.

definitions of identity—trends that, over time, erode our ability to discern truth from illusion. Instead of succumbing to the slow stain of alternative sexual and gender identities, we are invited to embrace an eternal perspective: one where every human being is created in the image of God, with a divinely prescribed gender identity, and that restricts sexual relations to male/female marriages. And as the world indulges delusion and affirms alternative lifestyles, we are called upon to "proclaim the truth"[20] and live not by lies.

---

20 D&C 75:3–4.

THE NORMALIZATION OF ABORTION

Monica was a teenager in high school when she became pregnant. With her boyfriend's encouragement, she decided to abort the baby. "I was so afraid of my dad being disappointed and angry with me," she explained. "I was afraid of people judging me and thinking I was a failure." Those fears led Monica to make the decision to kill her preborn child. "We secretly went to a clinic to get an abortion." She continued:

> After the procedure, I felt relief. I thought life would resume as normal, and it did for a while. I didn't count on years later, looking at the three children I have since carried and thinking of our baby that we selfishly aborted out of fear of facing our family. Who would they be now? Words can't express my regrets. Very few people know, and I carry shame for the mistake I made to mask what I thought was a mistake. I only hope that God has our child and I hope one day I will know who they were.[1]

---

1   "Abortion Regrets: Stories from Real Women," Sira, August 24, 2022, https://www.siragainesville.com/post/abortion-regrets-stories-from-real-women.

Monica's was one of some 73 million abortions performed globally every single year—on average, around 200,000 each day. In the United States, over one million abortions were recorded in the healthcare system (with more likely occurring informally and off the books).[2] With widespread legal sanction at varying levels among different governments, it entails systematic and state-sponsored violence against a specific (and defenseless) class of people. Of course, systematic and state-sponsored violence is widely condemned when involving already-born individuals—such as the Holocaust against the Jews, the Great Purges under Stalin, the mass murder in Mao's Great Leap Forward, and more. But when the violence is secretly conducted in the privacy of a medical facility against a preborn individual, few people raise an eyebrow.

Those who favor retaining the legal and cultural support for this practice resist calling it what it actually is. In their view, it is not murder of a preborn child. Instead, they call it a fetus or a "clump of cells"—intentional, dehumanizing terms designed to subdue the spiritual and emotional reaction people might otherwise have. Pro-abortionists even try to eliminate the term "abortion"; Planned Parenthood and the American College of Obstetricians and Gynecologists, for example, use phrases like "removing pregnancy tissue" or "removing the fetus."[3] Euphemisms like these are meant to reduce the

---

2   "Despite Bans, Number of Abortions in the United States Increased in 2023," Guttmacher Institute, March 2024, https://www.guttmacher.org/2024/03/despite-bans-number-abortions-united-states-increased-2023.

3   "America Fooled: Unraveling the Abortion Industry's Messaging," Human Coalition, accessed February 20, 2025,

emotional reaction to the underlying action. Sometimes this can be rather benign, such as saying someone "passed away" instead of bluntly saying that they died, in order to soften the language. In other cases, euphemisms are designed to hide the truth, such as calling the mass killing of a particular religious or cultural group an "ethnic cleansing," which is more vague and masks the underlying carnage. Like calling a growing baby a "clump of cells"—or describing this death-producing action as "reproductive health care" or "women's health"— these deceptive euphemisms are what condition people into tolerating this widespread assassination of defenseless human life. (The ending of a life is, by definition, the very opposite of health care.) As Neal A. Maxwell rightly observed, "As people become harder, they use softer words to describe darker deeds."[4]

Imagine Elon Musk and his crew successfully land humans on Mars, setting up camp in Chryse Planitia. The planetary settlers launch various research projects across the rusty terrain, and one hits paydirt. As the team digs into a crater, they unearth tiny, translucent worms—living, wriggling, feeding on subsurface minerals. Lab tests confirm they're methane-producing microbes, thriving in the cold, thin atmosphere. The settlers stare, awestruck, at undeniable Martian life. The find electrifies Earth, with humans overjoyed at the discovery

---

https://www.humancoalition.org/impact/blog/america-fooled-unraveling-the-abortion-industrys-messaging/.
4   Neal A. Maxwell, "Becometh As a Child," April 1996 General Conference, https://www.churchofjesuschrist.org/study/general-conference/1996/04/becometh-as-a-child.

of life. Back on Mars, great care is taken to preserve these tiny creatures as they are studied.

Yet this awe stands in stark contrast to our actions on Earth. If humanity would go to such lengths to protect a handful of alien microbes on a distant planet, celebrating their mere existence as a triumph, why are we so cavalier about destroying known, actual life in the human womb? The Martian worms, primitive as they are, spark wonder and preservation efforts, while millions of preborn children—each with beating hearts, unique DNA, and the potential to grow into someone like Monica's lost child—are extinguished yearly with legal sanction and cultural support. The disconnect is jarring: we'd marvel at life on Mars but discard it here, cloaking the act in euphemisms to dull the reality. What does it say about us that we'd cherish the alien unknown yet shrug at the familiar miracle within?

Members and allies of this death cult proudly wave the banner of "pro-choice," as if the label itself sanctifies the act. This can be quite insidious—even among Latter-day Saints who feel that since we believe in agency, we must be "pro-choice" on this issue. But let's peel that back a bit. Monica and her boyfriend chose to have sex—chose to dive into a hookup culture that shrugs at restraint and revels in fleeting pleasure. And yes, they even had the choice to end the life of their preborn child—just as someone can choose to murder an adult, rob a neighbor, or abuse a spouse. You can choose to beat up the kid down the street or pee in someone's lemonade. These choices all exist—nobody is denied choice. Agency is real, a sacred gift from God. But the existence of choices does not exempt one from the consequences. And that's what it boils down to—the "pro-choice" movement seeks legal sanction to exempt its participants from punitive consequences for killing a preborn child. Like secret combinations of old, they'd rather be ruled "according to the laws of their wickedness"[5] instead of being held accountable to God's law.

Connecting abortion advocates and actors to secret combinations is not as far-fetched as it might initially seem. Moroni warned of an end-time destruction that "shall come when the blood of saints shall cry unto the Lord, because of secret combinations and the works of darkness."[6] The time "soon cometh that he avengeth the blood of the saints upon you, for he will not suffer their cries any longer."[7] In a second warning, Moroni reiterates that "the Lord will not suffer that the blood of his saints, which shall be shed by them, shall always cry unto him from the ground for vengeance upon them and yet he avenge them not."[8] Nephi had previously warned of the same, noting that those whose "works shall be in the dark" cause that "the blood of the saints shall cry from the ground against them."[9] Nephi first used those words to describe the wickedness of the Nephites at the time of Christ's coming, saying that "the cry of the blood of the saints shall ascend up to God from the ground against them."[10] And Christ himself affirms that sixteen Nephite cities were destroyed so that "the

---

5   Helaman 6:24.
6   Mormon 8:27.
7   Mormon 8:41.
8   Ether 8:22–24.
9   2 Nephi 28:8–16.
10 2 Nephi 26:3.

blood of the... saints should not come up unto me any more against them."[11]

Who are these saints that, during the height of Nephite wickedness, and modern-day wickedness as well, are slain to such a profound degree that it moves God to impose carnage-heavy vengeance on a wicked people? Of course, secret combinations were slaying people in power who stood in their way; murder was part of how they acquired power. But murder has existed since the first family populated our planet and has not drawn this degree of divine retribution. Most would read these verses to envision that secret combinations and wicked people were and will be killing adult believers. That may be true in part, but Webster's 1828 dictionary reminds us that a saint is: "A person sanctified; a holy or godly person; one eminent for piety and virtue."[12] And who is more holy and pure than a little child, whether preborn or infant? No wonder Jesus said that unless we "become as little children, [we] shall not enter into the kingdom of heaven."[13] We fallen adults require the Atonement to be sanctified—to become holy—but a person who arrives in a perfect state from heaven, not yet corrupted by sin, is an actual saint. In short, it is likely that the high volume of blood of saints being spilled, provoking God's wrath, is the result of killing tens of millions of preborn children each year through abortion.

11   3 Nephi 9:9.
12   "Saint," American Dictionary of the English Language, accessed February 22, 2025, https://webstersdictionary1828.com/Dictionary/saint.
13   Matthew 18:1–6.

Consider further how this is referenced in the Book of Mormon. The term 'abortion' does not appear in the text. Instead, it seems that the term 'secret murder' was instead used by reference. Satan sharing his secret oaths with Gadianton involved carrying on "the work of darkness, and of secret murder."[14] The growing evil faction was supported by the wicked Nephites who decided to "join with them in their secret murders and combinations."[15] When Alma passed the Nephite records to Helaman, he noted that they included the secret oaths used by Satan to build secret combinations to "work secret murders and abominations."[16] And when Jacobugath was destroyed prior to Christ's arrival, He noted that it was "burned with fire because of their sins and their wickedness, which was above all the wickedness of the whole earth, because of their secret murders and combinations"—and that the inhabitants were destroyed to avenge the blood of the saints.[17] Murder is part and parcel of Satan's stratagem, and the scriptures are full of men killing one another—particularly political leaders and prophets. But *secret* murder seems different. Of course, abortion occurs inside the womb, a secret chamber of sorts where the killing can often be undetected and explained away as occurring due to natural causes, if it's even detected by others at all. Given the amount of saintly blood being spilled so as to trigger God's vengeance, and the astronomically high rate of death of preborn children

---

14 Helaman 6:29.
15 Helaman 6:38.
16 Alma 37:22.
17 3 Nephi 9:9.

compared to any adults who might be called saints, it would seem that abortion is a clearly offensive act in the sight of God requiring divine justice to ultimately be administered.[18]

And yet that offensive act has become normalized in a societal death cult that favors convenience over human life. It is culturally acceptable to "make the sacred womb a tomb," as Elder Maxwell said.[19] The numbers—in the tens of millions each year—make this the most egregious sin to have ever existed in the history of mankind. This widespread, normalized killing eclipses all wars and the mass murders committed by communist and other totalitarian regimes. Due to such precious innocents being the victims, it certainly ranks as the greatest evil of all human history.

One would hope that the watchmen on the warning tower would decry this deeply offensive act and vociferously oppose secret murder, yet Church leaders have been relatively silent on the topic. In 1991, the managing director of Public Communications for the Church put out a statement on behalf of its leaders, saying that "We have repeatedly counseled people everywhere to turn from the devastating practice of abortion for personal or social convenience."[20] And in the two decades prior, that was certainly the case. Due to the con-

---

18 For more analysis connecting abortion to secret murder, see Amberli Peterson, *Ripened: Why the Book of Mormon Damns America for Abortion* (Sa Sagesse Press, 2023).

19 Neal A. Maxwell, "The Women of God," *Ensign*, April 1978, https://www.churchofjesuschrist.org/study/general-conference/1978/04/the-women-of-god.

20 "Statement issued on abortion," Church News, January 19, 1991, https://www.thechurchnews.com/1991/1/19/23260986/statement-issued-on-abortion/.

troversy surrounding *Roe v. Wade* in the early 1970s, leaders discussed the topic frequently in general conference. In the 1970s, thirteen discourses substantively addressed the issue, with another twenty-three mentioning abortion.[21] This seems like "repeatedly counseling," yet extracting the actual text that is relevant to the topic from all these addresses results in around 1,900 words total during the decade—the average length of a single conference address. In the 1980s, a dozen discourses mentioned abortion, and only one significantly addressed the issue: a pointed, detailed address on abortion by Russell M. Nelson.[22] Excluding his powerful remarks—in which he strenuously warned that "those who advocate and practice abortion... incur the wrath of Almighty God"[23]—only 375 words total addressed abortion by leaders of the church during that entire decade. In the 1990s, fifteen talks mentioned abortion with four meaningfully focusing on the topic; the decade's worth of text yields only 603 words total. In the 2000s, abortion was not the focus of a single conference talk, and the word was mentioned only a single time as a passing reference in a list of "seditious evils."[24] In the 2010s, six talks briefly mentioned the issue, and none focused on it to any significant degree. And in the 2020s, at the time of this writing

21   This analysis of conference talks was the author's own, using lds-general-conference.org.

22   Russell M. Nelson, "Reverence for Life," April 1985 General Conference, https://www.churchofjesuschrist.org/study/general-conference/1985/04/reverence-for-life.

23   Ibid.

24   Russell M. Nelson, "Set in Order Thy House," October 2001 General Conference, https://www.churchofjesuschrist.org/study/general-conference/2001/10/set-in-order-thy-house.

in 2025, only two talks, both given by the same person, have touched on the issue.[25] This profound silence on so pervasive an evil has resulted in the rising generation becoming disconnected from the doctrine, leading one reporter to find, "Some of the Most Viral 'Pro-Choice' Instagram Content is Coming From Mormon Bloggers."[26] Left adrift without the anchor of divine doctrine, young members of the Church—like sheep without a shepherd—succumb to the world's seductive lies, their innocence eroded and their hearts indelibly marked by the pervasive stain of normalized wickedness.

If ever there was a reason to pound the pulpit, this is it. And while leaders should be more outspoken, lay members are certainly able to act independently—yet few do, fearing that because this issue is "political" or "contentious," it's best to be avoided. We abhor the child sacrifice of our pagan predecessors, yet navigate (and often excuse) a culture that embraces far worse—an institutionalized, legalized, culturally sanctioned practice happening daily. God's commandment is clear: "Thou shalt not... kill, nor do anything like unto it."[27] Abortion is clearly a modern stain of the world—a

---

25 Neal L. Andersen, "The Personal Journey of a Child of God," April 2021 General Conference, https://www.churchofjesuschrist.org/study/general-conference/2021/04/26andersen; Neal L. Andersen, "Cherishing Life" April 2025 General Conference, https://www.churchofjesuschrist.org/study/general-conference/2025/04/21andersen.

26 "Some of the Most Viral 'Pro-Choice' Instagram Content is Coming From Mormon Bloggers," Buzzfeed, May 6, 2022, https://www.buzzfeednews.com/article/stephaniemcneal/mormon-bloggers-abortion-pro-choice.

27 D&C 59:6.

dark blot seeping into the fabric of our society, and sadly into the Church as well, cloaked in euphemisms and excused by convenience. As God's chosen people, we cannot meet this abomination with timid silence; we must become His fiercest champions of life, raising our voices in strident opposition, wielding truth as a sword to cut through the lies, and standing as a bulwark against the tide of death that so freely spills the blood of millions of saints.

THE RISE OF FEMINISM

Seven decades after the American Revolution, another revolution ignited in the small town of Seneca Falls, New York. Elizabeth Cady Stanton, a young mother fueled by a fierce resolve, gathered with a handful of determined associates—women who were frustrated at a world that they felt silenced half its population. They had grown weary of being denied a vote, a voice, or any semblance of equality under the law. Something had to be done to address what Stanton called "my long-accumulating discontent."[1] So, they decided to call a convention to demand what they felt society refused to grant. But words alone wouldn't suffice—Stanton and her friends wanted a declaration, a resounding statement to echo their cause. So they turned to Jefferson's words to inspire their own.

Using the Declaration of Independence as their base text, Stanton and the women crafted the "Declaration of Sentiments," a manifesto that mirrored the colonists' grievances against King George III but spoke to their own struggle—a document for "the first organized protest against the injustice

---

1   Carrie Gress, *The End of Woman: How Smashing the Patriarchy Has Destroyed Us* (Washington, D.C.: Regnery Publishing, 2023), 48.

which has brooded for ages over the character and destiny of one-half the race."[2] "We hold these truths to be self-evident," Stanton proclaimed, "that all men *and women* are created equal." And then it came time to list the grievances, but these upper-class women struggled; theirs was a life of relative privilege and comfort. So they enlisted the help of some men to articulate problems faced by less fortunate women. Soon, Stanton "rejoiced to find that we could make out as good a bill of impeachment against our sires and sons as [the colonists] had against old King George."[3] One of the men teased her, noting after their long labor in creating the list, "Your grievances must be very grievous indeed, if it takes you so long to find them."[4]

Stories like Stanton's form the foundation of feminism—often hailed as the ushering in of women's liberation, such as securing voting rights, equal pay, and endless opportunities alongside those of men. But peel back the polished veneer and whitewashed historical accounts, and a troubling reality emerges: feminism's goal was never to simply lift women up. It's about wielding them as weapons to dismantle society's foundations. And feminism's heroes aren't the flawless trailblazers we're sold. Many were broken figures whose personal turmoil birthed radical agendas. Kate Millett, a staunch feminist and author of *Sexual Politics*, epitomized this. Struggling with mental instability and rejecting family life, she declared, "The complete destruction of traditional marriage and

2   Ibid., 49.
3   Ibid., 50.
4   Ibid.

the nuclear family is the 'revolutionary' or 'utopian' goal of feminism."[5] That's not empowerment—it's demolition.

Known as the "Female Marx" and later as the "high priestess of feminism," Millet rallied radical women to promote promiscuity, eroticism, prostitution, abortion, and homosexuality—all as a strategic effort to destroy monogamy in an effort to destroy the "Patriarchy" and further a cultural revolution.[6] The originator of the term patriarchy, as used in the pejorative sense by today's feminists, was one of the original Marxists—Karl's colleague, Friedrich Engels. In his 1884 book *The Origin of the Family, Private Property and the State*, Engels wrote that "The man took command in the home also; the woman was degraded and reduced to servitude, she became the slave of his lust and a mere instrument for the production of children."[7] This was the cause championed by early feminists—a way to upend culture and disrupt the family, not simply empower women with greater equality within the existing social construct.

Consequently, it's little surprise that feminism's roots were entangled not only with communism but also with its spiritual progenitor, Satan. Christianity, like capitalism, was seen by these communist feminists as the source of women's enslavement. Thus, once her Declaration of Sentiments was complete, Stanton set out to write her own Bible, recasting

---

5   Kimberly Ellis, *The Invincible Family: Why the Global Campaign to Crush Motherhood and Fatherhood Can't Win* (Washington, D.C.: Regnery Publishing, 2023), 24.

6   Gress, *The End of Woman*, 77–8.

7   Friedrich Engels, *The Origin of the Family, Private Property and the State* (New York: Verso, 2021), 56.

many of the book's stories in a way that eliminates perceived patriarchy. Stanton felt, as she wrote in the book's introduction, that church and clergy were "the very powers that make [women's] emancipation impossible"—that the woman's "political and social degradation are but an outgrowth of your status in the Bible."[8] Among other edits, Stanton's book turns Eve into a heroine and Satan into "a charitable philosophical instructor of woman." Satanism, and so-called "spiritualism," were central to the worldview of feminism's early pioneers. Thus did Bella Dodd, a communist activist who helped establish the Congress of American Women, write that "I retreated from God and went forth to meet the world, the flesh, and the devil... I'd join the devil himself. There is no doubt that I traveled with him at my side and that he extorted a great price for his company."[9]

Feminism's central tenet—building off of the communist sentiments of its founders—was that women would only be free once they are in the workforce, earning income independent of any man. Homemaking was seen as slavish servitude—a "comfortable concentration camp," in the words of Betty Friedan, a feminist activist in the mid-twentieth century.[10] Friedan knew that simply telling women to abandon their homes in order to realize Marx's dream of women entering the workforce would not resonate broadly in a culture that

---

8   Gress, *The End of Woman*, 51–2.
9   Mary Nicholes and Paul Kengor, *The Devil and Bella Dodd: One Woman's Struggle against Communism and Her Redemption* (Gastonia: TAN Books, 2022), 2.
10   Betty Friedan, *The Feminine Mystique* (New York: W.W. Norton & Co., 2013), 337.

valued motherhood and all its many benefits. So in order to succeed, Friedan and her associates needed to persuade them that remaining home was a bad thing.

To achieve this persuasion, feminists strategically recast motherhood and domestic life not as fulfilling callings but as forms of oppressive bondage. Friedan's influential book, *The Feminine Mystique*, depicted the homemaker as trapped in boredom and despair, her potential wasted, her ambitions crushed. This deliberate reframing wasn't merely about liberating women from supposed domestic drudgery; it was about severing them from family and faith—institutions feminists saw as fundamental barriers to their radical agenda. By stigmatizing motherhood and elevating career achievement as the true measure of a woman's worth, feminism began to reshape society from within, convincing generations of women to trade the sacred for the secular, and the family hearth for the cold comfort of corporate offices. Thus children—dependents—were cast as a hindrance, their termination via abortion an acceptable option to preserve the independence of the would-be mother.[11]

And the strategy worked—spectacularly so. Abortion has dramatically surged in a post-*Roe* world, with some 200,000 preborn babies killed daily, as mentioned in the previous chapter.[12] Women delay (if not abstain from) marriage at much higher rates, contributing to a steady decline in fertility

---

11   Gress, *The End of Woman*, 61.
12   "Despite Bans, Number of Abortions in the United States Increased in 2023."

rates.[13] Men's desire for sex is fulfilled with casual hookups with women who relish their independence and "free love" lifestyle secured by abortion as a backstop. Children (if they're born) are increasingly raised by day cares and government schools, all of them led by feminine authority figures.[14] Dual incomes in a marriage or sexual partnership create golden handcuffs, with women resisting losing the revenue and the luxuries it funds. And rather than caring for women, men increasingly have to compete with them—for college admission and for jobs—thus emasculating men and contributing to a decline in male labor force participation, dropping seven percentage points over the last half-century, from 96 to 89 percent.[15] Men want to be providers, yet feminism tells women to abandon their pedestal to share the man's with him. This, we're told, represents equality—proving that men and women are the same. But we're not the same, and thus, competition creates conflict; there isn't enough room on the pedestal for both. So feminists opt for pushing men off to make room for themselves—the original cause favored by feminism's founders.

Yet none of this has produced great outcomes for women writ large, let alone society as a whole. Early feminists felt

---

13 "U.S. Fertility Is Declining Due to Delayed Marriage and Child-bearing," The Heritage Foundation, March 4, 2025, https://www.heritage.org/marriage-and-family/report/us-fertility-declining-due-delayed-marriage-and-childbearing.

14 "The U.S. Teaching Population Is Getting Bigger, and More Female," The Atlantic, February 20, 2019, https://www.theatlantic.com/education/archive/2019/02/the-explosion-of-women-teachers/582622/.

15 U.S. Bureau of Labor Statistics, Series ID: LNS11300061Q.

that securing the right to vote, own property, and get an education would liberate them; second-wave feminists in the mid-twentieth century focused on pursuing higher education and employment to achieve personal satisfaction, along with their sexual liberation with the pill and abortion to facilitate it. But survey after survey reveals deep dissatisfaction with the results. The most comprehensive of them, the United States General Social Survey, has for over half a century asked Americans each year how happy they are. The statistically significant results reveal that since 1972, "women's overall level of happiness has dropped, both relative to where they were [when the survey began], and relative to men."[16] Similar multidecade surveys conducted around the world, asking over a million people the same question, result in the same finding: "greater educational, political, and employment opportunities have corresponded to decreases in life happiness for women, as compared to men."[17] Perhaps it's no surprise, then, that one in five women between ages forty and fifty-nine are taking antidepressants, at a rate more than double that of men[18]—or that more than half of women say they find it difficult to balance work and home life responsibilities.[19] As it turns out,

---

16   "What's Happening To Women's Happiness?" HuffPost, November 17, 2009, https://www.huffpost.com/entry/whats-happening-to-womens_b_289511.

17   Ibid.

18   "Why So Many Women in Middle Age Are on Antidepressants," *The Wall Street Journal*, April 2, 2022, https://www.wsj.com/articles/why-so-many-middle-aged-women-are-on-antidepressants-11648906393.

19   "Modern Parenthood," Pew Research Center, March 14, 2013, https://www.pewresearch.org/social-trends/2013/03/14/modern-parenthood-roles-of-moms-and-dads-converge-as-they-balance-work-and-family/.

happiness doesn't come from earning your own paycheck or being a "boss girl." And deprioritization (or abandonment) of a woman's maternal potential leaves her morally adrift and deeply unfulfilled. No wonder only 12 percent of liberal women—those who champion the feminist cause today—report being satisfied with their lives.[20] (Conservative women, by contrast, are over three times more likely to be satisfied with their lives.) The "have it all" mantra has left many burned out. It seems women are far more likely to feel fulfilled and happy if, instead of competing with men for their pedestal, they recognize and value their own.

Early communists were focused on eliminating class privilege and distinction, tearing down the wealthy, and redistributing their goods in common with workers. Second-wave feminists utilized the same strategy for society more broadly. Shulamith Firestone, a feminist activist and author, wrote that "the end goal of feminist revolution must be... not just the elimination of male *privilege* but of the sex *distinction* itself: genital differences between human beings would no longer matter culturally."[21] But there are more differences between men and women than mere genitals. As the Proclamation notes, a "divine design" appoints distinct roles for each—fathers presiding, providing and protecting, and mothers nurturing and caring for children. And in these roles, col-

---

20 "Why So Blue: Liberal Women are Less Happy, More Lonely. But Why?" Institute for Family Studies, February 13, 2025, https://ifstudies.org/blog/why-so-blue-liberal-women-are-less-happy-more-lonely-but-why.

21 Shulamith Firestone, *The Dialectic of Sex: The Case for Feminist Revolution* (London: Paladin, 1972), 19.

laboration—not competition—is key; "fathers and mothers are obligated to help one another as equal partners."[22] We don't swap pedestals or push the patriarch off his—we elevate each other's pedestal and embrace the divine design in which we operate. Kicking against the pricks might be a *cause célèbre* for communists and feminist activists, but the results speak louder than any rallying cry: broken families, declining happiness, and a profound loss of identity among the very women it claimed to liberate.

Ultimately, feminism has built its own great and spacious building, filled with communist-fueled arrogance and animosity toward man—an edifice that purports to lift women up, yet can only do so by tearing men down. Its core deception lies hidden within the mists of darkness: the widely embraced but false belief that feminism simply means "women's empowerment." Yet few realize the ideological poison seeping from its roots or fully recognize its bitter, destructive fruits. True empowerment is never achieved through division, resentment, or devaluing a woman's sacred role. Genuine strength arises from embracing our divinely designed differences and fostering unity and collaboration—not friction and competition—in our most sacred and societally important relationships.

---

22 Hinckley, "Stand Strong against the Wiles of the World."

PERVASIVE PORNOGRAPHY

At the age of eleven, Shaun Flores stumbled into the world of pornography, guided by a friend's introduction. "I was hooked almost immediately," reflects the now thirty-one-year-old. "It was just like, wow, what is this that people are doing where they look like they're just having the time of their lives?"[1] What began as innocent curiosity soon spiraled into a habit Shaun struggled to break. He recalls indulging in it morning, noon, and night, noting that it grew as routine as "common as brushing your teeth."

We think of porn as a modern problem, but in many ancient cultures, it was quite common as well. Numerous artifacts from Ancient Greece reveal phallic objects, sexual aids, and erotic mosaics, sculptures, and paintings.[2] Erotic art was also a prominent part of the Roman Empire, with frescoes, mosaics, and sculptures featuring explicit sexual imagery. The ruins of Pompeii, for example, include a number of art pieces depicting sex scenes that suggest a high level of tolerance for sexual expression as part of everyday life and public

1   "'I couldn't stop watching': Personal stories of how porn obsession takes over lives," BBC, November 29, 2024, https://www.bbc.com/news/articles/cg57r337rvzo.
2   "Classical Depravity: A Guide to the Perverted Past," Atlas Obscura, March 24, 2014, https://www.atlasobscura.com/articles/essential-guide-perverted-past.

discourse. These weren't puritanical cultures by any stretch of the imagination.

Yet despite a few select societies giving the nod to porn material, the whole of humanity has, for the most part, found it difficult (and taboo) to access. Historically, obtaining porn was no small feat. It often required facing another human being—perhaps a clerk at a dimly lit shop or a merchant in a back alley—someone who held the key to such forbidden material. The exchange was awkward, risky, and laden with shame, a transaction that demanded courage or desperation. Beyond that, the supply was limited: crude drawings, rare texts, or, later, photographs and films tucked away in secret stashes. For centuries, social stigma kept it underground, a whispered vice shunned by respectable society. Even in cultures less prudish than others, it was rarely flaunted openly outside specific contexts, like the elite gatherings of Rome or the private quarters of the wealthy. The taboo clung to it like a shadow, marking those who sought it as outliers, their pursuits cloaked in secrecy.

But the modern era has torn that veil apart. What once required effort, stealth, and a willingness to brave societal scorn is now a fingertip's reach away—free, instantaneous, and ubiquitous. The internet has unleashed a torrent of explicit content, flooding screens in homes, schools, and even churches. No longer must one face a knowing glance or risk exposure; anonymity reigns, and the barriers of access have crumbled. Shaun's story is a testament to this shift—what began as a stumble became a daily descent, fueled by an endless stream that no clerk or curtain could restrain. Today, porn is not just accessible—it is aggressive, seeping into advertisements, pop-ups, and social media feeds, a relentless whisper enticing God's people to partake of the stain that promises pleasure but delivers chains.

Free porn is readily available to anyone who wants it, and the rise of smartphones has allowed its consumption to increase dramatically. Today, one in five search queries on a mobile device is related to porn, which now comprises 4 percent of the entire Internet.[3] One of the leading websites is the fourteenth most trafficked site on the web, with 42 billion visits annually, or 115 million every single day.[4] The top three porn sites get more visits than sites like Amazon, Netflix, Yahoo, TikTok, and Zoom.[5] The top-ranked porn site had around a billion views more than these legacy, high-trafficked websites.[6] Through advertising, subscriptions, products, and more, these sites and the broader adult industry pull in $76 billion annually.[7]

---

3   "How Much of the Internet Consists of Porn?" Statista, February 11, 2019, https://www.statista.com/chart/16959/share-of-the-internet-that-is-porn/.

4   "The Digital Giant: Exploring Pornhub's Staggering 42 Billion Annual Visits," Fact Omelette, December 11, 2024, https://www.factomelette.com/p/the-digital-giant-exploring-porn-hub-s-staggering-42-billion-annual-visits.

5   P. J. Wright, R. Tokunaga, and D. Herbenick, "But Do Porn Sites Get More Traffic than TikTok, OpenAI, and Zoom?" *The Journal of Sex Research*, 60(6), 763–767. https://doi.org/10.1080/00224499.2023.2220690.

6   Ibid.

7   "Online Adult Entertainment Market to Exceed $118.1 Billion in Revenues by 2030 - Global and Country-Level Analysis by Content, Monetization Model, Interaction, Age Group, and End User," Research and Markets, December 16, 2024, https://finance.yahoo.com/news/online-adult-entertainment-market-exceed-100000487.html.

That pull is due in large part to the addictive nature of porn. Well over two-thirds of men regularly view it.[8] Its addictive nature is well-documented, with studies showing that it re-wires the brain, creating pathways that crave constant stimulation and novelty.[9] What begins as curiosity or a momentary lapse of discipline quickly escalates into a compulsive habit, consuming the viewer's thoughts and energy. It distorts his view of relationships and intimacy, reducing others to mere objects of desire and hollowing out the depth and meaning of genuine connection. This addiction not only isolates a man from his loved ones but also builds a barrier between him and God, making it difficult for him to feel the Spirit and hear divine promptings. In the words of Dr. William Struthers, a leading psychologist studying pornography:

> The on-demand availability of robust sexual stimuli presents a unique problem for developing and maintaining a healthy sexuality. The ease of access, variety of images, and the vigorous sensory constitution of this media go beyond the strength of mental imagery and fantasy. People can see whatever they want, whenever they want, however they want. In doing so they can generate, serve, and satisfy their sensual nature. Pornography creates a world today where the consumer (usually men) has the ability to bring up at their

8   R. Ballester-Arnal, M. García-Barba, J. Castro-Calvo, et al., "Pornography Consumption in People of Different Age Groups: an Analysis Based on Gender, Contents, and Consequences," *Sexuality Research and Social Policy*, 766–779 (2023).
9   Todd Love, et al. "Neuroscience of Internet Pornography Addiction: A Review and Update," *Behavioral Sciences* (Basel, Switzerland) vol. 5,3 388-433. 18 Sep. 2015.

whim graphic (and sometimes interactive) depictions of nudity and sexual encounters. Women are perpetually available for their pleasure with minimal immediate consequences. People become disposable.[10]

The internet has domesticated porn and normalized its consumption. And it's not just an adult problem; studies show that more than half of eleven to sixteen-year-olds have seen porn.[11] Youth are typically more tech-literate than their elders, and the pornography industry is at the bleeding edge of adopting any new technology that comes out. Since the invention of photography, followed by film, video, and digital media, then smartphones, AI and deepfakes, and virtual reality, porn is abundant and aggressive in its accessibility to the average individual—including adolescents. And what was before a centralized industry with sleazy producers and limited distribution has now exploded into something far more pervasive. Enter platforms like OnlyFans, which have democratized the production of porn and unleashed a tidal wave of explicit content tailored to every imaginable taste. No longer is the industry confined to shadowy studios or backroom deals; now, anyone with a smartphone can become a creator, churning out material for a global audience. This shift has flooded the

---

10   William M. Struthers, Ph.D, "The Effects of Porn on the Male Brain," Christian Research Institute, March 18, 2020, https://www.equip.org/articles/the-effects-of-porn-on-the-male-brain-3/.

11   "Pornography: The Public Health Crisis of the Digital Age," Psychology Today, April 15, 2021, https://www.psychologytoday.com/us/blog/end-human-trafficking/202104/pornography-the-public-health-crisis-the-digital-age.

digital landscape with an endless stream of porn, targeting not just the curious or the desperate, but anyone seeking a quick dopamine hit—especially the smartphone generation, always just a tap away from instant gratification. What was once a niche market controlled by a few has morphed into a grassroots deluge, where amateur producers and polished influencers alike vie for attention, bombarding users with personalized, addictive content. For Latter-day Saints striving to keep their minds and hearts pure, this relentless onslaught is a stark reminder of the adversary's cunning, dressing up sin as convenience and cloaking it in the guise of empowerment.

And one would hope that the Saints' leaders would be at the forefront of condemning this industry and cautioning everyone—the youth especially—about the addictive and destructive nature of porn. Certainly, there have been plenty of powerful addresses taking on the topic, such as Gordon B. Hinckley's 2004 talk "A Tragic Evil among Us" where he said that porn is "like a raging storm, destroying individuals and families, utterly ruining what was once wholesome and beautiful."[12] Another is Dallin H. Oaks's 2005 talk, simply titled "Pornography," where he said it "is sweeping over our society like an avalanche of evil."[13] But on this topic, as was the case with abortion, the talks have tapered off: In the 1970s there were eighteen substantive addresses about porn; in the

12 Gordon B. Hinckley, "A Tragic Evil among Us," October 2004 General Conference, https://www.churchofjesuschrist.org/study/general-conference/2004/10/a-tragic-evil-among-us.
13 Dallin H. Oaks, "Pornography," April 2005 General Conference, https://www.churchofjesuschrist.org/study/general-conference/2005/04/pornography.

1980s there were six; and in the 1990s, seventeen (no surprise given the rise of the Internet late in that decade).[14] But
in the 2000s, there were only nine, the same number as in the
2010s—on average, only one meaningful mention per year.
And in the 2020s thus far, only one discourse has substantively discussed the issue.

This quieting of prophetic voices is troubling, especially
now, when the avalanche of evil leaders previously warned
about has grown into a suffocating blizzard burying countless young people more than ever before. The adversary has
never had a more efficient tool, and yet the sustained, urgent
warnings from the pulpit seem to have dwindled just when we
need a clarion call the most. Where are the shepherds' cries
to pull our youth back from the edge? In decades past, leaders
spoke boldly and often, naming the sin and rallying the Saints
to resist. Now, as the storm rages fiercer than ever, the relative
silence feels deafening. What was once a slow stain is now
raging in full force, and we cannot afford to whisper when we
should be shouting.

---

14 This analysis of conference talks was the author's own, using
    lds-general-conference.org.

THE DUMBING DOWN OF SOCIETY

Few people have had as significant an impact on the modern educational system as John Dewey, a twentieth-century philosopher, psychologist, and education reformer. Best known perhaps for his book *My Pedagogic Creed*, Dewey was a passionate promoter of using schools to shape society. Consider this excerpt from the book:

> I believe that every teacher should realize the dignity of his calling; that he is a social servant set apart for the maintenance of proper social order and the securing of the right social growth. I believe that in this way the teacher always is the prophet of the true God and the usherer in of the true kingdom of God.[1]

Latter-day Saints might nod in response to that statement. After all, God has commanded us to "teach one another the doctrine of the kingdom"[2] and to "seek... out of the best books words of wisdom."[3] Further, "Whatever principle of intelligence we attain unto in this life, it will rise with us in the resurrection."[4] This is important stuff, since "the glory of God

---

1   Jo Ann Boydston, ed., *The Early Works of John Dewey*, vol. 5 (Carbondale: Southern Illinois University Press, 2008), 95.
2   D&C 88:77.
3   D&C 88:118.
4   D&C 130:18.

is intelligence."[5] And the Church clearly prioritizes the importance of education, putting a billion dollars each year of tithing revenue into its four institutions of higher education.[6] So wouldn't we celebrate all those who want to usher in the true kingdom of God by increasing education?

One problem: Dewey was an atheist. His god was the state. His religion was secular humanism—a philosophy that denies the existence of God and emphasizes sensory perception in truth-seeking—and Dewey promoted it by wrapping it in flowery prose. He wanted to persuade Christians to overlook the ultimate goals of the "kingdom" his preferred "prophets" would really be building. Along with his contemporary counterparts, Dewey's views shaped the early development of the modern government education system—fashioning it into a tool for social engineering in pursuit of secular statism. No wonder, then, that in 1928 he heaped praise on the Soviets for their "marvelous developments" in promoting "progressive" education.[7]

Dewey also loved that the schools had a role "in building up forces... whose natural effect is to undermine the importance and uniqueness of family life."[8] He and his like-minded

---

5   D&C 93:36.
6   "Church says court ruling against Huntsman was a sign of its integrity in use of tithing donations," KSL, February 27, 2025, https://www.ksl.com/article/51263962/church-says-court-ruling-against-huntsman-was-a-sign-of-its-integrity-in-use-of-tithing-donations.
7   Joseph Ratner, ed., *Characters and Events: Popular Essays in Social and Political Philosophy* (New York: H. Holt and Co., 1929), 405.
8   Jo Ann Boydston, ed., *The Later Works of John Dewey*, vol. 3 (Carbondale: Southern Illinois University Press, 2008), 230.

pseudo-philosophers saw opportunity to apply these principles at home in America, where, he said, "the increase of importance of public schools has been at least coincident with the relaxation of older family ties."[9] This, to Dewey, was a successful accomplishment—for secular ideas to flourish, they had to suppress spiritual ones being shared in the home. Those who pioneered the modern educational system did not seek to establish intellectual rigor and academic integrity as a foundation. For them, as a prominent official in the National Education Association wrote, "the major function of the school is the social orientation of the individual. It must seek to give him understanding of the transition to a new social order."[10] That "new social order"—complete with its government-anointed "prophets" promoting a counterfeit "kingdom"—is one in which good is denigrated as evil, evil is promoted as good, and God is pushed to the sidelines through the elevation of secular, humanist, socialist principles.

All of this might be easier to swallow if the education being offered by these institutions was of a high quality. But it's not—it's flat-out awful. That was the conclusion of the National Commission on Excellence in Education, a recent project that spent eighteen months reviewing curricula, pedagogy, and assessments, and talking to students, teachers, and parents. In their report, titled *A Nation at Risk*, the group warned:

---

9   Ibid., 409.
10   Quoted in Rod Paige, *The War Against Hope: How Teacher Unions Hurt Children, Hinder Teachers, and Endanger Public Education* (Nashville: Thomas Nelson, 2006), 29.

The educational foundations of our society are presently being eroded by a rising tide of mediocrity that threatens our very future as a nation and a people. If an unfriendly foreign power had attempted to impose on America the mediocre educational performance that exists today, we might well have viewed it as an act of war. As it stands, we have allowed this to happen to ourselves.[11]

That's a bold claim, right? And yet it understates the problem because this was not actually a recent project—that was a fib. This group met and published their results clear back in 1983. Over four decades have since passed; do you think education outcomes have improved in the meantime? If so, you'd be dead wrong. Just 26 percent of eighth graders now perform math proficiently.[12] Reading scores are at their lowest levels in recorded history.[13] Only 13 percent of students scored proficient in history.[14] (Not a good look if we're trying to produce an informed electorate.) The average ACT score is 19.4—a failing grade at 55 percent of the total points possible.[15] Approximately one-third of high school gradu-

11 "A Nation at Risk: The Imperative for Educational Reform," The National Commision on Excellence in Education, April 1983.
12 "'Nation's Report Card': Two Decades of Growth Wiped Out by Two Years of Pandemic," The74, September 1, 2022, https:// www.the74million.org/article/nations-report-card-two-decades-of-growth-wiped-out-by-two-years-of-pandemic/.
13 Ibid.
14 "Latest national test results underscore declining knowledge of U.S. history and civics," EdSource, May 3, 2023, https:// edsource.org/2023/latest-test-results-underscore-declining-knowledge-of-u-s-history-and-civics/689766.
15 "Average ACT Scores by State (Most Recent)," PrepScholar,

ates "require remedial or developmental work before entering college-level courses"[16]—costing US taxpayers $7 billion to provide.[17] (What's the point of graduating if you haven't passed a particular level of proficiency?) And many of these students can't even handle the catch-up work: "Nearly 40 percent of students at two-year schools and a quarter of those at four-year schools failed to complete their remedial classes."[18] There's plenty more data to substantiate the thesis—that there's a progressive dumbing down of the rising generation in recent decades, leading to an educational decline and a rise of intellectual mediocrity.

Consider one final example. In the days of *Little House on the Prairie*, it was common for children to drop out of school after the eighth grade—that was deemed enough required education before young people were able to get on with their lives. It was good to get some schooling, but father needed help on the farm. Advanced schooling was not particularly conducive to checking off one's chore checklist. When looking at this period of history, children were typically well disciplined and had good character—they learned to be indus-

---

accessed February 26, 2025, https://blog.prepscholar.com/act-scores-by-state-averages-highs-and-lows.

16   "Addressing the needs of under-prepared students in Higher Education: Does college remediation work?" *Journal of Human Resources*, 44(3), 736-771.

17   "How To Fix America's College Remediation Issue," U.S. News and World Report, July 3, 2014, https://www.usnews.com/news/articles/2014/07/03/schools-and-colleges-still-struggle-to-reduce-the-need-for-remedial-education.

18   "Most colleges enroll students who aren't prepared for higher education," PBS, January 30, 2017, https://www.pbs.org/newshour/education/colleges-enroll-students-arent-prepared-higher-education.

trious and had more responsibilities than children today. But at the same time, given their relative lack of education, we would consider an eighth-grade education woefully insufficient. Right?

Not so. For example, consider the final exam given to eighth-grade students in Salina, Kansas, clear back in 1895. This five-hour test covered a wide variety of subject matter. For grammar, in addition to giving "nine rules for the use of Capital Letters" and naming "the Parts of Speech and defin[ing] those that have no modifications," students were told to "Write a composition of about 150 words and show therein that you understand the practical use of the rules of grammar."[19] Moving on to math, young students were required to "Name and define the Fundamental Rules of Arithmetic" as well as answer a variety of complicated questions such as:

> District No. 33 has a valuation of $35,000. What is the necessary levy to carry on a school seven months at $50 per month, and have $104 for incidentals?

> Find the interest of $512.60 for 8 months and 18 days at 7 percent.

> Find bank discount on $300 for 90 days (no grace) at 10 percent.[20]

---

19   "An 1895 8th Grade Final Exam: I Couldn't Pass It. Could You?"
     The New Republic, November 27, 2010, https://newrepublic.
     com/article/79470/1895-8th-grade-final-exam-i-couldnt-pass-
     it-could-you.
20   Ibid.

And that was without a calculator or artificial intelligence. For history, children were asked to "Relate the causes and results of the Revolutionary War," "Show the territorial growth of the United States," as well as describe prominent battles, events, and people.[21] And then there was orthography. (Do you know what that even is?) Students had to explain what elementary sounds are, diacritically mark a variety of words including their syllabication, and give four substitutes for caret 'u,' among many other questions. Fast forward a few years, and it wasn't any easier. An eighth-grade exam used in Bullitt County, Kentucky, in 1912 was similarly challenging. Arithmetic questions were difficult: "Find cost at 12.5 cents per square yard of kalsomining the walls of a room 20 feet long, 16 feet wide, and 9 feet high, deducting 1 door 8 feet by 4.5 feet and 2 windows 5 feet by 3.5 feet each."[22] The grammar section asked: "What properties have verbs?" and "How many parts of speech are there?"[23] There were also sections on civil government, history, and physiology—where students were asked: "How does the liver compare in size with other glands in the human body? What does it secrete?"

By contrast, eighth graders today are held to a far lower educational standard—what some might call the "soft bigotry of low expectations."[24] The National Assessment of Educa-

---

21 Ibid.

22 "Century-old 8th-grade exam: Can you pass a 1912 test?" *The Washington Post*, January 15, 2012, https://www.washingtonpost.com/blogs/answer-sheet/post/century-old-8th-grade-exam-can-you-pass-a-1912-test/2012/01/04/gIQAxjC00P_blog.html.

23 Ibid.

24 "Bush Warns Against the 'Soft Bigotry Of Low Expectations',"

tional Progress tests eighth graders on reading and math, asking such questions as: "The ratio of boys to girls to adults at a school party was 6 : 5 : 2. There were 78 people at the party. How many of them were adults?"[25] Or this one: "Tyler drinks 24 fluid ounces of milk each day for 7 days. How many quarts of milk does he drink in the 7 days?"[26] Most questions provide multiple choices for the answer. The reading section is full of doozies such as this one: "The author ends the essay with a childhood story. Does the childhood story do a better job persuading readers of the author's point than the other parts of the essay? Explain why or why not."[27] Mediocrity like this becomes far more apparent when compared to what was once expected of children of the same age.

One might argue that this dumbing down of education standards was intentional—after all, why would those in power favor developing critical thinking and intellectual curiosity? People asking questions is an annoyance to the ruler who prefers obedience and ineptitude; it is easier to govern an ignorant population than an educated one. If the glory of God is intelligence, then Satan's glory is ignorance—he wants us uninformed and disengaged, thus more easily influenced. When we allow our children to be steeped in a system that

EducationWeek, September 22, 1999, https://www.edweek. org/education/bush-warns-against-the-soft-bigotry-of-low-expectations/1999/09.

25 "What questions are students able to answer?" The Nation's Report Card, accessed February 26, 2025, https://www. nationsreportcard.gov/reading_math_2013/#/sample-questions.

26 Ibid.

27 Ibid.

prioritizes mediocrity over mastery, conformity over curiosity, and secular humanism over eternal principles, we're not just failing them academically—we're handing the adversary a victory in the war for their souls. We're commanded to "bring up [our] children in light and truth,"[28] not to consign them to a conveyor belt that stamps out their potential under the guise of education.

Remember, too, that this isn't about mere academics; government schools were built for and continue to focus on social engineering. As our children navigate their new lives and develop their own set of beliefs, we need to be extremely cautious about exposing them—during the most formative years of their life—to false ideas instilled by those trying to build a counterfeit kingdom. As one evangelical pastor said, we "cannot continue to send our children to Caesar for their education and be surprised when they come home as Romans."[29] And Adolf Hitler wasn't wrong when he said, "He alone who owns the youth, gains the future."[30] The adversary wants to control that future. Putting our children through an intellectually mediocre and spiritually destructive system is a great way to help him do just that.

---

28 D&C 93:40.

29 Voddie Baucham Jr., *Family Driven Faith: Doing What It Takes to Raise Sons and Daughters Who Walk with God* (Wheaton: Crossway, 2007), 202.

30 Jennifer Keeley, *Life in the Hitler Youth* (San Diego: Lucent Books, 1999), 8–10.

MONETARY MANIPULATION

If you were to ask someone for a list of "modern stains"—particularly those that threaten the family—chances are that money might not make the top ten list. After all, few people have reason to connect macroeconomic policies with family disintegration. But that connection becomes clear as day once you learn a little monetary history. Let's start with Rome. The downfall of the Roman Empire can be attributed to several factors, but the state's corruption of money is a primary factor affecting most others. It was the economic largess facilitated by this "easy money" that funded military adventurism, decreased productivity, financed sexual debauchery, fomented political intrigue, and necessitated increasing layers of economic interventionism to address the fiscal problems it produced, including wage controls, legal tender laws, and constant debasement of the currency. In short, the manipulation of the monetary system created a whole host of downstream ills.

Or take Spain's massive influx of silver from the New World, in the 16th and early 17th centuries, which flooded Europe with wealth, inadvertently triggering the Price Revolution. Massively increasing the supply of silver reduced its value, causing widespread inflation across the continent. In Spain and beyond, the cost of living rose sharply—grain prices, for instance, increased severalfold over decades. For ordinary families, this meant that wages, which often remained static, lost purchasing power. Artisans, laborers, and peasants faced growing poverty and social stratification as the wealthy hoarded resources. In England, King Henry VIII debased the currency to finance his extravagant court and military campaigns, a period known as the Great Debasement. By reducing the silver content in coins while maintaining their face value, the crown effectively diluted the currency's worth. This sparked significant inflation, with prices of goods rising as the real value of money fell. This eroded the common people's earnings, making it harder to afford food, rent, or other necessities. The resulting economic hardship contributed to increased poverty and social discontent. It's a story that has repeated again and again—whether through manageable inflation or periods of disastrous hyperinflation.

But this issue is sadly not a trend relegated to the history books. Modern states have created *fiat* money, from the Latin for 'let it be done'—a decree. This currency has value only because the government decrees that it be so and makes it official. Unlike gold or silver, which has a degree of scarcity, there is no limit to how much paper (or digital) currency the state can produce. Thus exists the continuous temptation to print new money to fund desired projects—including war, industrial subsidies, bank bailouts, welfare programs, and more. The pernicious part of this process is that those who spend the new money reap its full benefit before inflation kicks in. As the economy absorbs the new money, it slowly begins inflating prices in response since there are more banknotes chasing the same amount of goods. And who has the short end of the stick? We commoners—families trying to pay bills, provide for children, and deal with prices rising faster than our wages. Manipulating the money supply has a direct and significantly negative impact on the family.

The reason is rather simple. The home is a business; parents are partners. One's home is literally a microcosm of the broader economy. There's income and expenses—money coming in and going out. We buy and consume goods, earn income, hopefully save some, and constantly engage in trade of time or money with those within our microeconomy and others. Money is the social lubricant that moves forward this family machinery—it is the tool that facilitates our interpersonal transactions. And if you corrupt that tool, then everything it touches begins to break down. Money is the lifeblood of an economy—facilitating trade, creating opportunities for families, and enabling individuals to plan for a stable future. It's the medium by which we exchange our efforts, resources, and talents. When money retains its integrity, society benefits broadly as honest laborers see their efforts rewarded and families can confidently look forward to a stable, prosperous future. But when monetary policy becomes distorted, manipulated, and corrupted by powerful interests, money no longer serves the people—it becomes a mechanism of hidden oppression.

Consider the Federal Reserve, a central banking institution created in 1913 purportedly to stabilize America's economy. Since its inception, it has instead systematically undermined the value of the dollar through persistent inflation and monetary debasement. By creating more money, it effectively

steals from savers and transfers wealth upward to politically
connected elites, banks, and corporations. This silent theft of
purchasing power means that your grandparents' savings accounts, which once could comfortably support a modest retirement or provide a foundation for future generations, have
now dwindled to a shadow of their former value. In 1971,
President Nixon ended the last link between the US dollar
and gold, unleashing the Fed's unchecked power to print and
manipulate currency. Since 1913, the dollar has lost nearly
97 percent of its purchasing power.[1] Consequently, intergenerational wealth, which once provided security for families,
has evaporated, leaving younger generations struggling under
unprecedented financial burdens.

This engineered inflation also changes the dynamics within the home. Historically, a single income was sufficient to
sustain an average American family comfortably. Now, with
the dollar's diminished value and the skyrocketing cost of
housing, healthcare, education, and even basic goods, it has
become increasingly difficult—often impossible—for a single
wage-earner to provide for an entire family. This financial
pressure has driven mothers into the workforce out of necessity, reshaping the cultural fabric of families and entire communities. While employment opportunities for women are a
valuable social advancement, the coerced necessity of two-
income households has significantly altered family dynamics, weakened parental bonds, increased reliance on external

1   "The Death of the Dollar (in Perspective)," Discipline
     Funds, accessed February 27, 2025, https://disciplinefunds.
     com/2024/07/23/the-death-of-the-dollar-in-perspective/.

childcare and government schooling, and diluted the family's ability to transmit core values to children. The Proclamation rightly notes that "Parents have a sacred duty to rear their children";[2] outsourcing that responsibility to others only creates problems—and yet families are heavily incentivized to do so because of economic conditions that make it difficult to live off of only one breadwinner.

"The well-known phenomenon of the modern breakdown of the family cannot be understood," one economist wrote, "without recognizing the role of unsound money allowing the state to appropriate many of the essential roles the family has played for millennia, and reducing the incentives of all members of a family to invest in long-term familial relations."[3] Weak money means few people save for the long term to help their children and grandchildren. Why bother? Saved money devalues over time, so better to spend it now—or try to "save" by investing in risky assets. When long-term saving stops, long-term thinking dies with it. People lose the incentive to sacrifice today for a stronger family tomorrow. Inflation punishes prudence and rewards reckless spending, making family-centered investment seem pointless. Instead of parents and grandparents building stable foundations for future generations, each generation struggles on its own, borrowing heavily just to survive. Financial struggles produced by this corrupt system are a leading reason for marital conflict and divorce. One study of 4,500 couples examining this connec-

---

2   Hinckley, "Stand Strong against the Wiles of the World."
3   Saifedean Ammous, *The Bitcoin Standard* (New Jersey: John Wiley & Sons, 2018), 95.

tion unsurprisingly demonstrated, in the words of the study's author, "Arguments about money is by far the top predictor of divorce. It's not children, sex, in-laws or anything else. It's money—for both men and women."[4]

With weakened money comes weakened families—and with weakened families comes a weakened society. More families must rely on government aid, ceding independence and self-reliance to state-run programs. More still break apart under financial strain and the conflict it created. As the family is sidelined, the state expands its influence, empowering the elites and modern-day secret combinations who thrive on our dependency and economic bondage. No wonder so few Latter-day Saints have heeded the consistent counsel to store a financial and food reserve for a rainy day.

Monetary debasement is among the most insidious forms of the slow stain, precisely because so few recognize its effects until the damage is done. Like a silent leak behind the walls of a home, most families fail to see it until the structural integrity is compromised beyond repair. Investment accounts and retirement balances might rise nominally year after year, creating an illusion of growth and prosperity, yet their real purchasing power relentlessly declines beneath the surface. Families believe they are saving their hard-earned money for the future when, in reality, they are barely treading water against the hidden currents of inflation and manipula-

---

4   "Researcher finds correlation between financial arguments, decreased relationship satisfaction," Kansas State university, July 12, 2013, https://www.k-state.edu/media/newsreleases/jul13/predictingdivorce71113.html.

tion. Few pause to question the nature or source of the unseen forces weakening their economic foundation—and even fewer realize they are victims of a deliberate system designed to siphon wealth upward, quietly robbing them of the stability and security they've spent a lifetime trying to build.

In the end, God has entrusted us with abundant resources—"enough and to spare"[5]—to nurture our families and advance His divine purposes. These blessings are meant to be enjoyed prudently, cultivated gratefully, and generously shared with others. Yet, when our wealth is stealthily eroded through monetary manipulation, our ability to fulfill these sacred responsibilities is impaired. Families bear the brunt of unnecessary hardship, contention, and division, robbing parents of precious energy and peace meant for the home, and depriving children of a secure foundation for their future. To safeguard our homes and preserve our stewardship, we must recognize this subtle theft for what it truly is—not merely an economic inconvenience, but an assault on the stability, integrity, and sacred mission of the family itself.

---

5   D&C 104:17.

MATERIALISM AND CONSUMERISM

At the apex of their popularity in the 1990s, shopping malls were the temples of American culture. Families and teenagers alike flocked to these sprawling centers of commerce, where brightly lit stores showcased abundance, choice, and endless opportunity. Teenagers lingered outside trendy clothing stores, parents browsed department stores piled high with products promising convenience and comfort, and food courts buzzed with laughter and conversation. Every transaction promised fulfillment; every advertisement whispered happiness. Without realizing it, millions of people were worshipping daily at the altar of consumerism—an altar carefully constructed to encourage spending and consumption as the highest virtues. Even today, Black Friday serves as the high holy day of this consumer religion, when otherwise rational people participate in rituals of frantic buying—seeking meaning and value in allegedly limited-time deals. But how did we get here?

Consumerism came into its own during the twentieth century. After World War II, unprecedented prosperity swept the Western world, bringing with it an explosion of new consumer products and technologies. Advertisers, ever attuned to human impulses, rapidly tapped into people's desire for novelty, comfort, and status. This era birthed the shopping mall concept, as well as the dominance of television ads and the rapid spread of credit cards. But what began as the build-up of simple conveniences soon transformed into something far more insidious: a culture centered on acquiring, consuming, and displaying wealth as the hallmark of happiness and success.

Yet this drive to consume was no accident—it was deliberately engineered. Over a century ago, Edward Bernays—one of the pioneers of the public relations industry and the father of modern propaganda—put it this way:

> Mass production is profitable only if its rhythm can be maintained—that is if it can continue to sell its product in steady or increasing quantity.... Today supply must actively seek to create its corresponding demand ... [and] cannot afford to wait until the public asks for its product; it must maintain constant touch, through advertising and propaganda ... to assure itself the continuous demand which alone will make its costly plant profitable.[1]

One group of historians described this marketing engine for material goods as the "slow unleashing of the acquisitive instincts," a systematic reshaping of our values away from spiritual and communal goals toward individualistic, material desires.[2] To understand the spiritual danger behind ma-

1   Edward Bernays, *Propaganda* (New York: Ig Publishing, 2005), 84.
2   "How the world embraced consumerism," BBC, January 20,

terialism, we must first recognize its historical roots. Ancient Greek philosophers like Democritus and Epicurus taught that nothing exists beyond the material world—that reality is composed solely of matter, without a spiritual dimension. Centuries later, thinkers such as Thomas Hobbes echoed similar ideas, reducing humanity to mere "matter in motion." This secular worldview stripped life of spiritual depth and eternal purpose, subtly undermining humanity's connection to divinity. And it's the worldview upon which ancient and modern Babylon are built.

Of course, this perspective is at odds with God's. To Him, "all things... are spiritual."[3] Thus, our actions—including our attitudes toward consumption—are inseparable from our eternal progression. We are spiritual beings that are interacting with material goods in furtherance of our eternal journey during this mortal experience. Yet the allure and enticement of worldly treasures are such that many of God's people become seduced like those Lehi saw who "fell away into forbidden paths and were lost."[4] "[Men's] hearts are set so much upon the things of this world," Joseph Smith observed.[5] Yet the Savior taught, "Where your treasure is, there will your heart be also."[6] When we treasure worldly possessions, we risk placing our hearts—and, therefore, our faith—upon shifting sands. This doesn't usually happen overnight. It begins

---

2021, https://www.bbc.com/future/article/20210120-how-the-world-became-consumerist.

3   D&C 29:34.
4   1 Nephi 8:28.
5   D&C 121:35.
6   Matthew 6:21.

subtly: the well-meaning desire to provide comfort or security for ourselves and our families gradually transforms into a quest for bigger houses, newer cars, flashy toys, fancy clothing, and luxurious vacations. Over time, these things cease to serve us; instead, we begin serving them. Keeping up with the Joneses comes at a high cost.

Materialism also offers a seductive illusion: it promises happiness but typically delivers emptiness. The Lord was emphatic about the spiritual dangers of seeking earthly goods: "Seek not the things of this world but seek ye first to build up the kingdom of God, and to establish his righteousness."[7] He also said to "lay aside the things of this world, and seek for the things of a better."[8] Our possessions—no matter how impressive or desirable—pale into insignificance when viewed through the lens of eternity. Indeed, "the greatest of all the gifts of God,"[9] eternal life, can't be found in shopping malls or on online e-commerce sites. And obtaining that heavenly prize requires us to resist the carnal pull of what these meccas of materialism offer. No man can serve two masters,[10] yet Mammon's material abundance is a constant distraction and influential tempter.

The Church itself is not immune from the slow stain of consumerism. Consider, for instance, its investment in the City Creek shopping mall in Salt Lake City. Over a billion dollars in funds originating from tithing and sacred contribu-

---

7   Matthew 6:21.
8   D&C 25:10.
9   D&C 14:7.
10 Matthew 6:24.

tions were diverted to create a 20-acre series of luxury stores promoting consumerism, including advertisements depicting women in a low-cut dress drinking wine—hardly an environment one can imagine Christ cheering on. The stated intention may have been to revitalize downtown Salt Lake City, but the symbolism is strikingly problematic. Babylon is enticing precisely because it offers worldly comfort, prestige, and pleasure. Its overtures appear rational: people need jobs; communities need gathering places; businesses need customers; and cities need thriving economies. On the surface, these arguments feel sensible, even virtuous, and thus become compelling justifications for participating in consumerist culture. But the spiritual risk emerges when these worldly purposes overshadow—or worse, displace—our eternal mission. Babylon seduces us by wrapping spiritual distractions in practical packaging, subtly shifting our focus from eternal truth to temporary convenience and persuading us to rationalize worldly choices rather than seek first the kingdom of God.

Ultimately, the problem with materialism is that it blinds us to what truly matters. Our earthly possessions will decay, fashions will fade, gadgets will become obsolete, and the riches of the world will offer no lasting security. But a relationship with God endures forever. The treasures of eternity are invisible to consumer culture, yet they're infinitely more valuable than anything offered by the mall or marketed on Black Friday. Ultimately, overcoming consumerism and materialism requires a conscious effort to rediscover simplicity. It demands prioritizing experiences over possessions, relationships over status symbols, and spiritual growth over

worldly acclaim. It requires learning, like Job, to find content-
ment even in minimal circumstances, and discovering peace
through reliance on the Savior rather than possessions. "Be
still, and know that I am God," the scriptures teach.[11] In this
stillness, freed from the relentless pressure of endless consumption, we can clearly see our purpose: to love God, to
serve others, and to focus our hearts on that which truly lasts.

---

11   Psalm 46:10.

THE FALSE GODS WE WORSHIP

Fifty-six years after the Declaration of Independence was signed, the Mormon community in Missouri was viciously attacked by a mob consisting of their disgruntled neighbors. Speaking of this event, Joseph Smith wrote that "July, which once dawned upon the virtue and independence of the United States, now dawned upon the savage barbarity and mobocracy of Missouri."[1] Having lost their homes, their loved ones, and their possessions, the remaining Latter-day Saints understandably felt a desire for retaliation and revenge. After all, this latest bout of persecution was not a unique occurrence; time and time again, the Saints were subjected to similar oppression to some degree.

In the midst of such intense feelings and contentious circumstances, the Lord gave a revelation in response. Despite a strong desire to strike back, God's instructions were to instead "renounce war and proclaim peace."[2] The Lord intended this pursuit of peace to be a persistent effort, for the Saints were told to thrice "lift a standard of peace" to whoever tried to do them harm. Then, and only then, would the Lord justify their retaliatory attack. This wasn't a new concept, despite

---

1   B. H. Roberts, ed., *History of the Church of Jesus Christ of Latter-day Saints.* vol. 1 (Salt Lake City: Deseret Book, 1978), 372.
2   D&C 98:16.

how poorly past peoples had adhered to it. It was "the law that I gave unto mine ancients," God explained, and "is an ensample unto all people... for justification before me."[3]

This high bar for justified warfare is one below which God's people have routinely remained. In a world of constant conflict and strong support for military interventionism, how well have we so-called Christians fared in renouncing the status quo of destruction and death and proclaiming peace? Do the self-proclaimed followers of the Prince of Peace carry His standard in the face of war, or do they gladly parade around with the flags and insignia of their respective Caesars? Consider one data point from the war in Iraq in the mid-2000s. Out of any religious group in America, Gallup pollsters found that "Mormons are the most likely to favor" the war.[4] An astounding 72 percent of American Latter-day Saints supported sending troops to Iraq to fight a war that had no justifiable basis—not only were Saddam Hussein's supposed weapons of mass destruction a fabrication on the part of those in the US government who wanted to start the war, but even if they existed, God's clear standard was completely ignored by those who claim to follow Him.

And even when one leader attempted to draw attention to this standard, the Church threw him under the bus. Just as the war began, Russell M. Nelson gave a general conference talk that any faithful Christian would consider gospel

3   D&C 98:33–38.
4   "Among Religious Groups, Jewish Americans Most Strongly Oppose War," Gallup, February 23, 2007, https://news.gallup.com/poll/26677/among-religious-groups-jewish-americans-most-strongly-oppose-war.aspx.

truth. He drew attention to our living in the last days, full of prophesied turmoil. He referenced our mandate to follow the Prince of Peace and noted that He taught, "Blessed are the peacemakers: for they shall be called the children of God."[5] Then-Elder Nelson next highlighted the Golden Rule, noting that it applies to nations as much as individuals. He rightly taught that the scriptures "condemn wars of aggression" and that despite conflict, "Peace is a prime priority that pleads for our pursuit." Nelson unabashedly affirmed that Jesus Christ's teachings would bring actual and welcome peace:

> These prophecies of hope could materialize if leaders and citizens of nations would apply the teachings of Jesus Christ. Ours could then be an age of unparalleled peace and progress. Barbarism of the past would be buried. War, with its horrors, would be relegated to the realm of maudlin memory. Aims of nations would be mutually supportive. Peacemakers could lead in the art of arbitration, give relief to the needy, and bring hope to those who fear. Of such patriots, future generations would shout praises, and our Eternal God would pass judgments of glory.

> The hope of the world is the Prince of Peace—our Creator, Savior, Jehovah, and Judge. He offers us the good life, the abundant life, and eternal life. Peaceful—even prosperous—living can come to those who abide His precepts and follow His pathway to peace. This I declare to all the world.[6]

---

5   Matthew 5:9.
6   Russell M. Nelson, "Blessed Are the Peacemakers," *Ensign*, November 2002.

Concluding his remarks, Elder Nelson reminded us that God has commanded us to "renounce war and proclaim peace."[7] While objecting to aggressive war is part of the equation, it is only a part. We should also, he said, "follow after the things which make for peace. We should be personal peacemakers." These, he says, are the true patriots. And lip service is insufficient—"we should live by the Golden Rule."

Media backlash came quickly. The Associated Press published a brief report, stating that the "Mormon church issued a strong anti-war message... clearly referring to current hostilities in the Middle East."[8] One newspaper's headline announced Elder Nelson had "railed" against war,[9] despite his remarks expressing not a shred of anger or contention at all. The Church was quick to respond to the growing media portrayal of Nelson's messaging being "anti-war" in a cultural environment where people were extremely supportive of retributive war. Someone, Americans largely felt, had to pay for the 9/11 attacks.

One day after the conference ended, the Church's public relations division issued a media advisory, stating that some news outlets had "misinterpreted" the address and encourag-

---

7 D&C 98:16.
8 "Mormons issue strong anti-war statement directed at Middle East," *Associated Press*, October 7, 2002, https://www.mississippivalleypublishing.com/mormons-issue-strong-anti-war-statement-directed-at-middle-east/article_cbb68d23-eaa4-5d7e-a9e2-939698c48083.html.
9 "Mormon church rails against war," *Spokesman-Review*, October 6, 2002, https://news.google.com/newspapers?nid=1314&dat=20021006&id=5LszAAAAIBAJ&sjid=rPIDAAAAIBAJ&pg=6758,3918474.

ing reporters and editors to "consider the full text."[10] The advisory emphasized a minor part of the text, in which Nelson noted that the Church "[urges] its members fully to render... loyalty to their country,"[11] including military service—even when fighting against others of their same faith. Notwithstanding this exception, Elder Nelson correctly condemned wars of aggression and justified war in cases of legitimate self-defense, all the while repeatedly emphasizing that peace is possible, peace is optimal, and peace is what we should all be striving for—even (and especially) during the run-up to full-blown military intervention. But the Church's PR move worked. The Associated Press issued a follow-up report titled, "Mormons Back Bush Middle East Policy," explaining the Church had "qualified" Nelson's remarks and "offered support for President Bush's policy in the Middle East"[12] in the form of an editorial in the Church-owned *Deseret News*. That editorial, issued the following Wednesday, completely contradicted the substance of Elder Nelson's address. "Saddam Hussein and the threat he represents to the United States and her allies will not go away on his own," it read. "This time, the nation may well have to strike first." It concluded that

---

10 "Message of Peace Misinterpreted," The Church of Jesus Christ of Latter-day Saints, October 7, 2002, https://web.archive. org/web/20030203035754/http://www.lds.org/media2/ letters/0,10599,1592-1,00.html.

11 Nelson, "Blessed Are the Peacemakers."

12 "Mormons Back Bush Middle East Policy," Associated Press, October 10, 2002, https://wwrn.org/ articles/5994/?&place=united-states&section=christianity.

"Americans have known they must face Saddam again sooner or later. It appears the time has come."[13]

This was a tragic failure and missed opportunity to boldly affirm Christ's teachings, even if unpopular with the blood-thirsty public, who was eager to go to war. The Church's back-pedaling and the theologically barren op-ed in its newspaper completely undermined the power and potency of reminding countless Christians, who had been caught up in hoping to see their enemies killed, that the Golden Rule still applied to their modern-day circumstances. Jesus did not back down when challenged,[14] even when confronted with a hostile majority—should we?

It would appear that most Christians reject the Golden Rule—loving others, including our enemies—upon which all of God's law is predicated. It is another example of how many supposed disciples "draw near [to God] with their mouth, and with their lips do honor [Him], but have removed their heart far from [Him]."[15] As a result, "we are, on the whole, an idolatrous people," Spencer W. Kimball noted, saying he was "appalled and frightened" at how poorly God's people were following His expectations. He continued:

> We are a warlike people, easily distracted from our assignment of preparing for the coming of the Lord.

---

13   "A clear and simple case," *Deseret News*, October 9, 2002, https://www.deseret.com/2002/10/9/19682020/a-clear-and-simple-case.

14   For example, when charged with blasphemy—a "crime" for which capital punishment was mandated—the high priest demanded of Jesus, "Art thou the Christ, the Son of the Blessed?" His simple but direct response: "I am." See Mark 14:61–62.

15   Isaiah 29:13.

When enemies rise up, we commit vast resources to the fabrication of gods of stone and steel—ships, planes, missiles, fortifications—and depend on them for protection and deliverance. When threatened, we become anti-enemy instead of pro-kingdom of God; we train a man in the art of war and call him a patriot, thus, in the manner of Satan's counterfeit of true patriotism, perverting the Savior's teaching:

"Love your enemies, bless them that curse you, do good to them that hate you, and pray for them which despitefully use you, and persecute you; That ye may be the children of your Father which is in heaven." (Matthew 5:44–45.)

We forget that if we are righteous, the Lord will either not suffer our enemies to come upon us—and this is the special promise to the inhabitants of the land of the Americas (see 2 Nephi 1:7)—or he will fight our battles for us (Exodus 14:14; D&C 98:37, to name only two references of many). This he is able to do.[16]

Society's reliance upon the natural man and these gods of stone and steel has become so deep that most of us fail to even see how thoroughly we have allowed our hearts and minds to become stained by the philosophies and priorities of worldly power. Most of us not only tolerate Caesar's culture of militarism—we celebrate it, *more than those of any other religion!*—cheerfully pledging allegiance to the very symbols of

---

16 Spencer W. Kimball, "The False Gods We Worship," *Ensign*, June 1976, 3.

empire that so often stand in opposition to the teachings of Christ. We offer unqualified praise to warriors, treating them as sacred heroes, even as we neglect or disparage those who humbly advocate for peace and reconciliation.

Yet God's law remains clear: we must renounce war and proclaim peace. This message has never been more counter-cultural, more difficult, or more urgently needed than in our time of unending geopolitical conflict. While the nations rage, our challenge is to rise above the partisan hatred, propaganda, and fear that saturate our world. If we are to truly follow Christ, our identity must never be found in flags, armies, or political ideologies—it must be found in Him alone. As disciples, we must cultivate a radically different worldview, one that is rooted not in military might but in the enduring power of love, forgiveness, and peacemaking. Easier said than done, to be sure—but it is crucially and eternally important.

This path may not be popular or easy—it may invite ridicule, criticism, and even rejection—but it is precisely the path Christ has asked us to walk. Only by rejecting the false security of worldly power and embracing the principles of His kingdom can we truly become His disciples, citizens of His kingdom, bringing hope and healing to a world that desperately needs it.

SECRET COMBINATIONS

When George W. Bush obtained the Republican Party's nomination for his reelection campaign in the 2004 presidential election, his main challenger was John Kerry, a US senator and Democratic nominee. Naturally, one would think that these two individuals were worlds apart—leaders of clashing political parties with opposing outlooks resulting in public clashes in a war of words. And that's certainly how it appeared to voters; one major press outlet said the sparring candidates went "toe-to-toe in [a] quarrelsome debate."[1] Bush said that Kerry "changes positions a lot, because he does"; Kerry said Bush was making the world more dangerous "because [he] didn't make the right judgments."[2] But for all the spectacle and sportsmanship, these two individuals shared a private bond—one that few voters were ever even aware of.

Few voters, that is, except those who happened to see *Meet the Press* host Tim Russert interview both candidates. On February 4, 2004, Russert took occasion to ask President Bush about his membership in a secret society known as Skull

---

1   "Bush, Kerry go toe-to-toe in quarrelsome debate," NBC News, October 8, 2004, https://www.nbcnews.com/id/wbna6191353.
2   Ibid.

and Bones—a group in which Kerry also happened to be a member.

> **RUSSERT:** You were both in Skull and Bones, the secret society.
>
> **BUSH:** It's so secret we can't talk about it.
>
> **RUSSERT:** What does that mean for America? The conspiracy theorists are going to go wild.
>
> **BUSH:** I'm sure they are. (Laughs) I don't know. I haven't seen the Web pages yet.
>
> **RUSSERT:** Number 322...?
>
> **BUSH:** (Laughs)[3]

From there, Bush pivoted to talking about the race—clearly uncomfortable with Russert's direct questioning about something that had not been spoken about publicly before. And in August, when Russert hosted Kerry just months prior to the election, he proceeded with a similar line of questioning:

> **RUSSERT:** You both were members in Skull and Bones, a secret society at Yale. What does that tell us?
>
> **KERRY:** Not much, because it's a secret. (Laughs)
>
> **RUSSERT:** Is there a secret handshake? Is there a secret code?

---

3   "Interview With Tim Russert Broadcast on NBC's 'Meet the Press,'" The American Presidency Project, February 7, 2004, https://www.presidency.ucsb.edu/documents/interview-with-tim-russert-broadcast-nbcs-meet-the-press.

KERRY: I wish there were something secret I could manifest.

RUSSERT: 322? A secret number?

KERRY: There are all kinds of secrets, Tim.[4]

And from there, Kerry likewise pivoted to talking about the race—also visibly uncomfortable with having to deal with such questions. Both Bush and Kerry were graduates of Yale in the 1960s and were one of only fifteen candidates admitted to Skull and Bones in their respective years. The group has bonded diplomats, media moguls, bankers, and spies into a lifelong, multigenerational fellowship far more influential than your average fraternity. After all, what are the odds that the two leading candidates for the most powerful political position on the planet both happened to be members of a tiny club whose membership only includes around 600 living persons at any given time? The odds are low, which means the likelihood of corruption is high.

The Book of Mormon's descriptions of secret combinations highlight a few common characteristics: Their members place one another "in power and authority among the people";[5] they become "partners of all [their] substance,"[6] luring others to "believe in their works and partake of their spoils";[7] they "protect and preserve one another," helping members

---

4   "Bush/Kerry Skull and Bones Avoidance," YouTube, accessed March 1, 2025, https://www.youtube.com/watch?v=gwJDs1cg9Eo.

5   Helaman 2:5.

6   3 Nephi 3:7.

7   Helaman 6:38.

evade criminal consequences;[8] they operate subject to "the laws of their wickedness," according to the "oaths and covenants" handed down by Satan;[9] and they are "built up to get power and gain."[10] After acquiring sufficient power to "obtain the sole management of the government,"[11] their evil activities cause societal destruction.[12] So what groups today qualify as the secret combinations? The Lord clearly commanded us, through Moroni, that "when ye shall see these things come among you that ye shall awake to a sense of your awful situation, because of this secret combination which shall be among you."[13] If we're supposed to "suffer not that these murderous combinations shall get above [us],"[14] we first need to understand who we're actually talking about. We cannot fight an enemy whose characteristics and motives and location we do not know.

Many attempts to list possible secret combinations fall short. One BYU religion professor said his students "struggle to grasp why communism, the Mafia, or even street gangs" constitute secret combinations.[15] "I rarely offer corrections to my students' suggestions," he noted, "primarily because I

---

8   Helaman 6:21.
9   Helaman 6:24–25.
10   Ether 8:23.
11   Helaman 6:39.
12   Ether 8:21.
13   Ether 8:24.
14   Ether 8:23.
15   Nicholas J. Frederick, "'When Ye Shall See These Things Come among You': A Survey of Teachings on Modern Secret Combinations," *Religious Educator*, vol. 25 no. 1, 2024, https://rsc.byu.edu/vol-25-no-1-2024/when-ye-shall-see-these-things-come-among-you.

don't feel like I'm able to provide a sufficient answer." (Cue Jesus: "if the blind lead the blind, both shall fall into the ditch."[16]) Hugh Nibley argued that secret combinations were organized crime, such as "the Mafia and Cosa Nostra."[17] M. Russell Ballard once said, "Among today's secret combinations are gangs, drug cartels, and organized crime families."[18] No doubt these conclusions are true, in part. Certainly, organized crime syndicates murder to acquire power and gain. Some have secret codes or handshakes. They aim to "protect and preserve one another."[19] But the most pernicious combinations—the ones that deserve our attention and opposition—are those that infest the government. Crime has existed since Cain slew Abel, and countless people have conspired to rob or murder people. These activities, whether one-offs or organized, pale in comparison to the combinations whose goal is to "overthrow the freedom of all lands, nations, and countries."[20] And you can't do that without controlling the levers of power in government.

On April 10, 1953, Allen Dulles shocked the nation by warning them of a new Soviet program that would threaten their freedom and even their sense of what is true. Only weeks into his new position as the first civilian director of the Central Intelligence Agency (CIA), Dulles warned his audi-

---

16 Matthew 15:14.
17 Hugh Nibley, *The Collected Works of Hugh Nibley*, vol. 7, Since Cumorah, 2nd ed. (Provo, UT: FARMS, 1988), 395–96.
18 M. Russell Ballard, "Standing for Truth and Right," *Ensign*, Nov. 1997, 38.
19 Helaman 6:21.
20 Ether 8:25.

ence, and the American people more broadly, about a new "mind control" system the Soviets were developing. "Its aim," he said, "is to condition the mind so that it no longer reacts on a free will or rational basis but responds to impulses implanted from outside."[21] He continued:

> If we are to counter this kind of warfare we must understand the techniques the Soviet is adopting to control men's minds...
>
> The human mind is the most delicate of all instruments. It is so finely adjusted, so susceptible to the impact of outside influences that it is proving a malleable tool in the hands of sinister men... We in the West are somewhat handicapped in brain warfare.[22]

Dulles further claimed that "it is hard for us to realize that in the great area behind the Iron Curtain a vast experiment is underway to change men's minds, working on them continuously from youth to old age."[23] What Dulles didn't reveal is that plans were already underway within the CIA to enter the mind control business as well. Known as Project MK-Ultra, this top-secret government program involved mind control experiments using drugs, electroshock therapy, toxins, hypnosis, radiation, and more. Some participants had volunteered

---

21 "Summary Of Remarks By Dr. Allen W. Dulles At The National Alumni Conference Of The Graduate Council Of Princeton University Hot Springs, Va., April 10, 1953 - Brain Warfare," Central Intelligence Agency, accessed March 2, 2025, https://www.cia.gov/readingroom/document/00146077.
22 Ibid.
23 Ibid.

freely for the program, but most were enrolled under coercion or without any knowledge that they were human guinea pigs for the CIA's activities. Soldiers, prisoners, mentally impaired individuals, and other vulnerable members of society were lab rats for Dulles's project.

For over a decade, MK-Ultra involved 149 projects using drug experimentation and other tactics, often on unsuspecting individuals. To avoid scrutiny, the CIA set up secret detention facilities in areas under American control, such as in Japan, Germany, and the Philippines, so that they could avoid criminal prosecution if they were discovered. CIA officers captured people suspected of being "enemy agents" and other people they felt were "expendable" and began experimenting on and torturing them. Where was the oversight, you might wonder? The CIA's own Inspector General—typically tasked with investigations, audits, and addressing any abuses at the agency they oversee—warned CIA officials, "Precautions must be taken not only to protect operations from exposure to enemy forces but also to conceal these activities from the American public in general. The knowledge that the [CIA] is engaging in unethical and illicit activities would have serious repercussions in political and diplomatic circles and would be detrimental to the accomplishment of its mission."[24]

---

24 "Project MKULTRA, the CIA's Program of Research in Behavioral Modification," Joint Hearing Before the Select Committee on Intelligence and the Subcommittee on Health and Scientific Research of the Committee on Human Resources, August 3, 1977, https://www.google.com/books/edition/Project_MKULTRA_the_CIA_s_Program_of_Res/TEqhqtrF3XEC.

This wasn't a rogue group within the CIA or a one-off project. It was part and parcel of how this shadow government has operated since its post-WWII inception. It is a lawless group of people whose covert activities are operated independent of oversight and scrutiny by the formal government of which it is a part. Its power, according to one of its former members, "derives from its vast intergovernmental undercover infrastructure and its direct relationship with great private industries, mutual funds and investment houses, universities, and the news media, including foreign and domestic publishing houses."[25] It is "able when it chooses to topple governments, to create governments, and to influence governments almost anywhere in the world."[26] That was clearly the case in Operation Ajax when CIA officials orchestrated a coup against the democratically elected leader in Iran to topple his government and install a puppet they could control. In addition to toppling and influencing governments, the CIA steals resources, murders innocent people, manipulates the media, traffics drugs, and shields itself behind layers of classified secrecy to evade accountability.

Perhaps it seems shocking to call an agency of the US government a "shadow government" that constitutes a secret combination. Let's address that head-on, point by point. The CIA places its people "in power and authority among the people"[27] by routinely elevating individuals from within

---

25 L. Fletcher Prouty, *The Secret Team: The CIA and its Allies in Control of the United States and the World* (New York: Skyhorse Publishing, 2011), 3.

26 Ibid.

27 Helaman 2:5.

its own ranks or closely connected circles to influential positions in government, military, and diplomatic service. For instance, former CIA Director George H.W. Bush later became
Vice President and President of the United States, positioning
agency loyalists in strategic roles to consolidate power and
influence. The CIA, often using front groups, entices corporations and governments to become "partners of all [their]
substance"[28] through arms trades, drug trafficking, and financial manipulations, as was evident in operations such as
the Iran-Contra scandal. They lure others to "believe in their
works and partake of their spoils"[29] by manipulating media
narratives to gain public support for morally questionable operations, convincing citizens and allies that their actions are
necessary for national security—for example, as was the case
in Operation Mockingbird. By sharing wealth, influence, and
immunity from legal repercussions with political, media, and
industry partners, the agency has enticed many influential
groups to support and justify their covert operations. Those
in power at the upper echelons of the CIA "protect and preserve one another,"[30] helping members evade criminal consequences. They have persistently evaded any accountability
for crimes ranging from torture and assassination plots to
illegal surveillance of American citizens. No senior CIA officials were ever prosecuted for any of its crimes that were
made public (nor, of course, for those yet to be made public).
This systemic shielding of personnel perpetuates impunity

---

28   3 Nephi 3:7.
29   Helaman 6:38.
30   Helaman 6:21.

within their ranks. The CIA operates under "the laws of their wickedness"[31] by adhering to a code of secrecy and deception, justifying morally reprehensible actions as part of their job description. Former agents and whistleblowers have openly described an internal culture based on secrecy, manipulation, and ruthless pragmatism, indicating moral decay embedded deeply within the agency's operational philosophy. In a confession near the end of his life, the former chief of counter-intelligence for the CIA, who had that prominent position for two decades, revealed:

> Fundamentally, the founding fathers of US intelligence were liars. The better you lied and the more you betrayed, the more likely you would be promoted. These people attracted and promoted each other. Outside of their duplicity, the only thing they had in common was a desire for absolute power. I did things that, in looking back on my life, I regret. But I was part of it and loved being in it... Allen Dulles [and other early CIA leaders] were the grand masters. If you were in a room with them you were in a room full of people that you had to believe would deservedly end up in hell. I guess I will see them there soon.[32]

The laws that we citizens have to follow—and for which we'll be prosecuted should we violate them—simply are not applied to the CIA's members. The agency is "built up to get power and gain,"[33] using coups such as those orchestrated in

---

31   Helaman 6:24–25.
32   Joseph J. Trento, *The Secret History of the CIA* (New York: MJF Books, 2001), 479.
33   Ether 8:23.

Guatemala, Iran, Chile, and elsewhere to control governments and secure resources for American corporate and political interests. And by carrying out their evil deeds free from legal consequence or public awareness, the CIA effectively has become an autonomous shadow government—its power enabling it to "obtain the sole management of the government."[34]

This is where the reasonable reader will no doubt push back. Surely the CIA's elite have not obtained the sole management of the US government, right? One investigative reporter who obtained unprecedented access into the CIA's activities concluded, "Presidents come and go, but the intelligence bureaucracy remains in place as the real ruling class in our political system."[35] Shocking, right? But why else would a sitting US senator warn the sitting president, on camera, "Let me tell you—you take on the intelligence community, they have six ways from Sunday to get back at you."[36] Clearly, Bruce R. McConkie was right: "Gadianton robbers fill the judgment seats in many nations."[37]

Sometimes called the deep state, this shadow government includes institutions beyond the CIA: intelligence and law enforcement institutions such as the Federal Bureau of Investigations or the National Security Agency; extra-governmental

---

34 Helaman 6:39.
35 Trento, *The Secret History of the CIA*, xii.
36 "Schumer warns Trump: Intel officials 'have six ways from Sunday at getting back at you,'" *Washington Examiner*, January 4, 2017, https://www.washingtonexaminer.com/news/1866424/schumer-warns-trump-intel-officials-have-six-ways-from-sunday-at-getting-back-at-you/.
37 Bruce R. McConkie, "The Coming Tests and Trials and Glory," *Ensign*, May 1980, 73.

coordinating groups like the Council on Foreign Relations, the Trilateral Commission, or the World Economic Forum; industry associations and major corporations including those associated with Big Tech, the Military Industrial Complex, or Big Pharma; economic actors like the Federal Reserve; and counterpart corporations and governmental bodies across the world. These interconnected groups form a web of influence and power, operating beyond public accountability or transparency, steering policies and outcomes toward their own gain. Organized crime is amateur hour; the real masters of societal destruction are these politically embedded secret combinations, quietly orchestrating chaos at the highest levels.

Ultimately, recognizing these combinations as a clear fulfillment of scriptural warnings compels us to confront an uncomfortable truth: the slow stain of corruption has spread widely through society, embedding itself deeply into institutions once designed to protect freedom, uphold justice, and promote the public good. We have repeatedly been warned to "suffer not that these murderous combinations shall get above [us]";[38] yet, for decades, many have chosen ignorance or complacency rather than vigilance and courage. The slow stain can be cleansed only through conscious awakening, deliberate resistance, and an uncompromising commitment to truth.

---

38 Ether 8:23.

THE ALL-SEEING EYE

Imagine a world where every step you take, every word you speak, and every purchase you make is monitored, evaluated, and scored. In China, this isn't a far-off dystopian fantasy—it's daily life under the social credit system, a sprawling web of surveillance and control launched in 2014, first as an opt-in system, and expanding ever since, without the ability to opt out or the need to opt in at all. By blending advanced technology—facial recognition, AI, and vast databases—with a network of over 600 million cameras, the Chinese Communist Party now tracks its citizens' behavior whether they consent or not, assigning each a score that dictates their place in society. Pay your bills on time or donate to charity, and your score rises, unlocking perks like easier travel or better school access. Jaywalk, criticize the government online or even associate with low-scorers, and your rating plummets, barring you from jobs, flights, or high-speed trains.[1] This system touches nearly every aspect of life for over a billion people.

The mechanics are chillingly precise. Data pours in from public records, social media, bank transactions, and "smart" city infrastructure with data-gathering cameras and devices,

---

1   "Discipline and Punish: The Birth of China's Social-Credit System," *The Nation*, January 23, 2019, https://www.thenation.com/article/archive/china-social-credit-system/.

feeding algorithms that churn out real-time scores. By 2020, pilot programs had already penalized millions—banning over 17.5 million plane ticket purchases and 5.5 million train trips for infractions as minor as smoking in public.[2] Rewards and punishments twist incentives, nudging citizens to conform not out of conviction but fear. A father might skip a protest to protect his child's school admission; a friend might shun another to preserve her own rating. When Liu Hu recently attempted to book a flight, airline employees explained he was banned from flying because he had been placed on a list of untrustworthy people. Liu, a journalist, had previously been ordered by a Chinese court to apologize for some social media posts he wrote and was then told his apology was insincere. "I can't buy property. My child can't go to a private school," Liu said. "You feel you're being controlled by the list all the time."[3] This isn't an effort to increase safety—it's coercion dressed as care, a paternalistic state claiming to shepherd its flock while tightening the reins on thought and action. "A feeling of security is the best gift a country can give its people," President Xi Jinping once told his people. Perhaps it's no surprise, then, that 42 percent of the world's video surveillance cameras are in China.[4]

---

2   "China banned millions of people with poor social credit from transportation in 2018," The Verge, March 1, 2019, https://www.theverge.com/2019/3/1/18246297/china-transportation-people-banned-poor-social-credit-planes-trains-2018.

3   "China's behavior monitoring system bars some from travel, purchasing property," CBS News, April 24, 2018, https://www.cbsnews.com/news/china-social-credit-system-surveillance-cameras/.

4   "Discipline and Punish," *The Nation.*

The United States—the so-called "land of the free"—may lack a full-fledged social credit system (for now?), but don't assume privacy thrives here. The National Security Agency vacuums up phone records, emails, and internet activity without a warrant, amassing data on ordinary citizens under the guise of national security. That information is accessed (and often abused) by a wide range of government officials who can now dig up dirt on anyone they wish to target. At airports, the Transportation Security Administration subjects millions of travelers to invasive screenings—pat-downs, full-body scanners, and humiliating searches in what is rightly called "security theater"—a performance designed to reassure the public without meaningfully reducing threats. Much like China's cameras, these procedures rarely catch actual threats; instead, they condition Americans to tolerate the loss of personal privacy in exchange for a false sense of safety. (Undercover tests of airport security checkpoints have demonstrated that TSA agents failed to catch weapons and explosives up to 95 percent of the time.[5]) Local police departments regularly deploy facial recognition technology, license plate readers, drones, and surveillance software, quietly monitoring individuals without meaningful oversight. Our smartphones, "smart" appliances, and even social media posts supply corporations—and through them, the state—with unprecedented insights into our private lives. Each new security measure, each new surveillance tool, chips away at the sacred space of private thought and action, gradually eroding the very liber-

---

5   "Abolish the TSA," *Reason*, December 2024, https://reason.com/2024/11/14/abolish-the-tsa/.

ties that form the bedrock of our ability to worship and act according to our convictions.

Throughout history, privacy has been essential to religious worship, individual conscience, and meaningful action. Before Christianity was legalized under Constantine, early Christians sometimes faced brutal persecution under Roman rule. To worship freely, they retreated to private homes and underground catacombs, holding secret services away from the state's watchful eye. In prerevolutionary France, underground presses churned out pamphlets criticizing the monarchy and church, distributed under cover of darkness. Without the protective veil of privacy, Thomas Paine's incendiary tract, *Common Sense*, might never have dared to challenge a king and spark the American Revolution. Fleeing persecution for rejecting the Church of England's doctrines, Puritans in premigration England clung to their faith by holding covert worship services in private homes and secluded fields, meeting in small, trusted groups to evade the Crown's informants.

True worship requires space to contemplate, communicate with God, and freely act on convictions without fearing that our prayers, conversations, or sermons might be secretly recorded, analyzed, and weaponized against believers. Consider Daniel, who openly defied the state decree forbidding prayer by continuing his worship privately within his home.[6] He understood that true discipleship often necessitates resistance to oppressive laws, but the ever-growing surveillance state severely restricts the ability to stand up against evil.

---

6   Daniel 6:10.

When an oppressive government wields invasive surveillance powers, we face an impossible dilemma: either compromise beliefs to remain safe and acceptable in the eyes of state authorities or risk persecution, ostracism, and punishment by openly resisting unjust policies. Those who bravely speak truth to power, fight oppression, or preach doctrines opposed by the state quickly find themselves labeled as threats. An oppressive surveillance state is not one that remains friendly to religious worship. An all-seeing eye quickly gives rise to the all-punishing fist.

The paternalistic (and hollow) promise of safety through surveillance is in clear contrast to the scriptures, where God reveals that "it is not meet that I should command in all things."[7] He expects us to act freely, taking responsibility and becoming spiritually mature. Yet modern governments increasingly operate on the opposite principle, implying that citizens cannot be trusted to manage their own safety, morality, or relationships. By monitoring our purchases, online interactions, and daily activities, the state infantilizes individuals, fostering dependency rather than self-reliance. As we surrender responsibility for our safety to authorities promising security, we lose not only liberty but also the opportunity for spiritual growth through independent action. Surveillance states promise freedom from danger by exerting total control, but true security is found only through trusting in God's protection. Rather than relying on the futile assurances of an ever-watchful government, Christians must instead build

---

7   D&C 58:26.

their lives upon the Rock of Ages. Caesar's technology and
tactics promise a superficial peace—one purchased through
surrendering our liberty—but the gospel provides lasting ref-
uge. Human surveillance and divine salvation are at odds with
one another. No man can be protected by two masters.

The state's quest to monitor every action mimics God's
omniscience—"the eyes of the Lord are in every place"[8]—but
lacks His divine love and mercy. Where God sees our hearts
and desires to redeem us,[9] surveillance systems mercilessly
judge us to control and punish, assigning scores or flags based
on cold data. This turns the state into a counterfeit deity, demanding obedience not to eternal principles but to its own
shifting rules. Put simply, this is idolatry—a modern golden
calf where technology promises safety but delivers bondage.
We must recognize surveillance for what it truly is: a spiritual
counterfeit that enslaves us under the guise of protection.

---

8   Proverbs 15:3.
9   1 Samuel 16:7.

THE POPULARITY OF SOCIALISM

In January 1959, Fidel Castro rolled into Havana, greeted by throngs of Cubans ecstatic to see Fulgencio Batista—a dictator who'd looted $700 million in cash, art, and gold as he fled to the Dominican Republic—finally toppled. Batista's regime was a cesspool of corruption, propped up by US mafia muscle and brutal thuggery, leaving even his American backers lukewarm. The cheering masses saw Castro's revolution as a golden ticket: a chance to ditch crony capitalism's elite enrichment for a system promising progress for all. Castro played it coy on economics—muttering about land reform, democracy, and schools—while appointing liberals to high posts and swearing, "I am not a communist." But six months in, with land reform floundering and allies bickering, he needed a plan—and fast. Enter Che Guevara, his deputy with zero economic chops but a head full of Marxist dreams, tapped to remake Cuba's destiny.[1]

Guevara's idea was to nationalize everything—farms, factories, and shops—to set prices, wages, and egg rations from Havana, vowing to double incomes, end unemployment, and birth a "New Man" who would toil joyfully for socialism's glory. Literacy initially soared, clinics quickly multiplied, but

---

1   "Cuba: a story of socialist failure," IEA, February 13, 2020, https://iea.org.uk/cuba-a-story-of-socialist-failure/.

the price was steep. Cuba's economy flatlined at 1 percent annual growth, leaning on Soviet and Venezuelan crutches until they snapped.[2] Sugar withered, food imports spiked to two-thirds of the diet, and when the USSR collapsed, GDP tanked by a third, leaving Cuban stomachs empty. Education and healthcare ate 20 percent of GDP combined, yet housing rotted, and growth stayed a fantasy.[3] Castro's liberation became a straitjacket, proving socialism's grand vows crumble under its own dead weight—leaving Cuba a stark warning of progress derailed.

Cuba's economic failure is no outlier. Socialism's history is littered with shattered dreams and human wreckage. The Soviet Union's iron-fisted planning choked innovation, stranding citizens in breadlines and shadow markets.[4] Venezuela, once a Latin American jewel, crashed under Chávez and Maduro, its hyperinflation soaring to 1,000,000 percent as millions fled starvation.[5] North Korea's Juche ideology forged a national prison where famines claimed millions while the regime polished its nukes.[6] East Germany's gray inefficiency

2   "The Fall and Recovery of the Cuban Economy in the 1990's," IMF Working Papers, 2001(048), A001, https://doi.org/10.5089/9781451846744.001.A001.
3   "The Economic Cost of Cuban Socialism," Foundation for Economic Education, August 2, 2019, https://fee.org/articles/the-economic-cost-of-cuban-socialism/?gad_source=1.
4   "Why Communism Failed," Foundation for Economic Education, March 1, 1991, https://fee.org/articles/why-communism-failed/.
5   "As Venezuela Collapses, Inflation Careens Toward 1 Million Percent," Foundation for Economic Education, August 1, 2018, https://fee.org/articles/as-venezuela-collapses-inflation-careens-toward-1-million-percent/.
6   "Juche, the state ideology that makes North Koreans revere

pushed desperate souls to brave the Berlin Wall's bullets.[7] Zimbabwe's Mugabe turned a fertile breadbasket into a wasteland, printing $100 trillion notes that bought nothing.[8] Mao's Great Leap Forward unleashed a famine that devoured 30–45 million Chinese lives.[9] Cambodia's Khmer Rouge butchered 2 million in a mad purge of markets and minds.[10] These aren't flukes—they're socialism's brutal signature, and Cuba's decay is just another grim echo.

Reviewing this destruction and death toll leads many people in Western nations to conclude that *their* country is different—surely these barbaric regimes and thuggish dictators are to blame, while respectable republics such as ours are not guilty of such crimes. This ignorance rests in large part upon a misunderstanding of what socialism actually is. Traditionally defined, socialism refers to the collective ownership or state control of the means of production—factories, land, resources, and businesses—managed centrally rather than through

Kim Jong Un, explained," Vox, June 18, 2018, https://www.vox.com/world/2018/6/18/17441296/north-korea-propaganda-ideology-juche.

7   "The Berlin Wall: Its Rise, Fall, and Legacy," Foundation for Economic Education, November 5, 2019, https://fee.org/articles/the-berlin-wall-its-rise-fall-and-legacy/.

8   "Zimbabwe's Dictator Fell but the Country Is Still In Trouble," Foundation for Economic Education, November 17, 2017, https://fee.org/articles/zimbabwes-dictator-fell-but-the-country-is-still-in-trouble/.

9   "Hungry Ghosts: Mao's Secret Famine by Jasper Becker," Foundation for Economic Education, December 1, 1997, https://fee.org/articles/hungry-ghosts-maos-secret-famine-by-jasper-becker/.

10   "Visiting the Killing Fields," Foundation for Economic Education, August 1, 2000, https://fee.org/articles/visiting-the-killing-fields/.

individual choice and free-market competition. This version of socialism consistently proves disastrous, as demonstrated by the catastrophic failures listed previously. Central planners arrogantly presume they can efficiently direct millions of economic choices from distant capitals, disregarding local knowledge, individual preferences, and the motivating power of incentives. It is a fatal conceit, where central planners believe they can make better decisions for the people than the people can for themselves. History repeatedly shows their grand designs lead not to prosperity but poverty, not equality but entrenched privilege for party elites.

But focusing narrowly on state ownership alone obscures a far more prevalent—and pernicious—form of socialism: the coercive redistribution of resources from one group of citizens to another. This approach leverages the power of the state, not to manage every economic decision directly, but to seize wealth and property through taxation, regulation, or inflation, redistributing them according to political rather than economic logic. Under such a system, the government becomes a central clearinghouse, forcibly socializing the costs of its programs among the many while concentrating benefits on the favored few. This subtle form of socialism gradually corrodes personal responsibility, incentivizes political corruption, and creates a dependent class of indolent citizens, all while disguising itself under the virtuous banners of fairness, equality, and compassion.

Many who bear the slow stain of socialism fail to recognize it, not because they've fully embraced its extremes, but because their own compromises blur the line. For example, while conservatives rightly decry socialist programs like Medicare for All and the Green New Deal, they usually defend sacred cows like Social Security, government schools, and public libraries—touch those, and these supposed critics of socialism swiftly transform into its most ardent champions. This selective outrage reveals how deeply socialism has quietly infiltrated our society, shaping the public's expectations of government's role and responsibility in caring for our neighbors. And despite its catastrophic track record, socialism remains very popular—particularly among the youth. Sixty-one percent of Americans ages eighteen to twenty-four support the concept,[11] many of them proudly (and ignorantly) wearing T-shirts featuring Che Guevara.[12] (With only 13 percent of US students having proficiency in American history,[13] even fewer are literate in world economic history—and thus we repeat the mistakes of the past because we fail to remember and teach them to the rising generation.)

Latter-day Saints are certainly not immune from this ignorance. A 2009 Pew Research Center poll found that nearly half (49 percent) of Church members "believed that the gov-

---

11 "Gen Z prefers 'socialism' to 'capitalism,'" Axios, January 27, 2019, https://www.axios.com/2019/01/27/socialism-capitalism-poll-generation-z-preference.

12 "How the Che Guevara t-shirt became a global phenomenon," Dazed, July 26. 2016, https://www.dazeddigital.com/fashion/article/32208/1/how-the-che-guevara-t-shirt-became-a-global-phenomenon.

13 "Eighth-Grade Scores Decline in Civics and U.S. History on the Nation's Report Card," National Assessment Governing Board, May 3, 2023, https://www.nagb.gov/news-and-events/news-releases/2023/eighth-grade-scores-decline-in-civics-and-us-history.html.

ernment should do more to help the needy."[14] This impulse is understandable—after all, approximately four billion people, nearly half of humanity, live on less than $7 per day.[15] God's commandments regarding poverty leave no room for ambiguity: we must "administer of [our] substance unto him that standeth in need,"[16] seek equality in "heavenly things, yea, and earthly things also,"[17] esteem others as we do ourselves,[18] and "remember the poor, and consecrate of [our] properties for their support."[19] Clearly, Christ finds our neglect unacceptable, warning that those who fail to aid the poor are not His disciples.[20] Yet the means by which we fulfill this sacred obligation matter profoundly. Positive ends—like alleviating poverty—do not justify coercive, immoral methods such as socialism. Christ and Caesar propose fundamentally different approaches to caring for the poor, yet many Latter-day Saints—and Christians more broadly—have outsourced this divine responsibility to a corrupt, inefficient, and secular state. Some are seduced by socialism's promises of benefits without personal sacrifice, masking the cost by spreading it across faceless others. After all, who doesn't find "free stuff"

14   "A Portrait of Mormons in the U.S.," Pew Research Center, July 24, 2009, https://www.pewresearch.org/religion/2009/07/24/a-portrait-of-mormons-in-the-us-social-and-political-views/.

15   "Poverty, Prosperity, and Planet Report," World Bank Group, accessed March 6, 2025, https://www.worldbank.org/en/publication/poverty-prosperity-and-planet.

16   Mosiah 4:16.

17   D&C 78:5–6.

18   D&C 38:24.

19   D&C 42:30.

20   D&C 52:40.

appealing? It's precisely this seductive offer that enticed ancient Nephites into partaking of the secret combination's spoils.[21]

Instead of voluntarily engaging in personal stewardship and charitable giving, many Christians have become comfortable relying on Caesar's arm of flesh, supporting welfare programs built on force rather than faith, and compulsion rather than compassion. Yet nowhere does God delegate charity to the coercive hand of government—taxing by threat, wasting resources through corruption, and funneling funds through inefficient bureaucracies. Instead, He invites direct, personal action driven by genuine love. And true charity is not merely a one-way transfer from rich to poor; rather, as Paul emphasized, "your abundance may be a supply for their want, that their abundance also may be a supply for your want: that there may be equality."[22] Unlike socialism's misguided aim of equalizing wealth by force, God's equality emerges voluntarily, from hearts freely giving time, talents, and resources. Zion doesn't demand uniformity in material possessions, but rather a free and mutual exchange—those rich in temporal resources sharing generously, and those spiritually abundant offering gratitude, humility, and love in return.

The seduction of others' spoils is real. One group of Church members created an organization dedicated to promoting socialism under the guise of gospel principles. Calling themselves "Mormons with Hope for a Better World," they claim to be "anxiously engaged in a good cause" to "bring forth and

---

21   Helaman 6:37–38.
22   2 Corinthians 8:13–14.

establish the cause of Zion"—yet announce they are "dedicated to socialist and leftist political theory grounded in the Mormon religious, spiritual, and historical tradition."[23] Like an attempt to mix oil and water, this effort inevitably fails. Undeterred, these individuals advocate for "collective ownership of the means of production" and for the "equitable distribution of resources."[24] Like Satan purporting to guarantee salvation no matter what one does, these misguided Mormon Marxists demand that governments guarantee them "free, accessible, and sustainable housing" and "free, accessible, and well-funded education," among many other entitlements.[25] They want the state to "ensure [that] every child of God [enjoys] a good life full of diverse and fulfilling experiences"[26]— living easy at the others' expense. But Zion cannot be built by force, nor righteousness legislated by compulsion. To seek God's kingdom through socialism's coercive methods is not merely misguided—it is spiritually dangerous, leading believers to trust in Caesar rather than Christ.

It's easy to look at advocates like these and say, "That's not me." Yet the slow stain of socialism is far subtler—and far more widespread—than many of us care to admit. Our trap is failing to recognize how often we ourselves quietly benefit from programs funded by coercive taxation, programs whose

---

23 "About Us," Mormons with Hope for a Better World, accessed March 6, 2025, https://www.mormonswithhope.org/about.

24 "10-Point Program for Mormons with Hope," Mormons with Hope for a Better World, accessed March 6, 2025, https://www.mormonswithhope.org/program.

25 Ibid.

26 Ibid.

costs are involuntarily borne by our neighbors. Consider honestly: What socialist policies or programs do you support, rely upon, or defend? How many times have we justified these compromises simply because we personally benefit, masking compulsion behind convenience? God's kingdom is built on persuasion, not force; voluntary sacrifice, not involuntary taxation. Socialism is a path that leads nowhere but away from Zion—and Latter-day Saints ought to be its fiercest critics.

EQUITY AND NEO–MARXISM

Karl Marx was more than a mere critic of capitalism—he sought to obliterate the very foundations of society by igniting class warfare. In his view, history was not a collection of individual choices but a brutal clash between oppressors and the oppressed: the "bourgeoisie," who owned the means of production, and the "proletariat," the exploited workers. To Marx, this conflict defined human existence, and only violent revolution could dismantle the old order and usher in his utopian vision. "The history of all hitherto existing society is the history of class struggles," he wrote in his infamous *Communist Manifesto*.[1] Unlike socialism's often gradual creep, Marxism demanded a radical rupture—seizing factories, land, and wealth to forge a stateless, classless society. But at its core, Marx's philosophy stripped away individual identity. People weren't unique souls with divine potential; they were either actors or pawns in a grand collective struggle, their worth measured solely by their class affiliation. A farmer wasn't a person with dreams or dignity—he was a "proletarian." A merchant wasn't a neighbor or friend—merely a "bourgeois" enemy.

---

1   Karl Marx and Friedrich Engels, *Communist Manifesto* (New York: Penguin Putnam Inc., 2002), 219.

This erasure of individuality wasn't accidental—it was Marxism's beating heart. Marx saw human nature as malleable clay to be molded by economic forces as a result of a never-ending stream of "contests between exploiting and exploited, ruling and oppressed classes."[2] Where socialism might redistribute wealth through state mechanisms, Marxism went further, aiming to dissolve the structures—family, religion, and property—that gave rise to the perceived problem of class disparity. The family was an incubator for inequality and slavery;[3] religion was the "opium of the people";[4] and property was public enemy number one, with Communism's theory being "summed up in one sentence: Abolish all private property."[5] The result of this ideology? A worldview that reduced God's children to faceless units in a revolutionary war machine, their lives valuable only as fuel for the collective cause.

Many people mistakenly believe that Marxism died with the fall of the Berlin Wall and the dramatic implosion of the Soviet Union. Tens of millions perished in Marxist revolutions throughout the twentieth century—a grim testament to the destructive and anti-Christian nature of Marx's ideology. Yet, Marxism didn't simply disappear. It's naïve to assume that ideas deeply embedded in human hearts and minds suddenly vanished. They didn't. Like a virus—like a slow stain—Marxist

---

2   Ibid., 203.
3   See Friedrich Engels, *The Origin of the Family, Private Property, and the State* (New York: Penguin Books Limited, 2010).
4   Karl Marx, *Critique of Hegel's Philosophy of Right* (New York: Cambridge University Press, 1982), 131.
5   Marx and Engels, *Communist Manifesto*, 138.

thought quietly seeped into the halls of academia, infiltrated mainstream media, and spread steadily through influential cultural institutions. Today, Marxism thrives not in its traditional guise of class warfare between economic groups and communist dictators, but in new ideological battles that have emerged through identity politics, Diversity, Equity, and Inclusion (DEI) initiatives, and "woke" cultural narratives. Neo-Marxists now pit groups against one another, not merely over wealth and property but across categories like race, gender, education, and even family structures. The modern "bourgeoisie" is no longer merely wealthy factory owners; they now include those who benefit from supposed advantages such as "white privilege," stable two-parent families, or traditional educational credentials. Thus, when Black Lives Matter rose to power after the riots in Ferguson, they declared that one of their end goals was to "disrupt the Western-prescribed nuclear family structure."[6] Like Marx and his communist comrades before them, this system was targeted as the root of oppression.

The same oppressor/oppressed narrative is utilized to attack personal merit, individual achievement, and accountability. In schools and workplaces, merit-based standards are increasingly dismissed as "racist" or inherently oppressive. Objective criteria—grades, test scores, workplace competence—are condemned as perpetuating systemic inequities.

---

6   "BLM site removes page on 'nuclear family structure' amid NFL vet's criticism,' *New York Post*, September 24, 2020, https://nypost.com/2020/09/24/blm-removes-website-language-blasting-nuclear-family-structure

Marxism is alive and well. Critical race theory instructs students to view themselves not as individuals with unique potential but as avatars of historical guilt or grievance—white children as oppressors, and minorities as victims. A straight-A student's effort is reframed as a product of so-called privilege, while a struggling student is told the system, not their choices, is to blame. This breeds resentment and lowers standards, as schools chase "equity" by diluting excellence. In workplaces, DEI initiatives impose quotas that prioritize identity over ability. A talented software developer is passed over for a promotion because the company needs to "balance" its racial metrics; a skilled surgeon or pilot faces hiring obstacles to meet gender targets, creating risk to customers who are forced to experience lower-quality services in the name of fairness.

Adherents of this false religion act like Pharisees—moral gatekeepers establishing purity tests, enforcing language codes, and policing thoughts. A professor challenges the data behind affirmative action, which gives preferential treatment to minority racial groups? He's labeled a bigot and fired. A worker refuses to use a colleague's preferred (though inaccurate) pronouns? He's ostracized or disciplined. This obsession with collective grievance clashes with the gospel's vision of individual worth and unity. Marx saw people as cogs in a class war; Christ sees us as children of God, each with divine potential. Where neo-Marxists divide us into warring tribes, the gospel calls us to love our neighbors as ourselves—across race, class, or creed;

all "are alike unto God."[7] Marxism demands coerced equality; Christianity invites voluntary service and personal accountability. As this ideology fractures society, the gospel offers a path to heal it—not through revolution, but through redemption. Instead of signaling virtue, we actually practice it.

It's critical to remember that the Zionic society after Christ's visit to the Americas saw an era of unprecedented peace and prosperity. As a result of the gospel permeating through society, "There were no robbers, nor murderers, neither were there Lamanites, nor any manner of -ites; but they were in one, the children of Christ, and heirs to the kingdom of God."[8] The previous monikers of Nephite or Lamanite washed away as they focused on a direct relationship with Christ. It was nearly two centuries later, when some fell prey to pride, that "they began to be divided into classes,"[9] causing "a great division among the people."[10] Striving for that Zionic ideal requires us to abandon all collectivist notions of class distinction. God holds each person accountable for their own choices; individuals are judged by their hearts and actions—not by group identity or perceived privilege. To resist the slow stain of Marxist thought, we must courageously defend individual initiative, merit, and personal accountability, teaching our children that their value and potential lie in their divine identity as a child of God—not their membership in socially constructed classes.

---

7   2 Nephi 26:33.
8   4 Nephi 1:17.
9   4 Nephi 1:26.
10   4 Nephi 1:35.

Too many Latter-day Saints today are unaware of the degree to which Marxist ideology quietly shapes their worldview. They absorb these corrosive narratives through media, education, and popular culture, mistakenly believing these ideas reflect fairness, kindness, or justice. Gradually, they begin to adopt class-based thinking—grouping others by race, economic background, or perceived privilege rather than seeing each soul as a unique child of God. Marxism in its modern variants thrives when we view each other through worldly filters—labeling privilege instead of seeing potential or oppression instead of opportunity. The slow stain of neo-Marxist class warfare thrives precisely because it appears virtuous, cloaked in appeals to equality and compassion. Saints must urgently awaken to this deception, firmly rejecting all forms of collectivism and reaffirming the divine principle of individual worth. Zion rises not by tearing others down but by lifting each soul toward Christ.

NEW AGE NONSENSE

After a spiritual experience that prompted her to seek God, Kelsea attempted to find Him—visiting several churches and eventually settling on New Age spiritualism. For years to come, she went deep into this path:

> I became a Reiki healer; I got "attuned," as it's called; and I offered it as a service to others. I got really into tarot, manifestation, and past lives. I had a spiritual business where I did energy healing and emotion code healing, and tarot readings. I was also really into crystals.[1]

Kelsea's journey led her to feel increasingly "enlightened" while at the same time developing deep resentments and rage toward those closest in her life. "I would have told anyone— and I truly believed this—that I was happier than ever," she explained. Yet she was truly miserable, experiencing suicidal thoughts and taking steps toward dismantling her family. Daily episodes of rage left her feeling out of control. "I turned into someone I had never been," she later realized.

---

1   "Kelsea's journey from the darkness of New Age to the Church of Jesus Christ of Latter-day Saints," Come Back Podcast, YouTube, October 20, 2024, https://www.youtube.com/watch?v=xE1FF79h8M4.

The experiences Kelsea navigated are certainly not unique to her, nor is she a rare exception in embracing New Age spirituality. In fact, many people embrace varying beliefs that fall under the New Age umbrella. Eighty-seven percent of Americans say they believe in at least one of twenty New Age concepts, and almost half say they believe in at least five.[2] And women like Kelsea are more likely than men to believe in New Age concepts.[3] But belief and behavior are different, and while a large number of people claim to conceptually agree with certain New Age ideas, far fewer actually incorporate them into their daily life.

One would think that these actual practitioners of New Age spirituality would have some sort of common identity or distinct set of doctrines. Unlike most formal religions, however, this movement has no holy scripture, centralized organization, membership, clergy, or creed. It is more like a loosely knit network of independent believers who share similar ideas that evolve over time, especially as they attempt to adapt them to whichever formal religion they might also choose to follow. There are, of course, some clear commonalities among those who embrace this spiritual path. These include:

---

2   "Most Americans endorse at least some aspects of the new-age spiritual movement," YouGov, November 29, 2022, https://today.yougov.com/health/articles/44581-most-americans-hold-some-new-age-beliefs-poll.

3   "'New Age' beliefs common among both religious and non-religious Americans," Pew Research Center, October 1, 2018, https://www.pewresearch.org/short-reads/2018/10/01/new-age-beliefs-common-among-both-religious-and-nonreligious-americans/.

1. **The Law of Attraction.** This concept holds that people can bring their desires into reality by focusing their thoughts. Adherents believe that positive thinking—like imagining wealth or good health—can attract those things into their lives, while negative thoughts draw unwanted outcomes. For example, someone might repeat affirmations like "I am abundant" to manifest prosperity. This concept emphasizes the mind's ability to influence one's circumstances through intention and visualization.

2. **Follow Your Heart.** This idea teaches that emotions and instincts are reliable guides for making decisions. Adherents trust their feelings over logic or outside opinions, often choosing paths that feel authentic to them. For instance, someone might quit a secure job because it doesn't resonate with their inner sense of purpose. This belief values personal intuition as a key to living a fulfilling life.

3. **All Roads Lead to Heaven.** This belief suggests that all spiritual paths lead to the same ultimate truth or state of enlightenment. Adherents believe that whether someone meditates, prays, or follows a personal philosophy all approaches are equally valid. For example, one person might say, "I find peace through nature, and you do through art—both work." This concept supports the freedom to pursue a unique spiritual journey. It is closely tied with subjective morality—no absolute right or wrong, only each person's "truth" they freely pursue.

4. **Fascination with the Supernatural.** New Age followers often explore mystical practices like tarot card readings, astrology, or energy work to connect with hidden forces. Adherents might use tools such as crystals to enhance their energy or consult psychics to gain clarity about their lives. For instance, someone might wear amethyst for calm or use a pendulum to answer questions. This belief centers on engaging with unseen energies that shape everyday experiences.

5. **Religious Pluralism.** In New Age belief, pluralism is the conviction that all religions are different yet equally valid paths to ultimate reality, with no single worldview capable of fully revealing the truth. New Agers hold that, despite their varied teachings and practices, all religions are fundamentally one, united as diverse expressions of the same spiritual essence. This perspective views figures like Jesus, Buddha, or other spiritual leaders as conveying a shared, universal truth—such as love or enlightenment—tailored to their unique cultural contexts, emphasizing a harmonious unity beneath the surface of religious diversity.

6. **An Impersonal God.** Many New Agers see God as an impersonal energy or force, often called "the Universe" or "Source." Adherents believe this universal energy supports and guides them, rather than acting as a distinct being. For instance, someone might say, "I'm letting the Universe handle it," trusting that this force will bring what they need.

7. **A Weak View of Satan and Sin.** In this belief, Satan
    is seen as a representation of negative energy rather
    than an actual entity, and sin is considered a lack of
    awareness of one's inner potential. Adherents focus on
    growth and self-discovery instead of guilt or wrongdo-
    ing. For example, someone might say, "I'm not bad—I
    just need to realign my energy." This perspective em-
    phasizes personal development over judgment.

To the committed Christian, it's clear how ideas such as
these are opposed to the gospel. Instead of following our own
heart, the Bible reminds us that, "He that trusteth in his own
heart is a fool,"[4] for the natural man's "heart is deceitful above
all things, and desperately wicked."[5] And instead of all roads
leading to heaven, "wide is the gate, and broad is the way,
that leadeth to destruction, and many there be which go in
thereat."[6] Jesus taught that He is "the way, the truth, and the
life: no man cometh unto the Father, but by me."[7] Further, we
aren't supposed to manifest our own will but pursue God's.[8]
And morality is not subjective; instead, "there is a law, irrevo-
cably decreed in heaven before the foundations of this world,
upon which all blessings are predicated."[9] Finally, God is not a
source of pure undifferentiated energy, consciousness, or life
force; Joseph Smith taught that "God himself was once as we

---

4   Proverbs 28:26.
5   Jeremiah 17:9.
6   Matthew 7:13.
7   John 14:6.
8   John 6:38, 7:17; Matthew 7:21; 2 Nephi 10:24.
9   D&C 130:20–L

are now, and is an exalted man, and sits enthroned in yonder heavens!"[10] We are His children, designed in His image.[11]

If New Age beliefs contrast so deeply against Christ's gospel, why then are so many disciples attracted to them? Forty percent of Christians believe in psychics; 29 percent believe in reincarnation; 26 percent believe in astrology.[12] Lump various New Age concepts together, and 62 percent of Christians believe in at least one of them. Kelsea offers an answer from her own experience after later converting to the restored gospel and, with the benefit of hindsight and spiritual eyes, discerning how she had been deceived:

> There's so much about New Age beliefs that are counterfeits of the restored gospel—so much about it that feels true and sounds true and you can convince yourself sounds true. I think that's why many Latter-day Saint women seem to gravitate toward it because it's so similar to what they already know and feel. That's what makes counterfeits so dangerous, is that they seem like the real thing.[13]

Mainstream Christians seemingly have more of an aversion toward New Age concepts than Latter-day Saints, perhaps due to restored doctrines that reveal concepts that are not dissimilar from certain New Age ideas. For example, the

---

10 "History, 1838–1856, volume E-1," Joseph Smith Papers, accessed March 12, 2025, https://www.josephsmithpapers.org/paper-summary/history-1838-1856-volume-e-1-1-july-1843-30-april-1844/342.

11 Genesis 1:26–27; Romans 8:16; Moses 3:5.

12 "'New Age' beliefs..." Pew Research Center.

13 "Kelsea's journey..." Come Back Podcast.

common New Age idea that natural objects have a spiritual essence—such as mountains, trees, and rocks—is not supported by conventional Christianity. But the restored gospel teaches that God "created all things... spiritually, before they were naturally upon the face of the earth."[14] New Agers often subscribe to a form of Monism—a philosophical view that sees all of existence as reducing to a single, ultimate essence. They thus say things like, "I am the universe. I am one with all things." Christians reject this idea, pointing out that "In the beginning, God created the heaven and the earth" and later made man in His image.[15] How can a creation be one with the same substance as its creator? But Latter-day Saints know that we are all made of a spiritual substance called intelligence, which "was not created or made, neither indeed can be."[16] It is "independent in that sphere in which God has placed it, to act for itself."[17] And God rules "over all the intelligences," which He "organized before the world was," into spirit children.[18] In this sense, we are all part of a similar, heavenly essence—and as probationary mortals we are "gods in embryo"[19] who need to "learn how to be a God."[20] New Age adherents often believe that all humans have a divine essence, giving rise to affirmations like, "I am God. You are God. We are all God." Christians reject these concepts, yet those who have the benefit of

---

14   Moses 3:5; see also D&C 29:31–32.
15   Genesis 1:1, 26–27.
16   D&C 93:29.
17   D&C 93:30.
18   Abraham 3:21–22.
19   *The Teachings of Spencer W. Kimball*, ed. Edward L. Kimball (Salt Lake City, 1982), 28.
20   Historian's Office, General Church Minutes, 7 Apr. 1844.

modern revelation see in them somewhat of a similarity with gospel truth.

And therein lies the problem—these concepts are often a corrupted counterfeit of true principles. But beyond that, they are completely divorced from their divine source. New Age practitioners manifest their way into a connection with an amorphous god blob—an abstract conceptual universe. The knowable and relational God is absent from the New Age equation. Individuals who follow this path perceive that there is no need for the Atonement, only enlightenment. By removing God from the picture, one's worship and pursuit of spiritual wisdom rely upon idols—crystals, energy, sorcery, astrology, and more. New Age followers embrace the Law of Attraction as a core fundamental; as explained in the famous film *The Secret*, which explains how the principle purportedly works, "the universe" will "rearrange itself" to provide for you that which you desire.[21] One should "have unwavering faith" in what one wants and "feel the way you'll feel once it arrives." The "positive energy" you are "sending out" will return to you whatever it is you want, "every time."[22] But this is wrong; it is God who provides. "Therefore, if you will ask of me you shall receive," He said. "If you will knock it shall be opened unto you."[23] We are the receivers, and God is the giver; there is a relationship that cannot be disregarded. "Every thing which inviteth to do good, *and to persuade to believe in Christ,*

---

21   "The Secret (is Stupid)," Connor's Conundrums, March 29, 2007, https://connorboyack.com/blog/the-secret-is-stupid/.
22   Ibid.
23   D&C 14:5.

is sent forth by the power and gift of Christ."[24] God's purpose is to provide us with the things we need and worthily desire, but to the end of worshiping Him and building His kingdom; the goal is not to obtain more worldly wealth and pleasures, but to believe in Christ. The New Age message bypasses God altogether, reducing spiritual practice to selfish demands for prosperity or pleasure. Its adherents worship created things rather than the Creator. Ultimately, this isn't spiritual enlightenment but idolatry cloaked in soothing affirmations, subtly and quietly leading believers into a counterfeit kingdom—a kingdom that mimics heaven but leads directly away from Christ, toward spiritual emptiness and bondage. Rather than peace, it breeds resentment; instead of genuine enlightenment, it fosters spiritual stupor. "There's nothing good in New Age spirituality that you can't find in the restored gospel," Kelsea explained. "There's nothing to gain and everything to lose."[25]

---

24 Moroni 7:16–17.
25 "Kelsea's journey ..." Come Back Podcast.

FOOD AND PHARMA

By every reasonable measure, we're getting sicker as a society. In less than half a century, youth obesity in the United States has more than tripled; more than a third of adults and nearly one-fifth of all children are obese.[1] One-fifth of children have a diagnosed mental health condition, a number that grows to half by the time they reach adulthood.[2] Nearly one-third of adults and a quarter of children have some form of allergy—an 18 percent increase in just over one decade.[3] Over 10 percent of individuals have diabetes, doubling the rate in the past few decades.[4] Millions of children are given psychotropic (mind-altering) medication.[5] 80 percent of adults fail

1   "Childhood and Adolescent Obesity in the United States: A Public Health Concern," Glob Pediatr Health, December 2019, https://pmc.ncbi.nlm.nih.gov/articles/PMC6887808/.
2   "Mental Illness," National Institute of Mental Health, accessed March 13, 2025, https://www.nimh.nih.gov/health/statistics/mental-illness.
3   "Diagnosed Allergic Conditions in Children Aged 0–17 Years: United States, 2021," National Center for Health Statistics, accessed March 13, 2025, https://www.cdc.gov/nchs/products/databriefs/db459.htm.
4   "The Increasing Incidence of Diabetes in the 21st Century," National Library of Medicine, accessed March 13, 2025, https://pmc.ncbi.nlm.nih.gov/articles/PMC2769839/.
5   "Psychotropic medication in children and adolescents in the United States in the year 2004 vs 2014," National Library of Medicine, accessed March 13, 2025, https://pmc.ncbi.nlm.nih.gov/articles/PMC6154488/.

to exercise regularly.[6] One in thirty-six children is diagnosed with autism, a five-fold increase since the year 2000.[7] Entire volumes could be (and are) filled with shocking statistics such as these, along with all sorts of explanations for why disease is on the rise. These discussions are important and necessary, but often unproductive.

Instead, consider a provocative question: Does the pharmaceutical industry prefer a healthy populace or one that is ravaged with disease? Framed this way, the answers take on a shade of economic rationality; systemic incentives entice certain behaviors over others. As Casey Means, a doctor-turned-whistleblower, wrote, "Every institution that impacts your health makes more money when you are sick and less when you are healthy—from hospitals and pharmacies to medical schools, and even insurance companies."[8] One would expect that spending trillions of dollars on "health care" would lead to a decline in chronic disease, and yet across the board, the rates are going up. We're spending more and yet at the same time are sicker.

The multibillion-dollar food industry has similar incentives. Their profits surge not by nourishing the public, but

---

6   "CDC: 80 percent of American adults don't get recommended exercise," CBS News, May 3, 2013, https://www.cbsnews.com/news/cdc-80-percent-of-american-adults-dont-get-recommended-exercise/.
7   "Autism Prevalence Higher, According to Data from 11 ADDM Communities," Centers for Disease Control, March 23, 2023, https://www.cdc.gov/media/releases/2023/p0323-autism.html.
8   Casey Means and Callie Means, *Good Energy: The Surprising Connection Between Metabolism and Limitless Health* (New York: Avery, 2024), 61.

by engineering addictive processed products packed with re-fined sugars, inflammatory seed oils, and artificial additives that stimulate overconsumption.[9] Scientists and marketing teams methodically design foods that manipulate taste buds and neurological reward systems, ensuring consumers keep coming back, craving more.[10] These hyperprocessed foods flood supermarket shelves, touted as "healthy" through de-ceptive labels, while chronic conditions like obesity, diabetes, and heart disease proliferate.

One would expect physicians to be watchmen on the med-ical tower, warning patients about the problems with what we eat and how we live. They would, we hope, sound the alarm about the growing crisis and point us to simple solutions—exercise, nutrition, and sunlight—that could resolve a whole host of medical complications. And yet, as Dr. Means wrote, "medical leaders are absolutely silent on the things that are actually making us sick: food and lifestyle."[11] Why recom-mend dietary changes or natural remedies when prescription drugs, surgeries, and other interventions offer a steady rev-enue stream? It's a subscription plan for medical services—a guarantee of a customer for life with frequent demands on the system for which they and their insurance provider pay generously. These massive industries and their influencers—

---

9   "Ultra-processed foods may be as addictive as smoking, study says," Medical News Today, October 18, 2023, https://www.medicalnewstoday.com/articles/ultra-processed-foods-may-be-as-addictive-as-smoking-study-says.

10 "How food is engineered to keep us eating," Citro, accessed March 14, 2025, https://www.joincitro.com.au/news/how-food-is-engineered-to-keep-us-eating.

11 Ibid., 67.

though they won't admit it, as they're perfectly nice people—ultimately prefer people be sick. There's profit in dependency, and nearly none to be had from an independent, healthy society.

This unhealthy system thrives not by accident but by design—fueled by massive lobbying expenditures and political influence. Pharmaceutical and food corporations spend lavishly each year to shape the regulatory environment in their favor, creating conditions that prioritize profit over public health. One recent watchdog report revealed that the health care industry donated $14 million to Congress in a single year, with contributions flowing directly into the campaign coffers of lawmakers tasked with regulating their industry. In fact, 72 US senators and 302 members of the House—more than two-thirds of Congress—accepted significant donations from Big Pharma, demonstrating just how deeply embedded this influence has become.[12] "It remains routine," the report concluded, "for the elected officials who regulate the health care industry to accept six-figure sums" from the very companies they purport to oversee.[13] As a result, laws and regulations meant in theory to protect public health instead protect profits for these industries, ensuring the continuous flow of cheap, addictive foods and the proliferation of pharmaceutical products, rather than genuine solutions that promote true health and eliminate chronic illness.

---

12   "More than two-thirds of Congress cashed a pharma campaign check in 2020, new STAT analysis shows," STAT, June 9, 2021, https://www.statnews.com/feature/prescription-politics/federal-full-data-set/.

13   Ibid.

No matter the amount of money spent on political influence or the saturation of advertising campaigns to create public demand for these industries' products—amounting to tens of billions of dollars in advertising each year[14]—what is far more persuasive is the psychological condition that leads us to implicitly trust those who claim to have special knowledge and ability to unlock the mysteries of health and life. In Ancient Egypt, priests served as both physicians and magicians, seen as guardians of secret knowledge given by the gods to humanity.[15] Across many indigenous societies, shamans have served as healers and spiritual leaders—believed to possess secret knowledge granted by spirits or ancestors, using it to cure illnesses through rituals, herbal remedies, and magical practices.[15] In ancient Celtic society, Druids were political, spiritual, and intellectual leaders. They were seen as possessing esoteric knowledge of nature, astronomy, and the supernatural.[17] And in our modern day, cultural deference is given to the elite few who proceed through years of medical

---

14 "Why Pharma and Healthcare Advertising Spending Continues to Rise," Health Union, February 12, 2025, https://health-union.com/blog/digital-ad-spend-increasing-in-healthcare/, and "Companies Spend Billions to Market Food & Beverages Harmful to Our Health — And They Are Succeeding," Burness, February 2, 2023, https://burness.com/blog/companies-spend-billions-to-market-food-and-beverages-harmful-to-our-health-and-they-are-succeeding.

15 "Ancient Egyptian Magic," BBC, February 17, 2011, https://www.bbc.co.uk/history/ancient/egyptians/magic_01.shtml.

16 "Shamanism," Wikipedia, accessed March 14, 2025, https://en.wikipedia.org/wiki/Shamanism.

17 "Understanding Druid Training in Ancient Celtic Society," Connect Paranormal Blog, September 25, 2024, https://connectparanormal.net/2024/09/25/understanding-druid-training-in-ancient-celtic-society/.

training to acquire specialized knowledge that the common-ers lack, creating the power imbalance you feel when in the doctor's office and at the mercy of whatever they observe and diagnose.

This reliance on authority figures regarding our own health is widespread and manifests in a variety of ways: advertising suggesting that "nine out of ten doctors" recommend the product being pushed on you; the steady stream of celebrity endorsements touting pharmaceuticals on television; or public health officials leveraging their supposed expertise to coerce acceptance of sweeping health mandates. Our conditioned trust in credentialed authorities has become deeply entrenched, nudged forward by an education system that prizes conformity to institutional experts over individual inquiry and informed skepticism. Physicians in white coats, government agencies, and health bureaucrats are presumed infallible—elevated to positions of near priesthood, whose pronouncements must not be questioned.

That presumption was evidenced in a communication sent to members of The Church of Jesus Christ of Latter-day Saints by the First Presidency regarding COVID-19. In it, President Nelson (a physician himself) and his colleagues said that "We know that protection from the diseases [COVID-19 causes] can only be achieved by immunizing a very high percentage of the population."[18] Thus, the claim was that no other solu-

---

18   "The First Presidency Urges Latter-day Saints to Wear Face Masks When Needed and Get Vaccinated Against COVID-19," The Church of Jesus Christ of Latter-day Saints, August 12, 2021, https://newsroom.churchofjesuschrist.org/article/first-presidency-message-covid-19-august-2021.

tion would reduce the impact of this virus—only a rushed and untested pharmaceutical product that the industry and its paid-for politicians and media allies universally championed as salvation. (President Nelson called the vaccine "a literal godsend."[19]) These Latter-day Saint leaders claimed that the vaccine—which they "urge[d] individuals" to receive—had been "proven to be both safe and effective," except neither characteristic turned out to be accurate.[20] Finally, members were instructed to "follow the wise and thoughtful recommendations of medical experts and government leaders"—an implicit assumption that such recommendations would be the best course of action. This appeal to religious authority compounded an already complex and troubling situation for many Latter-day Saints. On one hand stood Church leaders urging them to defer without question to medical and governmental authorities; on the other stood mounting evidence and personal experiences suggesting that these recommendations might be neither safe nor truly effective.

None of the above should be shocking to those familiar with scripture. The preface to the well-known Word of Wisdom, for example, explains the purpose for which it was given: "In consequence of evils and designs which do and will

---

19   "President Russell M. Nelson and the COVID-19 vaccine: What the church leader has said and done," *Deseret News*, April 29, 2021, https://www.deseret.com/faith/2021/4/29/22407953/president-nelson-on-on-covid-19-vaccine-comments-speeches-actions-prayers-shot-church-news/.

20   "COVID-19 Vaccines Revealed as 'Neither Safe, Nor Effective': Watchdog," *The Epoch Times*, September 17, 2023, https://www.theepochtimes.com/world/covid-19-vaccines-revealed-to-be-neither-safe-nor-effective-watchdog-5492986.

exist in the hearts of conspiring men in the last days."[21] Few pay attention to this purpose and what it implies—for doing so would lead us to confront the stark reality of how dysfunctional our approach to personal health has become. Indeed, the conspiracies of our modern age aren't always shadowy plots hatched in secret; often, they manifest openly as institutionalized profiteering, incentivized illness, and a relentless focus on symptom management rather than genuine healing. By treating superficial symptoms while ignoring or exacerbating root causes, these powerful industries secure customers for life, ensuring continued profit at the expense of human health. Can you imagine a more evil design than to craft a system whose success symbiotically depends on increasing and failing to resolve our illness?

Let's revisit and revise the provocative question asked earlier, but this time with a spiritual twist: Does Satan prefer a healthy populace or one that is ravaged with disease? Here, too, the question answers itself. Sick, obese, and malnourished individuals—burdened by chronic illness, fatigue, and mental fog—find themselves severely limited in their capacity to act, to serve, and to fulfill their divine potential. It's difficult to be "anxiously engaged in a good cause, and do many things of [our] own free will, and bring to pass much righteousness," when we're confined to our beds.[22] This modern "flaxen cord" of illness and incapacity gently but firmly binds people, robbing them of the physical and spiritual energy necessary to be productive agents on the Lord's errand. How can

---

21 D&C 89:4.
22 D&C 58:27.

one effectively build God's kingdom or serve others when suffering under the daily constraints of preventable disease and dependency on pharmaceuticals merely to function? A population tethered by physical limitations is one far easier to control, exploit, and pacify.

Latter-day Saints are often praised—and often praise themselves—for having a health code that requires them to abstain from things like drinking alcohol or using illicit drugs. Yet for all the benefits obtained by avoiding certain addictive items, members of the Church are by no means a peculiar people as it pertains to pharmaceutical usage, poor food consumption, weak exercise habits, and more. Utah—a state predominantly populated by Church members, thus serving as a proxy to look at Latter-day Saints generally—leads the nation in antidepressant prescriptions, issuing them at nearly twice the national average. The state also ranks seventh overall for prescription medications, including opioids.[23] One study reported that Latter-day Saints "were significantly less physically active" than nonmembers.[24] And while faithful members abstain from Starbucks, they are passionate patrons of institutions like Swig or Sodalicious, who pump customers full of caffeine and sugar; Utah children, for example, consume sugary drinks at a higher rate than the general population.[25]

---

23 "Study Finds Utah Leads Nation in Antidepressant Use," *Los Angeles Times*, February 20, 2002, https://www.latimes.com/archives/la-xpm-2002-feb-20-mn-28924-story.html.
24 "Religious preference, church activity, and physical exercise," National Library of Medicine, accessed March 14, 2025, https://pubmed.ncbi.nlm.nih.gov/11482994/.
25 "Utah kids drinking more sugar than the national average," KSL News Radio, March 16, 2023, https://kslnewsradio.com/health/utah-kids-drink-more-sugar-than-national-average/1993507/.

Utahns, and thus presumably Latter-day Saints more broadly, have no improved health outcomes compared to the general population for diabetes, obesity, heart disease, and more. We appear to be suffering from—and actively participating in— the "evils and designs" we were warned about. Unlike the general population, we can't plead ignorance.

God desires a healthy people—individuals physically capable and spiritually prepared to "act... according to the moral agency which [He has] given."[26] Avoiding the chronic illnesses and diseases that burden society is essential if we are to effectively "waste and wear out our lives in bringing to light all the hidden things of darkness"[27]—including the "evils and designs" that thrive in the hearts of conspiring men, who prefer and profit off of a sickly society of dependent, deferential people. Of course, pharmaceutical products are not inherently problematic—many are obviously life-saving and beneficial. Nearly half of pharmaceutical drugs are derived from compounds first identified or isolated from plants or other natural sources[28]—effectively industrializing the healing properties found in the "many plants and roots which God had prepared to remove the cause of diseases."[29] Nature, and nature's God, offers many ways to health—and many of them at nearly no cost.

---

26   D&C 101:78.
27   D&C 123:13.
28   "Natural products derived from plants as a source of drugs," National Library of Medicine, accessed March 14, 2025, https://pmc.ncbi.nlm.nih.gov/articles/PMC3560124/.
29   Alma 46:40

Saints, who should understand and honor the sacred connection between physical health and spiritual capacity, have increasingly fallen prey to trusting in prescriptions over prevention, thus unknowingly surrendering their freedom to act, serve, and thrive as God intended. If today's medical, political, and religious leaders fail to serve as vigilant watchmen, guarding against the evils and designs threatening our physical and, therefore, spiritual well-being, then we must rise to the occasion ourselves—embracing personal responsibility, informed discernment, and deliberate action to preserve our health and safeguard our agency.

CONCLUSION

Slavery has been a persistent feature of human society since ancient times. It is, tragically, as old as civilization itself—ancient Sumerians codified laws governing it; Egyptian pharaohs built monuments through it; Roman emperors leveraged it to fuel their sprawling empire; and even revered philosophers in Greece and Rome casually justified its existence. Whether prisoners captured in war, debtors sold by creditors, or defeated warriors taken in conquest, slaves formed the foundation of many early economies. The practice spread steadily, from ancient Babylonian ziggurats to Greek and Roman marketplaces, normalizing a horrific commerce in human souls. Yet even these terrible injustices pale next to the scale and brutality of later slave systems—like the transatlantic slave trade, where the British Empire alone forcibly transported millions of Africans across oceans, commodifying human life itself to fuel economic ambition. This particular slow stain of wickedness had spread so deeply that society itself seemed permanently dyed by its cruelty.

There were, of course, exceptions—people who resisted the spread of this evil and sought to check its advance. People like John Newton, an English sailor who himself actively participated in the slave trade, captaining ships that carried human cargo across the ocean. After experiencing a profound spiritual conversion during a violent storm at sea, Newton began to deeply question the morality of his actions. Overwhelmed by the realization of his own complicity in perpetuating human suffering, he became an outspoken abolitionist, passionately urging others to reject the very system from which he had previously profited.[1] His widely popular hymn, "Amazing Grace," poignantly reflects his profound repentance and the transformative power of God's mercy—serving as a timeless reminder that even in a society saturated by wickedness, individuals can choose to stand courageously against evil and alter its course.

That's what William Wilberforce, a friend and mentee of Newton's, chose to do. While a Member of Parliament, Wilberforce went through a spiritual journey and learning process that led him to join the side—and become the face—of the abolitionists in Great Britain. His first major speech on the topic, and the beginning of his parliamentary campaign against the slave trade, was in 1789.[2] And in the seventeen years that followed, Wilberforce unsuccessfully attempted each year to advance antislavery motions designed to abolish the slave trade.[3] Finally, in 1807, after persistent efforts building up opposition to its establishment, Wilberforce had enough political support to pass the bill and finally abolish the slave trade. Tears streamed down his face as colleagues paid

---

1   See William E. Phipps, *Amazing Grace in John Newton: Slave-Ship Captain, Hymnwriter, and Abolitionist* (Macon: Mercer University Press, 2001).

2   "William Wilberforce," Wikipedia, accessed March 15, 2025, https://en.wikipedia.org/wiki/William_Wilberforce.

3   Ibid.

tribute to him as they voted, with 283 votes in favor of his motion and only 16 against, as "even the recalcitrant recognized the inevitable."[4] It was a monumental achievement that was decades in the making.

But the fight was not over; abolishing the slave trade did not end slavery itself. The stain had penetrated too deeply to be easily removed—hundreds of thousands remained enslaved throughout the British Empire, continuing to endure bondage and abuse. Wilberforce understood this painful reality and refused to relent; he tirelessly devoted the remainder of his life to achieving full emancipation. Even as his health deteriorated, he remained a tireless advocate, rallying public opinion and marshaling political allies in pursuit of this final moral victory. Finally, in 1833—just three days before Wilberforce's death—Parliament passed the Slavery Abolition Act, outlawing slavery throughout most of the British Empire and bringing freedom to over 800,000 enslaved individuals. The slow stain of slavery, so deeply embedded into society, was finally beginning to fade, thanks in large part to Wilberforce's unwavering moral courage and perseverance.

Our own resistance to today's slow stains can be informed and inspired by stories such as these. Samuel the Lamanite boldly preached from the walls of Zarahemla despite arrows aimed at his life—fearlessly calling a prideful people to repentance.[5] Abinadi, whose unyielding testimony before King

---

4 William Hague, *William Wilberforce: The Life of the Great Anti-Slave Trade Campaigner* (Orlando: Houghton Mifflin Harcourt, 2007), 354.
5 Helaman 13–15.

Noah cost him his life, planted seeds of conversion that transformed generations.[6] Daniel courageously defied Babylonian
decree, choosing obedience to God over loyalty to an oppressive king, willingly entering the lions' den rather than compromise his faith.[7] Likewise, Shadrach, Meshach, and Abedne-
go faced the fiery furnace rather than bow to a false idol, their
devotion unwavering even in the face of certain death.[8] Each
resisted the allurement and enticement of worldly comforts
and conformity, understanding clearly the subtle yet dangerous nature of the slow stain of wickedness.

John Newton's conversion and behavioral about-face
came after a life-threatening experience aboard his ship. Saul
was converted and turned from a Christian persecutor into a
promoter after a spiritual experience on the road to Damas-
cus.[9] Alma the Younger was paralyzed for three days after an
angelic rebuke, awakening as a converted disciple committed to righting the wrongs he had caused.[10] The Lamanites
who sought Nephi and Lehi's deaths were converted and repented after witnessing a miraculous deliverance in prison.[11]
Throughout history, we can find exceptional circumstances
such as these that result in a powerful conversion. But they
are just that—exceptions. What we find for the majority is a
consistent overtaking by the slow stain of the world. Again
and again, people who should know better find themselves

---

6   Mosiah 11–17.
7   Daniel 6.
8   Daniel 3.
9   Acts 9:1–31.
10   Mosiah 27.
11   Helaman 5:20–52.

enticed by the culture around them enough to justify embracing it. As Hugh Nibley wrote:

> Important in the record of the dispensations is that when men depart from God's way and substitute their own ways in its place they usually do not admit that that is what they are doing; often they do not deliberately or even consciously substitute their ways for God's ways; on the contrary, they easily and largely convince themselves that *their way is God's way.*[12]

This is the pattern—the frequent and persistent outcome of past societies that succumbed to worldly evils. God's people rarely reject him outright but rather slowly embrace idolatrous alternatives that pollute their faith. Avraham Gileadi noted this trend:

> Among the Lord's people, worship of the true God is rarely done away with. Rather, they often worship the true God alongside the false Gods. They maintain careful equilibrium in order to preserve an identity with the national God, the God of Israel or of the Fathers. At the same time, the people follow their own Gods as they please. This compromise enables people to satisfy both their carnal instincts and their spiritual aspirations.[13]

---

12 Hugh Nibley, "Beyond Politics," *Review of Books on the Book of Mormon 1989-2011*, vol. 23, no. 1, https://scholarsarchive.byu.edu/cgi/viewcontent.cgi?article=1841&context=msr.

13 Avraham Gileadi, 'Twelve Diatribes of Modern Israel," accessed March 15, 2025, https://web.archive.org/web/20160401084009/http://publications.mi.byu.edu/fullscreen?pub=1129&index=12.

We are not immune from this condition simply because we live in the last dispensation; no prophecy exists promising that there will not be a latter-day apostasy.[14] To the contrary, tares exist among the wheat, even in the Church—even among the "elect" in leadership. "Religious history testifies," wrote H. Verlan Anderson, "that with the single exception of the inhabitants of the City of Enoch, no people to whom the gospel has been given have remained faithful to their covenants for more than a few generations." He continued:

> This cycle of human folly which so many prophets have noted, has repeated itself with such consistent regularity that any group which finds itself to be the favored recipients of the gospel would do well to assume that their apostasy is certain, and the only question about it is how long it will take.
>
> It is also true that people who conform to the outward ordinances, ceremonies, and practices of Christ's

---

14 Daniel 2:44 (and D&C 138:44 which references it) mentions a latter-day "kingdom, which shall never be destroyed"—and some leaders of the Church have relied on this scripture to assert that the institutional Church (and therefore its leaders and/or members) will not apostatize. Summarizing these views—and relying on the aforementioned prophecy by Daniel—an article on apostasy published by the Church says that "unlike the Church in times past, The Church of Jesus Christ of Latter-day Saints will not be overcome by general apostasy." But this is not what Daniel said; God's kingdom can avoid destruction, as he noted, while still having the majority of Latter-day Saints (including those in leadership) be so stained by the world that they are in truth building up the devil's kingdom instead. It is hubris to say that because God's kingdom will avoid destruction, that therefore we in the Church will never generally stray from His path no matter what we say or do. Foolish virgins and Saints both falsely assume that their compromised discipleship is sufficient to merit God's approval.

Church tend to assume that such activities assure them a place in His kingdom. This assumption, according to the scriptures is likewise false.[15]

We should recognize that we are just as susceptible to embracing the slow stain of the world as were people throughout history. We can—we must—learn from their mistakes so as not to repeat them. Simply being aware of the problem means it's that much closer to being resolved. As dangerous cultural currents swirl around us, we should reflect soberly upon our own "awful situation." What slow stains have silently seeped into our beliefs and behaviors? Like the proverbial frog gradually boiled alive, have we grown comfortable in water that's slowly been heating, unaware of how close we are to spiritual peril?

President Hinckley's warning three decades ago was not enough to prevent God's people from casually accepting worldly philosophies and practices, believing them to be compatible with the gospel. Recognizing the stain, however, is only the beginning—awareness alone changes nothing unless accompanied by courageous action. Each of us is called to be a Samuel, an Abinadi, or a Wilberforce—boldly standing as a watchman against the many slow stains of our day. The battle ahead demands vigilance and conviction, but through small and simple acts of resistance, and unwavering devotion to God's revealed truths, we can reverse this incremental apostasy and halt the stain's spread.

---

15 H. Verlan Andersen, *The Great and Abominable Church of the Devil* (Self-published, 1972), 178–180.

ABOUT THE AUTHOR

Connor Boyack is the author of several dozen books, founder of a think tank that has changed over 100 laws, frequent public speaker, and outlaw beekeeper.

Connor is best known as author of the acclaimed Tuttle Twins book series which has sold over six million copies. The Tuttle Twins books teach kids (and their parents!) the ideas of a free society. He is also executive producer of the Tuttle Twins animated cartoon series inspired by the books.

A self-made entrepreneur, Connor not only talks the talk, but walks the walk as the founder and president of the Libertas Network, a series of initiatives that change hearts, minds, and laws to create a freer future. His leadership has led Libertas to innovate over a dozen legal reforms that were the first of their kind, changing the lives of millions of people.

Connor lives near Salt Lake City, Utah, with his wife and two homeschooled children.

Find his religious books for sale at SocialHarmony.org and all his other books at LibertasPress.com.